COMMUNITY ORGANIZING

SOCIAL WORK AND SOCIAL ISSUES
COLUMBIA UNIVERSITY SCHOOL OF SOCIAL WORK

Community Organizing

GEORGE BRAGER
and
HARRY SPECHT

COLUMBIA UNIVERSITY PRESS
NEW YORK AND LONDON

1973

The Columbia University School of Social Work Publication Series, "Social Work and Social Issues," is concerned with the implications of social work practice and social welfare policy for solving problems. Each volume is an independent work. The Series is intended to contribute to the knowledge base of social work education, to facilitate communication with related disciplines, and to serve as a background for public policy discussion. This is the second book to be published in the Series. The first book was

SHIRLEY JENKINS, *editor*
Social Security in International Perspective 1969

LIBRARY OF CONGRESS CATALOGING IN PUBLICATION DATA

Brager, George A
  Community organizing.

  Includes bibliographical references.
  1. Community organization. I. Specht, Harry,
joint author. II. Title.
HV41.B653   352   72-8947
ISBN 0-231-03393-1

PREFACE

CONTEMPORARY COMMUNITY ORGANIZATION practice is the spawn of currents of change which gathered force in the last two decades. Sometimes, the sounds of change had the ring of faith and hope ("We shall overcome. . . ." "I'll hammer out love between my brothers and my sisters. . . ."). And sometimes, the sounds resounded with notes of bitterness ("Up against the wall. . . ." "Off the pigs!"). As might be expected of the issue of the union of faith and cynicism, of love and discord, community work is a complex offspring—a method of social intervention filled with contradictions, controversy, and conflict.

The presentation, at this time, of a text on community organization practice places something of a burden on its authors. For one thing, this is a time in history when expectations about "what can be done" vacillate between extremes. There have been recent moments when the horizons of reform seemed limitless; while at other times within the same decade, belief in orderly social change was perilously shaken. A responsible assessment of professional practice must deal with hazards as well as hopes, and we endeavor, in this book, both to reflect the turbulence of community organization and to provide what intellectual order we can for those who practice it.

For another thing, the great social changes of the last decade have resulted in the redefinition of community work and shifting emphases in its practice. A wide-ranging method, community organization incorporates work with the poor and the rich, the disenfranchised and the powerful. It includes working in and/or influencing "established" institutions, "cause" organizations, neighborhood groups, community councils, planning agencies, as well as public and private organizations with regional, state, and national boundaries. A volume that attempts to explore a professional practice which covers such a multitude of differences cannot do justice to them all.

As a matter of fact, this book was begun with an emphasis on community work with a low-income constituency. It soon became clear, however, that the principles we were articulating were relevant for other population groups and other contexts as well. Although much of the material and many of our examples are still especially pertinent to organizing the poor, in the process of writing, the applicability of the volume was broadened. At the same time, we have dealt with the problem of the diversity in practice by focusing most sharply on the "people" component of community work.

This is a book about *how* individuals, groups, and organizations develop the means to deal with problems in their interaction with institutions. We recognize that many of the issues for which solutions are sought have nothing to do with the *how* of problem solving. Rather, these require answers to questions about *what* should be done to solve problems. Such questions begin with the words: "What kind of program will decrease (or increase)————?" To complete the phrase, add the issue of specific concern, such as racial discrimination, poor housing, unemployment, juvenile delinquency, student autonomy, male chauvinism, and so forth. However, this is not a book about social problems or the social programs that provide solutions to them. Our intention is to explore methods of practice rather than to explicate specific problems and solutions.

Although it is theoretically possible to separate method from substantive policy and program, in actual practice they are not separable, nor should they be. Essentially, we view community organizing as an activity in which participants attempt to accomplish a substantive objective (i.e., the development of a particular policy or program). Only secondarily is it valuable *by itself* as a process. Important parts of community organization methodology deal with technical matters such as problem analysis, clarification of program objectives and development of strategy, and the explication of practice requires that the relationships among them be made clear. Nonetheless, our attention is directed to the *how* rather than the *what* of community organization. Numerous works deal with the analysis of social problems and their solutions, whereas what the practitioner *does* and the knowledge he needs to *do* it have been relatively neglected (even in the community work literature).

Our focus, then, is on process and interaction. The book will be most useful, we expect, to organizers, urban planners, and administrators who are most interested in these practice variables. Our aim has been to build on the existent body of community organization literature, with primary attention to the description of how it is (or might be) practiced.

We have tried to include practical instruction to organizers, and thus the volume risks being "cookbookish." On the other hand, we base this instruction on theoretical ideas about groups, organizations, and behavior, which, for some readers, may seem "too theoretical." In other words, we have tried to maintain a balance between the practical and the theoretical, which is inherently tenuous, and the reader will have to judge with what degree of success we have managed it. We believe that an important characteristic which distinguishes the professional from the nonprofessional is his ability to utilize knowledge and theory in his work. However, knowledge and theory are relevant to professional practice only when they can be integrated by the worker, and embodied in what he *does*. Although we have relied heavily on selected social science theory, our test for its inclusion has been its direct applicability to worker activity.

In the turmoil of the "real world," community workers will not put the knowledge and theory we discuss in this book to use in anything resembling the way we have ordered it. People who work with community groups are likely to find that from the moment they begin to work they are flooded with the questions, issues, problems, and activities we explore in a sequential fashion. We will deem our efforts a success if we have selected some of what is significant in these dynamic experiences, and placed it in an analytic framework that makes it more accessible for use by organizers and planners.

GEORGE BRAGER
HARRY SPECHT

New York
July, 1972

ACKNOWLEDGMENTS

Two AUTHORS have a doubly difficult job in acknowledging those to whom they are indebted for assistance. Many of them are our friends, some of the primary actors in community organization who appear in this book. That is, many of the psuedonyms in the case examples are people with whom we've worked, professionals, students, community residents. Some of the intellectual contributions of our friends are acknowledged in footnotes. But it is difficult to separate out the ideas of colleagues with whom we have worked closely for long years. For Brager, Charles Grosser of the Columbia University School of Social Work and Simon Slavin of Temple University call for particular mention; for Specht, Neil Gilbert, Ralph Kramer, and Robert Pruger, of the Berkeley School of Social Work, the University of California. We owe a great deal too to Neil Gilbert and Stephen Holloway for reading several chapters and making helpful suggestions.

We are indebted to our students who have, over the years, provided the crucial test of the clarity of our ideas. Good students are creative thinkers who generate new concepts and who are challenging critics. Much that is included in this volume reflects our "rare moments" in teaching—those exciting occasions when teacher and student discover something together which is new.

The authors are grateful to The Lois and Samuel Silberman Fund for its support of the "Social Work and Social Issues" publication series of the Columbia University School of Social Work, of which this volume is a part.

But the last is first. More than to anyone, our gratitude belongs to our wives, Lennie and Riva, for their encouragement, criticism, patience, support, and—most of all—for their love. Without them, the book could not have been written.

G.B.

H.S.

CONTENTS

Part I

CONTEMPORARY COMMUNITY
ORGANIZATION PRACTICE

CHAPTER ONE

A TIME OF FERMENT:
COMPETING VALUES IN
COMMUNITY WORK

NATIONAL INTEREST IN COMMUNITY WORK evolved in the 1960's. "Burst forth" is perhaps more precise than "evolved," for there has not been an orderly or measured development of the profound changes that have taken place in our conceptions of the role of the consumer of social services in planning, policy making, and programming. New ideas about organizing low-income people have fairly tumbled forth, so that almost as soon as one ostensibly radical proposal was being put to the test, another and newer conception was introduced that made the first seem conservative.

For example, in 1964, when some organizations were struggling to defend the rights of local groups of the poor to mobilize on their own behalf, the Economic Opportunity Act introduced a more advanced notion into federal statutes which required federally supported agencies themselves to assure "maximum feasible participation" of the poor in community action. And hardly had some ways to involve the poor maximally under the Economic Opportunity Act been conceived, much less tested, when, in 1966, the Model Cities program was propounded in the Demonstration Cities and Metropolitan Redevelopment Act, introducing yet newer conceptions of citizen participation that outdated the Economic Opportunity Act. And the Model Neighborhood Area scheme, which implied that there must be some sharing of power among city hall, residents, and agencies, was hardly announced before it too was challenged by newer ideas about community control, "Black Capitalism," and "alternative institutions." Indeed, by 1970, although things would never be quite the same again, there were those who felt that the notion of participation had come full circle, that there were "strong tendencies leading toward the stalemate of citizen groups and political elites . . . (with) an inability of social policy to provide solutions by the mutual adjustment of the interests involved." [1]

It is undoubtedly true that in the early 1960's as hopes burgeoned that something might be done about poverty in America, as idealism was stirred and found channels for action in programs such as the Peace Corps, VISTA, and Model Cities, enthusiasm for community work with the poor oriented to changing institutions and righting social wrongs was at a crest. By the early 1970's much of the idealism had become frustration, and, more importantly, the opportunities to act on social injustices (through federal and other programs, the activities of "cause" organizations, etc.) had considerably diminished. Inevitably, however, community organizing undergoes an ebb and flow, an ascending and descending interest on the part of both elites and the poor themselves. Those who support its values and purposes, or who are among its participants, serve, by their commitments and activities to keep opportunities alive during fallow periods— opportunities which may then be accelerated as the social climate becomes more fertile for their effort.

In beginning this discussion of community work practice, it is necessary to place the events—and more importantly, the ideas—of the recent past in an historical context, if only so that the practitioner has some awareness of how the larger forces that shape the society affect his own perceptions and the perceptions of others.

*   *   *

From the 1960's to the 1970's the entire country was torn asunder over questions about the efficacy of American government to deal

---

[1] Jon Van Til and Sally Bould Van Til, "Citizen Participation in Social Policy: The End of the Cycle?" *Social Problems,* Vol. 17, No. 3 (Winter 1970), pp. 320–21.

with change demanded by large sections of the population which had heretofore been relatively quiescent. Few Americans were untouched in some way by the great social upheavals related to protests against the war in Vietnam, the marches and demonstrations launched by the civil rights movement, the disruption and even violence associated with the student revolt, the black revolution and developing movements of other minority groups, the welfare rights movement, and the women's liberation front, to mention only those groups which most occupied the attention of the news media during the decade.

While the dissatisfaction and goals of these movements were often quite different, their interests and activities coalesced at many points. Often, they were accompanied by disruption and violence, although studies indicate that the agencies of government bore a major share of the responsibility for the violence more often than the dissidents.[2] Disruption occurred because, in the belief of many protesters, the American system of government does not allow for orderly change processes in response to the needs of these many groups—of the poor, blacks and other minorities, and students. This view has considerable justification in reality, and finds support in such official statements as a report to the National Commission on the Causes and Prevention of Violence.[3]

Thus, many believe that the electoral system of government, while theoretically equalitarian, excludes too many citizens in practice, and does not allow them sufficient power to influence the political and administrative agencies of society that determine their destinies. Furthermore, it is believed, the agencies that serve the disadvantaged are governed by a system of prestige and privilege that serves best the interests of those who manage these systems and their constituents in white middle class America. Leadership in this system has tended toward elitism where, authority increasingly is centralized in the hands of a few who serve, in the vocabulary of dissent, "the power structure," "the military-industrial complex," and the "welfare colonialists."

[2] Jerome H. Skolnick, *The Politics of Protest,* A Report to the National Commission on the Causes and Prevention of Violence (New York: Ballantine Books, 1969), p. 3.

[3] *Ibid.,* p. 344.

PARTICIPATION, EXPERTISE, AND
LEADERSHIP IN GOVERNMENT

The more than three-hundred-year history of the American community has been marked by a continuing search for, and struggle over,
the means by which to reconcile three important and competing values which are at stake in many of these conflicts. These are the values of *participation, expertise,* and *leadership.* Each of these values
can be supported by theoretical arguments, and each of them constitutes the basic assumptions which underlie arguments against the others.[4]

Citizen participation refers to the belief that government should be
a means by which the governed can express their wishes and choose
their programs. The value is best captured in the slogan "one
man—one vote," and programmatically it was seen in the attempt of
organizations, particularly those sponsored by the young, to achieve
"participatory democracy." Theoretically, those who champion the
value of citizen participation in government believe that communities
will be served best when every man participates *directly* in making
decisions that affect him. There is countervailing theory which asserts that because there are such vast differences among men in their
interests, needs, resources, motivations and abilities, participation
can be, at best, only fragmented and partial.

Expertise is a value which grows out of our belief in the use of
technical know-how and scientific rationality as a means of solving
problems. It often arises as a reaction to waste and corruption in re-
gimes which have allowed the notions of participation and leadership
untrammeled sway. Expertise is viewed as nonpartisan. The conception implies that in an environment protected from the vagaries of
political partisanship the technical expert provides the most efficient
means for resolving community problems. Theoretically, the unfet-
tered freedom of the expert, being based on the most advanced uses
of knowledge, achieves the most rational and economic use of com-

[4] Herbert Kaufman, *Politics and Policies in State and Local Governments*
(Englewood Cliffs, N.J.: Prentice-Hall, 1964), pp. 35—43.

munity resources. Conversely, it is argued that expertise cannot be value-free and is itself a social resource, access to which is unevenly distributed and which has been used by privileged groups to the disadvantage of the wider citizenry.

The value of *leadership* is one which elevates the chief executive —be it the president, the mayor, the university chancellor, or the chairman of the community council—to an extraordinary level of power, centralizing decision making and control of resources in the hands of one or a few people. It suggests that "our leader" can get things done quickly and effectively, and that the people will know to whom they can turn or whom they can hold answerable for their problems. Its rationale is that the complexity of a pluralistic industrialized civilization requires centralization of authority, so that decisions can be made and resources distributed with equity and dispatch. The arguments used to support the values of participation and expertise are the same ones used to attack strong reliance on leadership—that is, centralization leads to corruption and to the alienation of those who are unable to control leadership.

American history reflects an interplay of these values, with one or another of them in the ascendency at different times. So, for example, the Revolutionary War and the Populist movement in the late 1800's were times in which the question of the representativeness of government was paramount to the nation. The movement against the "spoils system," the introduction of the merit system in civil service, and of government by technical experts, such as city managers and appointed independent commissions, are examples of times when the value of expertise was dominant in our society. There are, finally, instances of social movements which sought to give greater power to the chief executive, for example, the movement against the "long ballot" in the nineteenth century and charter reform movements in the twentieth century, both aimed at granting mayors and governors powers to appoint their administrative officials.

There are currently, in our complex system of government, examples that represent each of these values carried to the extreme. The city manager form of government used in many cities developed as a result of an earlier distaste for the technical incompetence of elected city councils. County government in the United States usually reflects the epitome of the belief that "that government is best which governs least." Highly representative, it is a form of government which eschews both expertise and leadership (and is usually ineffectual). And, as an example of government by leadership, there is the office of the President of the United States in which, in recent decades, extraordinary powers have been vested, much to the consternation of a large part of the Congress and many in the electorate.

In recent years the value of participation has risen to a new prominence in community life. This book is itself a reflection of that struggle, since it is concerned with the methods and processes by which the poor (and other citizens) can be better represented in community decision making. The quest for representative government is, of course, not an exclusive concern of the poor. The impulses which bring the poor to demand that government respond to their needs, and the dissatisfactions they feel with the way resources are distributed, have infected the poor, workers, ethnics, and others alike.

But the search for social mechanisms by which to achieve greater participation in community life is not without its dilemmas. One reason for this is that the other values—expertise and leadership—are present in our thinking, and demand attention. Even those who were strong supporters of the poverty program, for example, were not entirely enthusiastic about the quality of the programs and the lack of direction and leadership which seemed to result.[5] Although extremist groups may find it easy to assert one value over all others (e.g., "Power to the People" or "America Love It or Leave It"), the professional who is attempting to help constituents organize for action cannot avoid dealing with the contradictions inherent in all of the elixirs that provide simple solutions to complex problems.[6] Complex societies must also have specialization of function and hierarchy of command, so that the coordination and control of programs is main-

[5] For example, see Kenneth B. Clark, et al., *A Relevant War against Poverty: A Study of Community Action Programs and Observable Social Change* (New York: Harper and Row, 1968); Ralph M. Kramer, *Participation of the Poor: Comparative Case Studies in the War on Poverty* (Englewood Cliffs, N.J.: Prentice-Hall, 1968).

[6] The difficulties in integrating communiy organization, research, and political leadership in community action are described in Peter Marris and Martin Rein, *Dilemmas of Social Reform* (New York: Atherton Press, 1967).

tained. In effect, all people cannot be involved at all times in making all decisions, nor would it be wise for them to be, assuming that it was possible.

DEVELOPMENTS IN COMMUNITY
ORGANIZATION: A TIME OF FERMENT

Evident throughout the history of community organization in the United States is the ubiquitious tension among the three major values of participation expertise, and leadership. Three periods may be broadly identified, each of which has contributed to the present configuration of the field. Although we shall refer to the two earlier periods, our primary concern is with the present and more recent past. For those interested in the background and genealogy of their professional house, a number of historical accounts are available.[7]

The first period runs, roughly, from the beginning of the century to the 1930's. It is marked by the development of community welfare councils and councils of social agencies, which—in the tradition of the Charity Organization Societies—pressed for efficiency, centralization, and specialization within private philanthropy, and for effective leadership in planning for social services.

With the movement of social welfare from private to public auspices in the 1930's, the focus of community organization efforts, along with the rest of private philanthropy, shifted to those areas left for voluntary action—counseling and guidance, health, group services, recreation, and adult organization. During this period, community organization was clearly an elitist endeavor relying heavily on the leadership of politicians, bureaucrats, businessmen, and wealthy philanthropists.

The second major period of development, which terminated approximately in the late forties or early fifties, saw the dominance of

[7] See, for example: Meyer Schwartz, "Community Organization," *Encyclopedia of Social Work* (New York: National Association of Social Workers, 1965), pp. 177–90; Arthur Dunham, *The New Community Organization* (New York: Thomas Y. Crowell, 1970); Ralph M. Kramer and Harry Specht, eds., *Readings in Community Organization Practice* (Englewood Cliffs, N.J.: Prentice-Hall, 1969), pp. 12–19.

expertise, or technicism, in community work. It was a time of developing professionalization, and with the Lane Report to the National Conference of Social Work in 1939, the field became formally identified as a part of social work practice. Competing definitions and conceptions of practice were earnestly explored within the professional ranks. A primary issue, for example, was whether the aim of planning was to achieve a substantive end ("The articulation of resources and social needs," as suggested by the Lane Report) [8] or whether it was, as Murray Ross argued in 1955 in a seminal work, a *tool* to achieve cooperative and collaborative attitudes in the community.[9]

The issue is still being heatedly debated. Elitist planning—in which the problems addressed and methods used are palatable to the high status citizens who compose the effort—is very much a part of the current community organization scene. But the civil rights movement of the late 1950's and early 1960's, and the major federal programs in housing, redevelopment, urban renewal, and the war on poverty, dramatically signaled the broadening of community work practice. This, the third period, might be characterized as a "Time of Ferment."

In the 1950's came the damning realization that although the programs of the New Deal had aided the stable working class, which constituted a major component of the New Deal's constituency, they had failed to cope with the impact of major social problems of poverty, dependency, discrimination, and unemployment on many population groups. During this period, evidence began to mount that the redevelopment and urban renewal programs begun in the late 1940's were creating newer and greater social problems in their wake, just as the welfare, educational, and correctional systems also seemed to have created almost as many problems as they had been designed to solve.

A vast array of social programs and several new models of community organization emerged in the 1960's. Methods of "grass roots"

[8] Robert P. Lane, "The Field of Community Organization," *Proceedings, National Conference of Social Work, 1939* (New York: Columbia University Press, 1939).

[9] Murray G. Ross, *Community Organization: Theory and Principles* (New York: Harpers, 1955).

organization and "organizing the unaffiliated" were developed at Mobilization for Youth, the delinquency project which served as a model for the Community Action Program of the war on poverty. In the same period Saul Alinsky's model of the "Peoples' Organization," using conflict and confrontation tactics which had been developed by him a quarter century earlier, achieved voguishness among many organizations. Experience with "new careers" programs, whereby subprofessional positions in social services were created for the poor, accumulated rapidly. And with the advent of the poverty program in the middle sixties, the notion of the participation of the poor turned many organizers to policy development and program planning as points at which the increased mobilization of the poor would have effect. Many of these efforts represented the beginning attempts at a renewal of participation in planning, and often took the form of separatist organizations in competition with the established public and private community agencies.

City planners, community workers, and personnel of social welfare agencies came together to undertake joint planning in some of these newer attempts at community organization. The Model Cities Program, at least in conception, attempted to bring together the values of participation, expertise, and leadership. That is, by statute, the program required that cities "provide (for) widespread citizen participation in the program, make maximum possible use of new and improved technology and design . . . and programming systems" and that the administrative instrumentality, the City Demonstration Agency, be established by the local governing body of the city or county.[10]

In essence, the Model Cities program created an arena in which some especially difficult issues in planning in urban communities could be dealt with. Here, for the first time, was a planning mechanism through which residents of low income areas, emerging leadership (usually militants), technicians, city government, and established agencies could confront one another directly on issues of allocation of resources, centralization vs. decentralization, desegregation vs.

[10] Demonstration Cities and Metropolitan Development Act of 1966, Public Law 89–754, *Title I-Comprehensive City Demonstration Programs.*

ethnic communality, and so forth. The mechanism established a clear-cut means of communication among these actors and also brought a greater degree of equalization of the resources needed for planning among them.

In this context, it should not be at all surprising that in most instances the first encounters among the participants in planning were nasty and brief. Although the Department of Housing and Urban Development had general notions of who should be included in planning, no model existed of the processes by which to organize a planning system that could deal with the vastly divergent interests, values, and perceptions the participating actors brought to the planning effort.

The somewhat paradoxical emphasis on both self-help and institutional reorganization in this era was fed by several streams of thought. First, there was the developing theory concerning community power, along with the incorporation of organizational theory into community work practice. Second, the confrontation of racial and social class differences as a reality of American life was made inescapable by the civil rights movement. Martin Luther King, Jr.'s introduction of Gandhian conceptions of nonviolent resistance and civil disobedience was a major influence on the tactics of community work. Another was the style and tactics of Alinsky whose name had been anathema to intergroup relations workers for over 20 years. But with the advent of social ferment, civil rights organizers and others in community work found some of his organizing techniques useful in engaging the interests and energies of masses of unorganized ghetto dwellers.

Community development, which had been practiced in industrially underdeveloped countries and in rural areas of the United States, provided another source of practice knowledge for work with urban problems. After World War II, a vast number of community-based efforts were undertaken in the newly developing countries, many of which had been under colonial rule, as an organized attempt to overcome apathy through self-help and as a way of changing living conditions. In urban areas, this form of practice is utilized to develop a sense of community and solidarity, and to build mechanisms by which to encourage citizen self-help through participation.

In recent years the major contributions to the knowledge base of community organization practice have come from the theories of community structure and power, and analysis of organizational behavior. In contrast, both Saul Alinsky and the community development professionals operate largely on the basis of general principles, value considerations, and some operational instructions, which they induce from practice. In both cases, theory is not made explicit and is therefore weak. The first, Alinsky's, is supported by an ideology which says something like: "All groups are moved by self-interest, the poor and nonpoor alike; as soon as the poor and victimized learn to see it that way they'll be able to get power and control their destiny."[11] The community development view, equally doctrinaire, but relying more heavily on educational techniques and supported by a view which sees the appropriate mechanism for community change as a sort of neo-populist democracy, might be paraphrased as follows: "Most people are good and will cooperate in helping to change society; if one can release that goodness, the community will be able to deal with its problems." [12] Empirical evidence for the effectiveness of either of these approaches to organizing and planning is lacking and will have to wait upon systematic evaluation of these practice principles. To date, the large mobilization programs, Alinsky's Industrial Areas Foundation, community development, and the organizing and planning efforts growing out of the war on poverty and similar federal programs have made limited contributions on which to base theories of practice.

COMMUNITY WORK AND URBAN
DEVELOPMENTS

Every model of practice carries some view of the community which guides the practitioner, although it is often implicit and not well understood by those who use it. So, for example, in the traditional so-

---

[11] Saul Alinsky, *Reveille for Radicals* (Chicago: University of Chicago Press, 1946; reprinted by Vintage Books, 1969).

[12] William W. Biddle, *The Community Development Process* (New York: Holt, Rinehart and Winston, 1965).

cial planning model of the health and welfare councils, the "community" was frequently considered that social system to which the welfare councils had reference. Noncontroversial and noninflammatory issues tended to be addressed, since these held a higher potential for resolution among the more elite sections of the philanthropic and welfare community. Essentially, this constitutes a view of community organizing that is well suited to a congenial small town America or to some homogeneous sections of urban areas.

Similarly, the point of view implicit in the community development model is limited by its conception of the community as having identifiable geographic boundaries, as well as being homogeneous and underdeveloped. The Alinsky approach is a conceptualization of the community divided along social class lines, and Black Power advocates operate with the notion of the community as a "people" united by their common historical and ethnic experience. All of these are potentially useful ways to understand the meaning of "community," provided the organizer is aware of his conceptions, and is able to assess them in the context of current community trends and problems.

Contemporary community organization practice, as it is defined and described in the next chapter, is shaped by some of the forces which have been and are at work in urban America. The comments about trends which follow are not intended to be a definitive critique of the urban community—rather, they identify factors which are of particular salience in understanding the process and practice of community organization as explicated in this volume.

Three sets of factors are most important in this regard. One is the increase of publicly supported services in contrast to privately sponsored ones. A second factor is the pattern of growth of the American urban community; and the third is the differentials in social and political power which are at the base of a revolution in human relations.

PRIVATE PHILANTHROPY VS. PUBLIC PROGRAMS

The earlier model of community organization was based on a conception of the welfare community as a union of voluntary philanthropic services, and, prior to 1935, the role of private agencies in comparison to statutory programs in social welfare was considerably more significant than it is today. However, since the advent of the New Deal, the great bulk of the programs upon which the citizenry depend for their survival are publicly supported programs. Public expenditures for health, education, and welfare services were twenty-five times greater in 1967 than in 1929,[13] and the increase of public over private spending in public programs continues apace.

This shift in the sources of support for services and programs is the basic underlying cause of three interrelated characteristics of the American community that have influenced conceptions of organizing: (1) the increase of political decisions which affect people over personal/marketing decisions; (2) the growth of bureaucratic organizations; and (3) the increased development of "vertical" decision-making structures over "horizontal" ones.

Political Decisions vs. Market Decisions. As an increasing number of needs are met through public services, fewer of the decisions people make are personal and more of them become political.[14] That is, in a simpler society, each man and each family negotiate their own contracts for housing, medical care, recreation, employment, care of the needy and education. These are "market" decisions, in that each man "shops around" to find the best arrangements for himself and his family. But as societies become more complex, more of these decisions are made politically. That is, one man, or a small group of men, decides what kinds of arrangements can be made with doctors for all of us, or what kinds of housing shall be built in the city, or what kinds of welfare benefits the poor shall receive. There is only one Medicare program, one public school system, and one department of public welfare for each community. If citizens are to have a role in affecting the ways in which their needs are met in such a system, they must be able to participate in the political process by which these decisions are made. And although programmatic schemes have been advanced to reintroduce the "market" into social

[13] Pearl Peerbloom, "Major Trends in Health, Education, and Welfare," *Trends:* Part 1. National Trends (U.S. Department of Health, Education, and Welfare, U.S. Government Printing Office, Washington, D.C., 1967), p. 22.

[14] Sir Goeffrey Vickers, *The Art of Judgment: A Study of Policy Making* (New York: Basic Books, 1965), pp. 122–34.

welfare programs (e.g., an educational voucher system), decisions about these programs must be made in a political context.

While the political system is complex in all countries, it is a particularly difficult one to master in the United States because of our unique system of government. The jurisdiction over programs and services organized to meet the needs of people are distributed among municipal, county, state, and federal governments, in addition to specialized governmental units like school districts, housing authorities, and regional and metropolitan governments. Some services are under the exclusive jurisdiction of one level of government in some places and under another or several levels of government in other places. And the powers of any one particular level of government vary from program to program. Thus, in 1967, it was estimated that there were approximately 105,000 units of government in the United States.[15] This is a modest count and does not include many kinds of governmental agencies such as semiautonomous "authorities" and other special agencies.

Most of the benefits of programs which are available to the citizen under this system are statutorily defined legal entitlements. These legal-political arrangements provide a complicated system of remedies for dealing with grievances and inequities. That is, the dissatisfied consumer of services may use administrative appeal (through the executive system); he may seek the intervention of the courts (through the judicial system); or he may seek to change the law (through the legislative system). Community action, ultimately, aims to effect change through one or the other of these systems. Regardless of how community organizations begin their work, whether with demonstrations, public meetings, voter registration campaigns, or sewing circles, if change is to occur in the organization of community resources, community groups will have to succeed in utilizing one of these systems to achieve the change. The organizer, then, must guide the community group in moving toward the appropriate systems for achieving change.

The community organizer of the traditional school brought a dis-

[15] U.S. Department of Commerce, *Statistical Abstract of the United States, 1969* (Superintendent of Documents, U.S. Government Printing Office, Washington, D.C., 1969), pp. 405–6.

tinctively apolitical orientation to the question of the political nature of the decisions that affect peoples' lives. His view was that the electoral process provided the citizen with the opportunity to express his wishes in regard to public policy. Unrecognized were the number of factors which we have already mentioned which militate against the achievement of democracy in this classical sense, plus some other factors. For one thing, the representative process is often nonrepresentative, as tellingly illustrated by Adam Walinsky in the following quotation:

> Who . . . exercises "control" through the representative process? In the Bedford-Stuyvesant ghetto of New York there are 450,000 people. . . . Yet the area has only one high school, and 80 per cent of its teen-agers are drop-outs; the infant mortality rate is twice the national average; there are over 8000 buildings abandoned by everyone but the rats, yet the area received not one dollar of urban renewal funds during the entire first 15 years of that program's operation. . . .
>
> Clearly, Bedford-Stuyvesant has some special needs; yet it has been lost in the midst of the city's eight million. . . . In what sense can the representative system be said to have "spoken for" this community, during the long years of neglect and decay? [16]

Furthermore, even where communities are represented by a legislator (as Bedford-Stuyvesant accomplished through legal action), elections deal with a wide spectrum of issues, and the legislative process is protracted and complicated. For another thing, since authority is distributed among many units, the proper redress of grievances may be along any one of several lines of intervention, for example, an adminstrative rather than electoral route.

The conception of democracy in which the individual citizen makes his wishes known to his congressman, while not completely without value, is an oversimplification of how social policy can in fact be affected. It is through voluntary organizations—unions, civil rights groups, ethnic organizations, professional associations, and so forth —that the individual citizen exerts influence upon the legislative and

---

[16] Adam Walinsky, "Review of *Maximum Feasible Misunderstanding*," by Daniel P. Moynihan, *New York Times Book Review*, February 2, 1969, as quoted by Sherry R. Arnstein, "A Ladder of Citizen Participation," *Journal of the American Institute of Planners*, Vol. XXXV, No. 4 (July 1969), pp. 223–24.

elective processes. Thus, if citizens are to have even a modest effect upon the direction of social policy, they require organization. But to organize to affect political decisions—to build political leadership—is a long-term, arduous process requiring a depth of commitment which is, unfortunately, not characteristic of American social reform movements.

Growth of Bureaucracies. The delivery of publicly sponsored services to large numbers of people has resulted in the vast expansion of bureaucratic systems. Bureaucracies characteristically operate according to routine procedures that minimize personal response and preclude treatment of individuals as "special cases." To maximize reliability and efficiency, they are hierarchically organized, with each worker responsible to some other worker at a higher level. They encourage professionalization and specialization of function, so that organizational positions are filled on the basis of educational credentials or experience.[17]

Each characteristic of bureaucratic organization represents a potential disadvantage to the unorganized. For example, inflexible procedures, and authority diffused through a complicated and faceless organizational hierarchy, present serious difficulties for persons who need assistance with problems of living. These organizational characteristics pose formidable barriers for anyone, but particularly for people who do not have the knowledge, the time, and the style of life to negotiate their complexities. Thus, for some people and in some circumstances, bureaucracy is an inefficient mode of organization.

Hannah Arendt was not referring specifically to bureaucracy's impact upon the poor when she described it as the most formidable form of dominion:

The rule, by an intricate system of bureaus in which no men, neither one nor the best, neither the few nor the many can be held responsible . . . could be properly called the rule by Nobody. Indeed, if we identify tryanny as the government that is not held to give account of itself, rule by Nobody is clearly the most tyrannical of all, since there is no one left who could even be asked to answer for what is being done.[18]

[17] Robert K. Merton, *Social Theory and Social Structure* (New York: Free Press, 1957), pp. 195–206.

[18] Hannah Arendt, "Reflections on Violence," *New York Review of Books,* February 27, 1969, p. 23.

How much more imposing, then, is it to the people who depend on the bureaucracy for their very existence? The defensiveness and self-protectiveness which bureaucratic structure encourages has been well documented. In interaction with the poor, the least well-regarded segment of society, these strains are intensified. Policy challenges by impoverished persons, however weak and fleeting, call forth intense reaction and powerful counterattack.

Bureaucracies do, of course, function with greater or lesser equity and compassion. When they deliver the kinds of services people need or expect, they are rarely subject to the usual epithets, for example, "red tape," "hardening of the categories," "petty bureaucrats." When they do not, they frequently become the focus of movements for change. Comparisons of the Social Security Administration with departments of public welfare, for example, show the former to be highly regarded by its clients, while the latter is viewed with antipathy. The reasons for this go beyond the question of organizational factors by themselves. That is, the functioning of the respective organizations is related to the kinds of clientele they serve, societal attitudes toward social insurance versus attitudes toward public assistance, and the sociopolitical forces which act upon these organizations.

But there are characteristics shared by all large organizations that are supposed to meet the needs of citizens—the legally complicated and delicate balance between statutory authority and administrative discretion, the fact that they are administered by persons who are frequently unresponsive to the life styles and behaviors of the consumers of the service, and the fact that authority is vested in a complex legal-political system, control over which requires enormous financial, organizational, and technical resources. Therefore, when bureaucratic policy and program create dissatisfactions among their clients, there are significant barriers to applying corrective measures which are related to the nature of bureaucratic organization.

"Vertical" and "Horizontal" Decision-Making Structures. The traditional view of community organization, exemplified in the health and welfare councils, is based on the conception of the community as a local geographical entity, usually a city, in which various functional units come together for cooperative planning. Thus, in dealing with

the needs of an aging population, those agencies concerned with health, welfare, recreation, counseling and vocational guidance meet to work out ways to solve problems, with each agency making its unique contribution in expertise and resources. This is what Warren has called the "horizontal" community.[19] Implicitly, it is a conception of the community as a self-contained unit able to deal with all or most of its needs. However, in our complex society there has developed what Warren calls the "vertical" community structure. For any specific social function, whether employment, housing, social control, or medical care, there are many extracommunity agencies through which resources are distributed and authority assigned. For example, in regard to problems of aging, there may be local agencies which are concerned with the problem as well as county, state, and federal agencies.

Vertical patterns of planning and community organization are not new on the American scene but the attempt to deal with problems vertically has increased markedly through such structures as the President's Committee on Juvenile Delinquency and Youth Crime and the Office of Economic Opportunity. Between 1960 and 1970 nearly 100 new programs affecting urban communities were enacted by Congress, and two new departments and one new addition to the Office of the President had been created. The proliferation of such programs has been so rapid and vast that even today most urban communities do not have an inventory of the federal programs which operate within them.[20]

In a sense, what appears to have taken place is that the "mountain decided to go to Mohammed." The older forms of community work did not create the vertical organization whereby significant numbers of people in the core cities of metropolitan areas could utilize the resources of the federal government to change their life situations. In the absence of such organization, the federal government evolved new structures for doing this. The process by which these forms developed seems clear only in retrospect. Undoubtedly,

[19] Roland L. Warren, *The Community in America* (Chicago: Rand McNally, 1963), pp. 240–44.

[20] Federal Executive Board, Oakland Task Force, *An Analysis of Federal Decision-Making and Impact, The Federal Government in Oakland* (San Francisco: Federal Executive Board, 1968), pp. 3–5.

it was politically motivated, a reflection of the national administration's desire to reach beyond the states to its constituency in the cities. But the actual process was neither smooth nor clear, and it is certainly not complete.

PATTERNS OF GROWTH OF THE URBAN COMMUNITY

A second major factor which has influenced contemporary community organization practice has been the pattern of growth of the urban community. The city has been, for hundreds of years, a place of entry. As each new minority group arrived in this country, large numbers of them settled in the cities. Each had to fight, in its own way, for its place in the city's social and economic life.[21] It is not our purpose to recount here these successive adjustments of immigrant groups. But the conditions which immigrants confronted when they came to the cities in recent decades have made their problems of adjustment different from those of preceding groups. Earlier waves of immigrants arrived during periods when the economy was expanding at a rapid rate, and the need for unskilled workers was great.

Second, more recent waves of immigrants to metropolitan areas have been black and Spanish-speaking people. These in-migrants are not new Americans, but rather Americans moving within the country, largely to improve their social and economic opportunities. They differ from earlier arrivals to the city in several important (and tension-producing) respects. They are dark-skinned people, which in the light of the racism rooted in the American heritage makes them the victims of social and economic discrimination. The evidence that American institutions have developed standards, procedures, and rigidities which effectively discriminate against blacks and other minorities is so extensive as to need no citation. It has been put this way by one government-commissioned report:

It was as if a cruel joke had been played; the most liberally enshrined features of democracy served to block (black) aspirations to equality— local rule, trade unionism, referendums, the jury system, the neighborhood school. And to complete the irony, perhaps, the most elitist aspect of the constitutional system—the Supreme Court—was for a time the cutting edge of the established quest for equality, for which it came under populist fire.[22]

[21] Oscar Handlin, *The Uprooted*, (New York: Grosset and Dunlap, 1951).
[22] Skolnick, *Politics of Protest*, pp. 133–34.

In addition to discrimination, which itself makes the assimilation of these in-migrants into the mainstream a formidable task, the newcomers tend to come from rural backgrounds without the knowledge and skill to negotiate the urban environment. Moreover, as the economy develops ever more complex technology, mobility from unskilled labor to positions of higher socioeconomic status become more difficult to achieve. As unskilled jobs are eliminated, their occupants are left in a dependent status and must rely on the public welfare system for their means of sustenance. The inadequacies of our system of income maintenance and its impact upon the lives of the poor have been well documented.[23]

DIFFERENTIALS IN SOCIAL AND POLITICAL POWER

The last two decades have shocked American conscience and complacency. There was for many, perhaps a majority, of Americans a high degree of exhilaration initially in these shocks because the desire for social justice and the belief in our government's ability to deliver it run deep. But by the mid-1960's, much of this inspiration had turned into fear or despair with the realization that much of the poverty and social injustice from which many people suffer is supported by institutional arrangements from which others receive cherished benefits. The reasoned plea for redress of grievances fast became a white-hot anger in response to the intransigence of an unyielding system.

Change had been easy to consider only so long as it appeared that it would not have to be *us* that changed. The mixing of heretofore separated populations in the educational system, the replacement of a punitive and degrading welfare system with one which provided acceptable levels of living in a dignified way, the provision of decent and integrated housing, the guarantee of a job at an adequate wage for all those able and willing to work—the kinds of changes that spoke to what was wrong in America—all called for solutions that were far too radical for many Americans. And once the lid was off, there were many other groups besides the blacks and the poor who

[23] For example, see Herman Miller, *Rich Man Poor Man* (New York: Thomas Y. Crowell, 1964); and Jacobus tenBroek, ed., *The Law of the Poor* (San Francisco: Chandler, 1966).

saw and demanded changes in the injustices in their lives. Students, peace supporters, feminists, drug users, homosexuals, and others joined in what has become a general revolution in human relations, often in concert with the minorities. Each of these groups has a "backlash" counterpart composed of people who view the demand being made for change as unreasonable, immoral, or unpatriotic. Parents for Neighborhood Schools, the Minute Men, the John Birch Society, as well as the unorganized individuals of the "Great Silent Majority," mobilized in different degrees in response to demands for change. They too must be taken account of here as the counterrevolution in human relations.

The earlier model of community organization, the Health and Welfare Council, was based upon the belief that when people came to the round table of the community, they came as equals engaged in an enterprise which all recognized as useful and good. In an atmosphere of reasoned debate, mutual respect, and belief in the possibility of mutually satisfactory solutions to problems, the representatives of the community could work together.

However, the issues of the revolution in human relations challenge all of these assumptions. Those who were sitting at the table were *not* seen as representatives of any but specialized and select community interests. There were many people who never got to the table. When they did get there, they perceived that the planning was not so much in the "public interest" as in the interests of those who had money, power, and prestige. And the methods used by highly trained technicians, reasoned study and analysis of problems, were seen as methods used to serve the privileged of corporate America.

*   *   *

In contemporary community organizing, none of the values of participation, expertise, and leadership can be neglected. However contradictory these values may be, the organizer must, in our view, confront and resolve the dilemmas created by role responsibilities in which all three are manifest. He is called upon to be a "political" organizer, an expert, and an administrator. As organizer, he is concerned with the development of his constituency and the means by which

their interests are protected and advanced (i.e., the value of participation); as expert, he focuses on the tasks of organization building,
studying problems, developing strategies, and devising programs; and
as administrator, he undertakes the tasks of executive leadership
which are required if organizations are to grow and prosper. Staff
must be hired and trained, responsibilities delegated, operational
decisions made, and so forth.

Among the multitude of present-day social problems to which
these activities and values of community organization may be
directed—for example, racial discrimination, imperialism, war, the
liberation of women, ecology—one promises to endure beyond any
of the current movements for social change. This is the problem
which Arendt calls the "rule by Nobody," that is, depersonalization
of indispensable services through their organization in complex and
faceless bureaucracies. As long ago as 1887, Woodrow Wilson characterized the problem of large government as follows:

Like a lusty child, government with us has expanded in nature and grown
in stature, but has also become awkward in movement. The vigor and increase of its life has been altogether out of proportion to its skill in living. It has gained strength, but it has not acquired deportment.[24]

Wilson's words, as applicable today as when they were written,
will undoubtedly hold true in 1984 and after. Modern man cannot
live without the great organizations he has created but which simultaneously threaten his individuality and independence. All of the
community programs to which we have referred in this chapter—the
Office of Economic Opportunity, Model Cities, and so on—are essentially organizational efforts by which people attempt to deal with
the problems of living with organizations. It is not untoward, in such
a circumstance, to define a role for the state in protecting citizens
from the inequities of government itself. Nor is it surprising that the
age of the specialist and the bureaucrat should spawn programs in
which one specialist-bureaucrat (e.g., the organizer) defends people
against the power of other specialist-bureaucrats. In any case, it is

[24] Woodrow Wilson, "The Study of Administration," *Political Science Quarterly,* Vol. 56 (December 1941), p. 487.

because the problem of the complexity and facelessness of service-providing organizations is a major one, and likely to be enduring, that we accord it a central location as we define community work in the next chapter and detail its processes in succeeding portions of this volume.

CHAPTER TWO

DEFINING COMMUNITY WORK: PEOPLE, PROBLEMS, AND PARTICIPATION

DEFINING COMMUNITY ORGANIZATION is a mandatory, if unrewarding, activity. Widespread usage prescribes the use of certain words, although the words themselves are imprecise or at levels of abstraction which defy empirical referent. We use "community organization" and "community work" interchangeably, for example, but the word "community" may represent a multiplicity of levels of social organization with which organizers work. Their primary concern may be one small group in interaction with a single official. Or their practice may focus on an organization, a neighborhood, an institution, a community, or larger entity, such as a region or state.

Furthermore, the range of community organization practice, as it emerged in the 1960's, is too diverse for accurate categorization. Rothman, for example, has identified three distinct types which he calls "locality development," "social action," and "social planning." [1] Briefly, they may be described as follows:

Locality development typifies the methods of work with community groups used by settlement houses and in overseas community de-

[1] Jack Rothman, "Three Models of Community Organization Practice," *Social Work Practice 1968* (New York: Columbia University Press, 1968), pp. 16–47.

velopment work. A major focus is on the *process* of community building. Working with a broad, representative cross section of the community, the worker attempts to achieve change objectives by enabling the community to establish consensus via the identification of common interests. Leadership development and the education of the participants are important elements in the process. In this approach, great store is set by the values of both participation and leadership.

Social action is employed by groups and organizations which seek to alter institutional policies or to make changes in the distribution of power. Civil rights groups and social movements are examples. The participants are often some population group that feels disadvantaged by the institutional system it is trying to change, such as welfare mothers, tenants in public housing, or blacks. Their methods may be, often are, abrasive, and participation is the value most clearly articulated by those who use this approach. Both leadership and expertise may be challenged as the symbolic "enemies of the people."

Social planning is the method of community organization traditional to health and welfare councils, although its scope and arena were enlarged in the 1960's to encompass city planners, urban renewal authorities, and the large public bureaucracies. Effort is focused primarily on task goals and issues of resource allocation. Whereas the initial emphasis of this approach was on the coordination of social services, its attention has expanded to include program development and planning in all major social welfare institutions, for example, housing, public health, and education. Heavy reliance is placed on rational problem solving and the use of technical methods, such as research and systems analysis. Expertise is the cherished value in this approach, although leadership is accorded importance as well.

Rothman recognizes that he has drawn analytic extremes. The three models overlap, and within each there is considerable divergence. Thus any definition of community organization which is inclusive of these approaches must cast a wide net. With this qualification, we venture the following definition: *Community organization is a method of intervention whereby individuals, groups, and organizations engage in planned action to influence social problems. It is con-*

cerned with the enrichment, development, and/or change of social institutions, and involves two major related processes: planning (that is, identifying problem areas, diagnosing causes, and formulating solutions) and organizing (that is, developing the constituencies and devising the strategies necessary to effect action).

An inclusive definition has the disadvantage of its advantages. It incorporates diverse practices, and permits shifts in practice emphases as social circumstances and strategies change. But in including much, it excludes too little, so that the uniqueness of community work becomes partially blurred. For example, organizing is concerned with constituency development, but the constituency may be as diverse as the poor, ethnic Middle Americans, citizens-at-large, professionals with a stake in particular service outcomes, or other individuals or groups with interests to protect or promote. Organizing addresses a broad range of problems, and includes goals inhering in the values of process, as well as the achievement of task objectives. It employs widely varying tactics, ranging from the consensual to the conflictual, and the technical to the interactional, and such specific techniques as fact finding and research, program and policy analysis, legislative review and promotion, political maneuvering and pressure, fund raising, public interpretation, and administration.

To provide a focus for a discussion of community organization practice, then, requires a specification of the particular form or model of community work one has in mind. The focus of our interest in this volume is circumscribed by three elements: the nature of the participants, the type of problem, and the means used to reach objectives. That is, the priorities of our attention are on people as consumers of social welfare services, on the problems which stem from their interaction with social welfare institutions, and in their participation as a means of influencing these problems.

Much of what follows in subsequent chapters about the process and method of community organization, the influence of sponsoring agencies, and the tactics which may be employed is generic to all community organization—and indeed, in some measure to all of social work. Nevertheless, our concern with the participation of service consumers to deal with service institutions is purposely limiting. It is designed to give shape to our discussion of practice.

THE PARTICIPANTS

Our primary interest is in persons as they fill the social role of service users. Thus one boundary of community work, as it is discussed in this book, is its attention to people principally in their capacity as consumers of social welfare services.

Social role (that is, shared expectations concerning the behavior of persons who occupy particular positions, and the mutually understood rights and obligations which go along with these positions) is a significant analytic tool. Klein suggests its importance in community mental health:

. . . . It is at least as important to be familiar with the role of the superintendent [of schools] in modern American communities as to be aware of (a) particular superintendent's personality and characteristic ways of coping. For it is the *role* of the superintendent . . . that will determine, far more than will his personality, the ways in which he can respond to the mental health field.[2]

Since one's role is necessarily defined in relation to others in related positions, the concept is particularly relevant for community work in that it provides a link between the individual and the social structure. Its use may be illustrated by reference to the institution of education.[3] The notion that underachievement in the schools inheres in a social role which allows the underachiever relatively few privileges or rewards and subjects him to many constraints draws attention away from the singular personal characteristics of the student to

[2] Donald C. Klein, *Community Dynamics and Mental Health* (New York: Wiley, 1968), p. 35. (Emphasis in original)

[3] We use the term "institution" to refer to the system of patterned relationships through which a collectivity meets enduring needs, e.g., for education, production, consumption, distribution, social control, etc. "Institution" is sometimes used to connote a particular agency, e.g., "mental institution," and currently the term "alternative institutions" refers to experimental and innovative programs for meeting societal needs. Our usage is broader; thus, in discussing the educational institution, we mean the socially defined and patterned roles of teacher, pupil, parent, administrator, and others germane to a community's means of educating its young rather than to a specific school or program.

the social structure of which the student is a part. The distribution of power and rewards among the various actors in the social structure then becomes the salient variable. Some of the problems of the education system may be *manifest* in such conditions as underachievement or the disruptive behavior of children, but the arrangement of social roles within the institution may be the *source* of the problem.

We do not, by the above, suggest that the cause of problems is necessarily structural. Emotional "disturbance," family breakdown, *or* role arrangements within the institution may singly or in combination account for underachievement. The community worker's focus on the person as service user, however, requires that he sort out, for himself and his constituency, which problems are individual and idiosyncratic since these are of secondary concern to his function as an organizer. His primary focus is the role relationships of the actors in agency and institutional systems—the clients, agency personnel, policy makers, and community reference groups.

Our interest in the social role of service user is not bound by social class. The white worker, the lower middle-class homeowner, the black bourgeois, the middle-class student, the handicapped and the ill, all of these and others are the recipients of service in addition to the poor, and may constitute the focal point of organizing in our community work model. The possibility of successful action is increased, as a matter of fact, when common alliances can be forged between the poor and some of these others.

In so stating, we do not wish to imply that each does not have problems which are unique to their own role and status. The poor, particularly, are disadvantaged by the fact that in our individualistic society personal worth tends to be equated with material success, and this ethos permeates service giving. How the role of service user is defined, whether as citizen, consumer, patient, client, or victim, shapes how he is expected to behave, defines the "appropriate" responses of others to him, and limits the kind and quality of services to which he is "entitled." Few would quarrel, for example, with the observation of Keith-Lucas that

Persons who find themselves impelled to receive government assistance are not in general, or at least always, considered to have the same political and social rights as those who can provide for themselves and their families from their own economic effort and resources.[4]

Indeed, Briar has demonstrated that a majority of welfare recipients share the larger community's pejorative view of clients.[5]

Who it is that is considered to be poor is subject to relative social definitions. Although the absence of sufficient funds is the characteristic which defines the poor in this country, there are many persons of low income who are excluded from this definition. Thus college students and clergymen, because they live on small incomes only temporarily or because they *choose* a life of poverty are not perceived to be disadvantaged. Furthermore, even if level of income served as a precise indicator, it would obscure the fact that, like every other part of the urban community, the poor are not one solidary group. They are persons of varying ages, education, ethnic and racial backgrounds, who are beset by differing problems, whose differences often pose a major barrier to organizing.[6]

Nor do demographic differences exhaust the variations among subgroups of the poor. Although attitudinal differences are more difficult to define and identify, a wide diversity of world views exists even within demographically homogeneous populations. Thus, some poor are more alienated than others, some more upwardly aspiring, some angrier. Where they fall on these dimensions has a bearing on whether and in what types of organizing they will become involved.

[4] Alan Keith-Lucas, *Decisions about People in Need* (Chapel Hill: University of North Carolina Press, 1957), p. vii.

[5] Scott Briar, "Welfare from Below: Recipients' Views of the Public Welfare System," in Jacobus tenBroek, ed., *The Law of the Poor* (San Francisco: Chandler, 1966), pp. 46–61.

[6] To cite one example: Nearly half of all the people living under the Council of Economic Advisors' defined level of poverty are children. Burns reports, however, that of all these children, 3.5 million were receiving support from the Aid to Families with Dependent Children program, whereas 5 million were in families headed by a wage earner who was fully employed the previous year. Eveline M. Burns, "Childhood Poverty and the Children's Allowance," *Children's Allowances and the Economic Welfare of Children* (New York: Citizen's Committee for Children, 1968), p. 3. Obviously, those children who were poor *after* family incomes had been supplemented by public assistance and those who, though as poor, did not receive assistance, face different problems and develop different attitudes.

The proposition that different goals, issues, and programs attract and/or select a different clientele is a simple one. It tends to be overlooked, however as, for example, in the controversy within community social work regarding the extent to which a worker or agency may properly suggest or define the issue or program. The following statement from a community organization text thus obscures an important social fact:

(The worker does not) have the right, nor should he wish, to impose his conception of need or objective, nor to ask that it be explored to any greater extent than that of any problem, discontent, or objective suggested by any other individual in the community.[7]

Neglected in the statement is the fact that choice of problem, discontent, or objective effectively determines who in the community will or will not participate in the community work program.

THE PROBLEM

"To make an impact on social problems," as the definition of community organization directs, offers only a minimal limit to the practice arena. The focus may be sharpened, however, by reference to the developments in urban America which were noted in Chapter 1: the contraction of the free market, the increasing dependence on "political" as opposed to "market" decisions, the complexities of the political-administrative system, the pervasiveness and power of bureaucratic organizations, and the difficulties of understanding, negotiating, and managing these large-scale systems.

We are not—we hasten to note—so presumptuous as to suggest that the community organization method can solve the manifold problems of the urban milieu. Indeed, it is because we believe that community work can most effectively address problems of limited scope (or it may address larger problems only in their partial manifestation) that we believe it necessary to set priorities. A balance between problems which are consequential and those which are amena-

[7] Murray G. Ross, *Community Organization: Theory and Principles* (New York: Harper and Row, 1955), pp. 202–3.

ble to intervention is necessary, if only to protect practitioners from either excessive fantasy or frustration.

The problems of service users in their interaction with service-giving institutions constitutes a focal point of consequences for community work intervention.[8] The chairman of Great Britain's Citizen's Advice Bureaux defines these as crucial problems:

Protection of the individual is the heart of the matter in present day society. . . . People are faced with . . . a world in which impersonal forces operate over which they have no control—a vast complex of communal regulations that impinge on their lives. . . . We must give strength to the private individual even as we give the state a larger share of the responsibility.[9]

Our concern with the strength of the individual extends to the kinds and quality of services which are made available to him. The responsiveness of the institutions to the service user's needs—the protection of his rights—and his ability to use the services which are offered constitute related areas of interest. Central to strengthening the individual, as well, is his felt capacity to influence the decisions which shape his life.

We exclude from the above those problems that, as suggested earlier, are personal and idiosyncratic, not because they are unimportant, but because they lend themselves more appropriately to other forms of intervention. The distinction set forth by C. Wright Mills is relevant in this regard. He observed that:

Troubles . . . properly lie within the individual as a biographical entity and within the scope of his immediate milieu. . . .

Issues have to do with matters that transcend . . . the individual and the range of his inner life. They have to do with the organization of

[8] Although our primary attention is to public services, we do not mean by this to exclude the voluntary agency from our purview. They use "voluntary" dollars, true, but these are tax-exempt dollars, the large part of which are monies that have been channeled away from the public treasury. The public, rightfully, can and does establish the conditions of their use, i.e., as incorporated entities they are required to meet State specifications and must also adhere, in their internal operations, to constitutions and by-laws.

[9] Quoted in Mildred Zucker, "Citizen's Advice Bureaux," a paper presented for the Conference on the Extension of Legal Services to the Poor," Washington, D.C., November 1964, p. 1. (Mimeographed)

many such milieus into the institutions of a . . . society as a whole . . .
An issue is a public matter. . . .[10]

In the Mills context, the task of community work is to convert the
problems of service users from "private troubles" into "public issues."

CITIZEN PARTICIPATION

The participation of service users in institutional decision making is
one means of promoting consumer needs and protecting consumer interests. There are, we recognize, other methods as well, and we will
not argue here that participation is necessarily the most effective one.
It is, however, an underpinning of the mode of practice with which
this volume is concerned.

The concept of citizen participation emerged as the major idea, the
prized value, the great nuisance, and the center of interest of the war
against poverty and other social legislation of the late 1960's. Cu-
riously, however, this word about which so much has been written
and so many battles fought has been poorly defined by most who entered the lists to champion one or another view of it. The reason for
this, of course, is that the concept includes a congeries of ideas and
values. People participate in different degrees, in different roles, and
by different methods in a wide variety of happenings, experiences,
groups, and organizations.

In the remainder of this chapter, we shall describe what we mean
by participation in community work, particularly as the concept relates to the poor. We shall then explore the ways in which the poor
do participate, the degrees of participation which are possible, and
some of the considerations to be made in the allocation of decision-
making authority.

Participation: A Definition. For our purposes, participation refers
*to the means by which people who are not elected or appointed offi-
cials of agencies and of government influence decisions about programs and policies which affect their lives.* The definition excludes
concern with many types of participation, such as the kind that takes

[10] C. Wright Mills, *The Sociological Imagination* (New York: Grove Press,
1961), p. 8.

place within friendship groups and social clubs. Our interest in groups will be limited to the institutional ramifications of participation in them.

We shall discuss the forms and functions of group types bearing on the community work process in a subsequent chapter. We wish now, however, to make reference to one type of organization which is especially pertinent to community work, the *institutional-relations organization*. These are organizations whose major function is to mediate the relations between individuals and institutions. Examples are trade unions, professional associations, civil rights groups, social planning councils, and parent-teacher associations. Boards of education, city councils, and other elected and appointed bodies may also be included, since they too serve as mediating instruments between citizens and social systems. There are, of course, substantial differences in the functions, goals, and legal bases of these institutional-relations organizations. As a result, the ways in which they mediate the relations between individuals and institutions vary considerably. However, although the relationship of each to social change may be different—for example, to encourage reform, maintain the *status quo,* or to promote reaction—all of them function to protect the interests of their constituency vis-à-vis institutions.

A primary goal of community work as a professional process is to increase the capacity of service recipients to use and influence institutional-relations organizations in order to better meet their needs and protect their interests. Most often, this requires recasting the ways in which consumers participate in such organizations— redefining their roles, extending their access to a wider variety of roles within the organization, and increasing their control. This occurs, generally, in two distinct ways: (a) by the creation of *new* institutional-relations organizations, and (b) by organizing within existing ones. In the first instance—the creation of new institutional-relations organizations—groups of people are brought together outside the institutional framework in order to change existing patterns of authority and decision making. Civil rights organizations, community corporations, and neighborhood councils may be viewed as new constellations of community participants who attempt, in different ways, to modify the schools, the hospitals, and the social work agencies. In the second case—organizing within existing institutions—constituents are brought together to create new roles for themselves *within* the institution. Thus parents organized to demand community control of the schools are seeking to change their status within the institutional-relations organizations which make up the educational system.

One criterion for a healthy community is that opportunities for participation in its institutions is equally accessible to all of its social and interest groups. This is one reason why many newly created organizations are not sustained over long periods of time. (There are other reasons too, such as the scarcity of resources.) In effect, many of these organizations are not "the real thing" sought by people in community life. Rather, they are vehicles by which recipients of service strive to influence established institutional-relations organizations or attain meaningful participation in them.

The Participation of the Poor. Researchers have studied participation from two perspectives. One is the association of population characteristics with degrees and kind of participation. The second is the relationship between organizational characteristics and variations in participation.

Membership in voluntary associations is positively related to socioeconomic class, degree of education, and geographic residence.[11] That is, participation in voluntary associations is greater among higher-income persons, the better educated, and those who live in more affluent neighborhoods. Among working-class families, relatives constitute the most important source of relationship. Informal groups, in their rank order of importance to working-class

[11] For example, see the following studies: W. A. Anderson, "Family Social Participation and Social Status Self-Ratings," *American Sociological Review,* Vol. VII, No. 3 (June 1956), pp. 253–58; William G. Mather, "Income and Social Participation," *American Sociological Review,* Vol. VI, No. 3 (June 1941), pp. 380–83; Mirra Komarovsky, "A Comparative Study of Voluntary Organizations of Two Suburban Communities," *Sociological Problems and Methods,* Vol. XXVII, Publication of the American Sociological Society, (1933); Mirra Komarovsky, "The Voluntary Associations of Urban Dwellers," *American Sociological Review,* Vol. XI (December 1946), pp. 686–98; Gerhard E. Lensky, "Social Participation and Status Crystallization," *American Sociological Review,* Vol. XXI, No. 4 (August 1956), pp. 435–39; R. Clyde White, "Social Class Differences in Uses of Leisure," *American Journal of Sociology,* Vol. LXI, No. 2, (1955), pp. 145–50.

people, have been found to be: relatives, friends, neighbors, and co-workers. Among groups with higher status, income, or education, friends replace relatives as the group seen most frequently.[12]

Gans and others have suggested that low-income families meet many of their social and emotional needs in the "peer group," that is, a neighborhood-based type of extended kinship group.[13] Secondary or voluntary associations tend to bypass low-income groups; and because of this, voluntary organizations frequently do not reach their population targets.

Thus much of the literature on participation research has demonstrated that the poor do not participate in formal organizations as frequently as other segments of the population. These analyses, although correct, reflect a serious error in the conception of participation, however. That is, studies of participation, for the most part, count individuals' *voluntary* memberships in organizations, the formal positions they hold, or the number of meetings they attend. Account is not taken of the type of participation which most characterizes that of the poor—that is, *nonvoluntary* participation. The poor are involved in the public schools, welfare departments, departments of public health, the agencies of the correctional system, public housing, and so forth. Their participation in such organizations, although it is time-consuming, active, and enduring, is ordinarily not "voluntary" in the sense that they make the choice to join or attend or are elected. Rather, their participation is required by law or is mandatory for the acquisition of resources necessary to sustain life.

And what is most important about the nature of this active nonvoluntary participation of the poor in institutional-relations organizations is that *they exercise a relatively low degree of influence in or control over organizations in which they participate.* The organizations which occupy their energies and on which they are dependent usually are controlled by people who are *not* poor and are *not* recipients of the organization's services. In voluntary associations, the membership generally perceive (not always correctly) that the or-

[12] Morris Axelrod, "Urban Structure and Social Participation," in Paul K. Hatt and Albert Reiss, Jr., eds., *Cities and Society* (New York: Free Press, 1957), p. 737.

[13] Herbert Gans, *The Urban Villagers* (New York: Free Press, 1962).

ganization belongs to them, and that its officers represent the views of the majority. Similarly, middle-class consumers perceive (again, not always correctly) that the people who operate the public services tend to represent their interests.

This view of participation turns the problem around in an important way. Instead of asking, "Why don't the poor participate like other people?" or "How can they be made to participate like those others?", the question becomes, "*How* do the poor participate, and how can their participation be made of greatest use to them?" The issue then is not merely how to get the poor to participate more actively, but how to make their already active participation more beneficial and meaningful to them.

Degrees of Participation. Obviously, everyone does not participate in organizational decision making to the same degree. Even in the democratic model of the town hall meeting, there is need for a chairman who develops the agenda and conducts the meeting, officers to oversee the implementation of decisions, and staff to carry them out. With the myriad of organizations which impinge on one's life in a complex society, few have the time to become acquainted with the details of these organizations' operations, much less to contribute actively in their conduct of business. Individuals and organizations must make choices about their use of scarce resources.

Degrees of participation may be viewed schematically, as shown on page 39.[14]

Decision-making involvement is the important dimension in the above schema, with the extent of one's participation, as reflected in time spent, secondary. A service recipient may expend considerable time and energy "being informed," for example, and relatively little time in "planning jointly." It is in the latter case, however, that the person's degree of participation is higher, since he has more authority or power.[15]

[14] Material in this schema is adapted from Ralph Kramer, *Community Development in Israel and the Netherlands* (Berkeley: University of California, Institute of International Studies, Research Series 14, 1970), pp. 126–27.

[15] We use "authority" to mean legitimated power, i.e., those formally accepted roles to which the making of decisions and the application of sanctions are assigned. "Power" refers to the ability to affect the actions of others by means of actual or threatened sanctions; in an organizational context, it indicates a degree of control over the valued resources of the organization, e.g., money, staff, and facilities. "Control" is the maximization of power.

DEGREES OF PARTICIPATION, PARTICIPANT'S ACTION,
AND ILLUSTRATIVE MODES FOR ACHIEVING

DEGREE	PARTICIPANT'S ACTION	ILLUSTRATIVE MODE
Low	None	The community is told nothing.
	Receives information	The organization makes a plan and announces it. The community is convened for informational purposes; compliance is expected.
	Is consulted	The organization tries to promote a plan and seeks to develop the support which will facilitate acceptance or give sufficient sanction to the plan so that administrative compliance can be expected.
	Advises	The organization presents a plan and invites questions. It is prepared to modify the plan only if absolutely necessary.
	Plans jointly	The organization presents a tentative plan subject to change and invites recommendations from those affected. It expects to change the plan at least slightly and perhaps even more substantially.
	Has delegated authority	The organization identifies and presents a problem to the community; defines the limits and asks the community to make a series of decisions which can be embodied in a plan which it will accept.
High	Has control	The organization asks the community to identify the problem and to make all of the key decisions regarding goals and means. It is willing to help the community at each step accomplish its own goals, even to the extent of administrative control of the program.

One may conceive a major task of community work to be raising the degree of participation of service users from the low end of the scale (no responsibility for decision making) to the high end (control of decision making). Nevertheless, it is important to note that no single degree of participation is by itself intrinsically positive or negative. That is, "no participation" in one situation may be completely appropriate, whereas "having control" is desirable in another. For example, a tenants' organization has no basis for seeking participation in the affairs of the local religious fraternal association, may only claim representation in the neighborhood council, but legitimately demand delegated authority from the city rehabilitation agency. Or residents of a Model Neighborhood Area may assert the right to control the local City Demonstration Agency, while they expect only to participate in joint planning with the city-wide Human Resources Agency. In considering the degree of participation an organization may seek, therefore, complete control is not, *ipso facto,* to be desired.

Kramer has noted that these different degrees and modes of participation imply:

> . . . a set of implicit purposes or functions . . . that need to be differentiated in practice. . . . Clarity regarding the organizational rationale for seeking participation not only contributes to a more meaningful compact between the staff and clientele, but also helps the professional answer the fundamental questions concerning who should be involved, when, how, and for what purposes? [16]

Within a single organization, one may envision various degrees of consumer participation depending on the nature of the function or task. Of course, informal influence will bend and shape the formal structure, and in the real life of any institution, modifications in decision-making responsibility are more likely to be resolved following contention between the parties at least as much as they follow from considerations of organizational task. Authority is thus at least as apt to reflect the respective power positions of the actors as it does the thoughtful delegation of responsibility (actually more so, we believe). Nevertheless, rational considerations do operate (if most often, only secondarily). Even when a local community wins control over the operations of an institution, and there is a general shift in authority from the central office to the district, the problem of allocating decision-making prerogatives among administration, staff, elected officials, and residents still requires resolution.

Arguments against community control have been summarized as follows:

[16] Kramer, *Community Development in Israel and the Netherlands,* p. 127.

It supports separatism; it creates balkanization of public services; it is more costly and less efficient; it enables minority group "hustlers" to be just as opportunistic and disdainful of the have-nots as their white predecessors; it is incompatible with merit systems and professionalism; and ironically enough, it can turn out to be a new Mickey Mouse game for the have-nots by allowing them to gain control but not allowing them sufficient dollar resources to succeed.[17]

Some of these arguments are more telling than others, but none of them can be dismissed out of hand. Proponents of community control contend, in rebuttal, that conditions could hardly be worse for the inner-city poor than currently exist, and nothing else has worked. One might conclude, with Spiegel, that "neighborhoods can exercise power in a good many instances, control in some, but must occupy a subsidiary role in others. Neighborhood power and control do not eliminate the need for a central mechanism constituted on some representative basis." [18] He suggests that there are three factors which dictate the allocation of power among groups which live in the same locality. One is the level of government involved in, and the scope of impact of, the particular decision. Some decisions must be made at a higher level of government than the neighborhood; for example, those entailing the distribution of resources to the different neighborhoods of a city, or those setting minimum standards of performance for basic services. On the other hand, there are decisions in which the scope of impact is clearly limited, and which can be confined to a neighborhood; rehabilitation and urban renewal are examples.

Spiegel's second criterion is the functional area in which the decision must be made. Obviously some functional areas are more amenable to local control than others. Thus local control of education may be desirable, whereas local control of water resource development is impossible. And, as noted above, there may be varying degrees of resident control over the different decisions *within* a single functional area.

His third criterion is the degree of technicism involved, that is,

[17] Sherry R. Arnstein, "A Ladder of Citizen Participation," *Journal of the American Institute of Planners,* Vol. XXXV, No. 4 (July 1969), p. 224.

[18] Hans B. C. Spiegel et al., *Neighborhood Power and Control: Implications for Urban Planning* (New York: Columbia University, Institute of Urban Environment, November 1968), p. 157.

some decisions require a greater degree of technical ability than others. However, with resources to obtain technical assistance, there are few technical decisions for which local groups could not be responsible, and control might be accorded on the condition that standards of performance are met.[19]

Some interests of community residents and groups thus merit a higher degree of authority or control than others. Nevertheless, as we have indicated, the current participation of the poor (and many other service users) tends to be involuntary and passive, located at the "no participation" end of the scale. In effect, therefore, the poor must be helped to examine the arrangement of roles that make up their institutional lives and must be aided in the effort to "up-the-participation-ante;" that is, to move up the scale of participation—one step at a time, if that is all political circumstances permit, or to skip steps, as the opportunity presents itself.

As we shall specify in the following chapters, institutions and participants hold varying goals for engaging in community work. Service recipients come together to take action in regard to their problems in dealing with service institutions for many reasons. So too do the organizations which sponsor community activity. We wish, in the interests of emphasis, to restate the priorities of the professional as we conclude this discussion of people, problems, and participation. It is to increase the capacity of consumers to use and influence institutional-relations organizations in order to better meet their needs and protect their interests. Three professional goals, which may be pursued singly or in combination, can be extracted from the priorities statement: (1) the increased competence of community participants; (2) the greater responsiveness of service organizations to consumer needs, wants, and rights; and (3) small-scale or significant alterations in institutional policies and programs which impinge on consumer interests.

Although we have suggested that a critical task of community work practice with service recipients is to up-the-participation-ante, participation *by itself* is not enough. A study of 60 Community Action Programs concluded, as a matter of fact, that when the involvement of the poor became an end in itself, it served as "a skillful de-

[19] *Ibid.*, pp. 152–58.

vice for containment, obscuring the failure to achieve social change." [20] Participation may lead to community integration; it can be therapeutic for the participants; but it can not, of itself, assure institutional responsiveness or change. The competing claims of leadership and expertise, as noted in the prior chapter, must be integrated with the notion of participation. Community groups must, for example, develop leadership and other specialized roles among members —cultivate political acumen—mobilize resources—and devise tactics. And often, they must learn enough about specific issues to diagnose causes and formulate solutions in those problem areas. The commitment to participation is only a starting point in what the organizer must bring to his constituents.

[20] Kenneth B. Clark et al., *A Relevant War against Poverty: A Study of Community Action Programs and Observable Social Change* (New York: Harper and Row, 1968).

CHAPTER THREE

THE INSTITUTIONAL GOALS
OF COMMUNITY WORK

THE PROFESSIONAL GOALS of community organization oriented to work with people (in contrast to practice primarily concerned with organizational development or social planning) were suggested in chapter 2: to help the consumers of services to use and influence institutional-relations organizations in order to (1) increase their competence in community affairs, (2) insure that service organizations are responsive to their needs, and (3) promote alterations in policies and programs which impinge on their interests.

Clearly, these do not exhaust the purposes which induce individuals and agencies to engage in community organization. People participate in the group life of their communities for myriad reasons. They may find the activities educational or enjoyable. They may wish to overcome loneliness by seeking friendship and social contact. Often, they are moved to action because of disrespectful treatment, and their participation is an assertion of dignity. Some are motivated by the desire to serve; others crave prestige or power, or hope for financial reward. The incentives for participation may be as varied as the number of persons in the community group. Because, in attempting to foster group development, an organizer competes for scarce commodities (i.e., peoples' attention, time, and interest), sensitivity to individual motivation is required for group building, as well as to help individual constituents.

Furthermore, organizers must evaluate their own goals against those of their constituents and their sponsoring agencies[1] in order to define the perimeters of their effort. A hallmark of community work skill is the ability to draw upon those aims of constituents and sponsors which serve professional purposes—or to converge the goals of constituents, sponsors, and professionals into a coherent whole.

In this chapter, we explore the institutional goals of community work, that is, the societal goals adopted by organizations in the pursuit of community "health" or change. Although we devote a later section of this volume to some aspects of organizational sponsorship, we introduce institutional goals at this point because they inevitably set the boundaries to worker activity and importantly shape community practice. Ordinarily, in social work, aid to the client is believed to stem from his relationship to the worker. Thus the instrument of help is the worker himself, his capacity to listen and to hear, to understand and to empathize, to feel and to respond. Although these qualities are important to the community worker, the success of the community organization process more often rests on the ability of community action systems to marshal institutional sanction and influence. And in no respect do community workers function as individual entrepreneurs or free agents. The point has been put colorfully:

Whether the practitioner facilitates, fund-raises, foments or fumes— whether he plans, serves as a resource expert, counsels, or agitates—he is guided by the structure, aims, and operating procedures of the organization that pays the bills.[2]

[1] A sponsoring agency or organization ordinarily initiates, guides, and/or obtains support for community work. Although there is a distinction between funder and sponsor (the former are those who provide the financial support, whereas the latter receive the funds and are accountable for their use), we tend to treat the two as a single entity, and make distinctions throughout the volume only as they are significant to the discussion.

[2] Mayer N. Zald, "Toward a Sociology of Community Organization Practice," p. 10. Paper presented at the National Conference of Social Welfare, May 1965. (Mimeographed) For a revised version of this paper, see Mayer N. Zald, "Organizations as Polities: An Analysis of Community Organization Agencies," in Ralph M. Kramer and Harry Specht, eds., *Readings in Community Organization Practice* (Englewood Cliffs, N.J.: Prentice-Hall, 1969), pp. 143–54.

INTEGRATIVE, SOCIOTHERAPEUTIC,
AND ENVIRONMENTAL-CHANGE GOALS

Although all organizations develop a set of values and a culture which transcends their structural arrangements, the concept of an institutional value system is an elusive one. Reference to an agency's values and goals requires identifying the over-all objectives of a complex collectivity, that is, some merging of the possibly differing ends of its various participant groups. Thus, an agency's goals are more than the goals of its constituent parts, whether these be fund givers, boards of directors, executives, workers, members, clients, or outside reference groups. It is some combination of all of these, and therefore, necessarily amorphous. An organization's goals constitute its social contract binding the participants together in a common endeavor. It ordinarily results from an accomodation of the varying interests and influences of individual participants and subgroupings.

The concept of institutional goals is all the more elusive because the real goals of an organization may be unstated and the stated goals may be unreal. This obfuscation may be purposive or unintended; organizations may be aware of and hide their objectives for political reasons, or their goals may be undefined and implicit for lack of understanding, or because their complexity defies definition. In effect, goals are held by design and default. For example, the aims of a service program may be to offer specific help to particular people (its "design" goal). The program may also serve to advance social control, although its administrators, even behind closed doors, would not espouse client passivity or recognize the control objective (its "default" goal).

"Softness" in the concept of institutional values and goals has led some sociologists to avoid the study of goals in favor of the notion of "function." [3] Practitioners, in their need to act, cannot wait on preci-

---

[3] The term "function" refers to the vital social processes required by all human societies, and they are allocated to specific roles and systems. In community work, they are, in effect, the consequences of an organization's activities, which, when persistent, can be inferred as its "function."

sion, however, and community work, because it is purposeful, requires use of the concept of goals. Although, in the discussion which follows, we do not distinguish between "design" and "default" goals, community workers need to make the distinction—for if they ascribe motivation where none exists, they may go astray in their attempt to influence institutional direction. Whether by design or default, an organization's goals can be identified, not with precision or surety, but accurately enough to serve as a guide to practice.

Although there are many purposes for which sponsors undertake community work, we deal with only one broad, but important, goal dimension: the organization's relationship to equilibrium and change. Goals may be ranged along a continuum on this dimension, extending from purposes which maintain current arrangements to those which seek major environmental change. For purposes of analysis, the goals are grouped into three sets. The first, we call *integrative goals,* since the objective is social stability, or the improved juxtaposition of service givers and service users. The second may be termed *sociotherapeutic goals.* Here, the agency seeks the improved functioning or increased competence of citizens through community participation. The third set is *environmental-change goals,* the aim being the improvement of the environment of community residents.

Integrative goals are those designed to enhance agency and community services. One such objective is to broaden the use of available services, as when indigenous workers are employed to "reach out" and publicize the agency program or recruit clientele for it. Another is to gain acceptance for an established program or—on the other side of the coin—to avoid protest regarding some community plan. Agencies with integrative goals also organize participants as a means of providing channels for feedback between the users and implementers of the service. Although agencies may actually be interested in client reaction when they pursue this objective, the process is intended less to improve or reshape agency policies than as a means of maintaining cordial relations with recipients. Change, of either persons or their environment, figures no more than secondarily among integrative objectives.

Sociotherapeutic goals are those goals in which the primary aim is to change the participant. This includes a wide range of desired de-

velopmental states. One is to encourage persons to be upwardly mo-
bile, on the assumption that participation in community work can
spur the motivation and provide some of the necessary tools to "get
ahead." Another is to develop leadership and increase the competence of community residents to deal with issues, that is, to encourage them to assume responsibility for and to influence the social and
political life of their communities. The goal is the political sophistication of the participants, to help them learn the levers to press in
order to influence institutional decision making in their own interests.
The specific outcome of the community effort is less relevant than
whether the social and political development of the participants has
been advanced in the effort.

Another sociotherapeutic objective is pyschological in nature.
Through self-help, it seeks an improved sense of self, a feeling of
counting and contributing. On a group basis, the goal is peoplehood,
or pride in one's own social or ethnic group. Much of the organizing
in the black and other minority communities has, of course, been directed to this end.

Environmental-change goals are specific and concrete, focused on
a substantive change in some problem area. They may range from
modest local changes, such as obtaining a street-crossing guard or
improving neighborhood services, to changes of more significance
and scope. Other examples of modest change goals are those designed to obtain entitlements for the consumers of public services, or
the delivery of services in ways which insure the dignity of service
recipients. Although these goals are important to users of service,
they are modest in that they seek changes in the *administration* of
programs and policies, rather than in programs and policies themselves.

The environmental-change goals of community work often have a
citywide locus. The sights of neighborhood organizing may be set far
beyond neighborhood borders. An example is the press for "community control" in neighborhoods of large cities, which aims for
changes in the patterns of influence in the city-as-a-whole. Finally,
the reach may extend to the national community in the case of organizations interested in developing or contributing to the acceleration
of a social movement. Their hope is the basic alteration of the social
system.

Agencies may pursue several goals simultaneously, and we shall discuss at a later point how organizations manage some of the apparent contradictions. However, although one or another set is likely to dominate an agency's orientation, a mix of goals may be expected for several reasons. First, agencies dealing with a complex reality must attend to more than one problem at a time, no matter how well-defined or limited they might wish their objectives to be. For example, even the most aggressive environmental-change-oriented organization must have a constituency that supports its objectives, and thus integrative goals will be necessary if only for organizational maintenance purposes. Second, organizations appeal to different audiences on different grounds, and hold disparate goals to maintain the attachment of the various elements in their constituency. Finally, goals may be used to obfuscate as well as to clarify, and organizations adopt a mix of goals (by design or by default) to prevent others from understanding what it is they are or are not actually doing.

Each set of goals has both positive and negative features. In different ways, each is subject to the charge of deceiving or exploiting its constituency. Each presents problems and prospects.

The Problems and Prospects of Integrative Goals. Integrative programs stabilize and preserve existing institutional arrangements. Participation in community affairs is encouraged to promote a greater ego-investment in community life, in the hope that with greater ego-investment, an internalization of community values and traditions will follow, and that sources of challenge, conflict, and change will be muted. But the preservation of existing institutional arrangements is more likely to benefit the "haves" than the "have-nots," and is thus more often of advantage to established institutions than to recipients of service.

Efforts to gain the acceptance for an established program or avoid protest regarding an impending plan may not be seriously conceived to influence the program or plan. Often, they are designed to beguile participants into believing they can make an impact, when the plans are in fact predetermined. The intention, and frequently the result, is to "de-fuse" resistance and "cool out" the opposition.

The opening of communication channels to foster cooperative client-sponsor relations may also be a snare. As put by Selznick, when agencies use citizen participation "to fulfill both the political function of defending legitimacy and the administrative function of establishing reliable channels for communication, [they do not] envision the transfer of actual power." [4] Parent associations in public schools are an illustration. Set up to provide citizen support for administration —externally, to press for increased school budgets, and internally, to assure parent endorsement of school policies—they serve administrative rather than constituency interests. Only insofar as administrative and constituent interests overlap do they advance parental interests.

The cynicism of community workers in regard to integrative goals is expressed in this report of a line professional, hired to organize a patients advisory committee in a large municipal hospital:

Having an "outreach" program, involving the consumer in the planning of services (as advisor only) is a progressive and lucrative thing to do these days—it looks good in reports; and is an "innovative" concept that administrators involved in the conference circuit like to speak about. A hospital which professes to be primarily concerned with service, while in fact interested in research and training, can minimize conflictual policies by stressing its programmatic involvement with the consumer community. And, of course, it is far safer in terms of potential control of consumer demands to organize within the institutional structure than outside of it.

Nevertheless, sponsors which involve recipients of service in order to gain legitimacy and the acceptance of their programs may find that absorbing new elements into the organization has unintended consequences. To promote stability, organizations desire to make participants the prisoners of organizational policy. They may, however, end up having to pay a price. That is, preventing the coopted users of service from getting out of hand may require granting them some exercise of influence. Selznick, who is responsible for the authoritative work on cooptation, suggests that this means of neutralizing opposing forces creates a paradox which is "one of the sources of persistent tension between theory and practice in organizational behavior. The leadership . . . is committed to two conflicting goals: if it ignores the need for participation, the goal of cooperation may be jeopardized; if participation is allowed to go too far, the con-

[4] Philip Selznick, *TVA and the Grass Roots* (New York: Harper Torchbooks, 1966), p. 14.

tinuity of leadership and policy may be threatened." [5] In effect, the need to gain the cooperation of consumers provides them with opportunities as well as hazards.

Constituencies developed to support an organization's integrative goals may be able to extract more than a small "piece of the action." Some have been known to bite the supporting agency's hand and become the locus of opposition to its policies. Parent associations may be organized to promote the interests of educators, but it has been observed that "if these PTA organizations are captured by opponents of the existing educational system, as has occurred in some areas, then they provide a formidable vehicle for mobilizing opposition to school administrators—more effective, because of their semi-official status, than any other organizational resource at the disposal of critics of the educational establishment." [6]

Nor does agency absorption of indigenous leaders necessarily result in their being declawed. In a study of the development of antipoverty policy in Baltimore, Bachrach reports that there was no indication that black "militant moderates" appointed to various boards and commissions by the mayor had been coopted. However, there was evidence that some of them had used their new positions for leverage to continue building a power base in the ghetto. Bachrach suggests that black leaders were aware that a continued militant stance was essential to maintaining their leadership in the black community. He observes further that "a militant stance (was also) essential to them as a means of preserving their preferred position within the political system. Stripped of their militancy, they would be neither feared by the white elites nor regarded as symbolically useful in supporting the legitimacy of the system." [7]

This example represents cooptation in the best sense of the term. "Coopted" leaders who merely provide "window dressing" and who exert no influence are unlikely to serve either their constituency or the organization's quest for legitimacy, except in the short run. On

[5] *Ibid.,* p. 261.
[6] Francis E. Rourke, *Bureaucracy, Politics, and Public Policy* (Boston: Little, Brown, 1969), p. 18.
[7] Peter Bachrach, "A Power Analysis: The Shaping of Antipoverty Policy in Baltimore," *Public Policy,* Vol. XVIII, No. 2 (Winter 1970), p. 174.

the other hand, "coopted" leaders who provide "window dressing" and who are also influential may, over time, contribute to the development of new arrangements of power.

Indeed, it may be argued that one appropriate goal of organizing is to achieve a higher degree of political integration of specific subgroups. Successful organizing, in these terms, would result in the integration of constituents in the political life of the community, that is, residents holding public offices, serving on government commissions, having personal relationships with political leaders, and the like. There is some evidence to support the speculation that communities undergo an evolutionary process of this kind in the development of citizen participation structures.

A study of eleven Model Cities programs is suggestive.[8] In five of the cities, there was little organization of the residents of the Model Neighborhood Area, that is, resident cohesion and their involvement in the political structure was low. The City Demonstration Agency, organized to plan for the neighborhood, was dominated by the officials of established agencies, and there was little indication of change in the practices of these agencies; they pursued business-as-usual.

In two of the cities the residents of the Model Neighborhood Area were organized into several cohesive and militant organizations to represent their interests. In these cities the City Demonstration Agency was dominated by residents who were not, however, involved in the political life of the community. The planning environment was troubled by conflict, and the established agencies (and, more importantly, the resources which they controlled) were not significantly involved in the program.

In the other four cities, the Model Neighborhood Area residents were well organized and represented a cohesive force in planning. Although there had been conflict in these cities in the years prior to the Model Cities Program, accommodations had been reached and residents had achieved a higher degree of political integration than in the other cities. Thus an organizational structure was developed

<hr />

[8] Department of Housing and Urban Development, *The Model Cities Program: A Comparative Analysis of the Planning Process in Eleven Cities* (Washington, D.C., U.S. Government Printing Office, 1970).

which provided parity between residents and staff in control over planning, and, interestingly, it was in these four communities that residents and agencies together received more new money and effectuated more new programs than in the other seven cities.

There are four types of community behavior that may result from the interaction of varying degrees of community cohesion and political integration (although the study above illustrates only the first three). These are: (1) where cohesion and political integration are both low, residents may be alienated and respond with apathy; (2) when cohesion is high (perhaps as a result of community work efforts) but political integration remains low, residents may engage in social protest, with resultant conflict; (3) when cohesion and political integration are both high, there is an increased potential for cooperation between residents and government; (4) when cohesion is low, but integration is high, perhaps because resident leadership has been coopted, the consequence may be competition among residents (i.e., community "representatives" end up serving their own interests because there is no organized constituency).

The above suggests that political integration may be a desirable goal when it is accompanied by an organized and cohesive constituency of service recipients.

Some practitioners maintain critically that improving services to the poor via integrative organizing goals is intended to conduce to social stability and control. Gruber says, for example, that "If you give them services, and this is all you do, then you narrow the frustration gap—the gap between what people want and what they have. This dilutes the potential for more radical realignments in the system." [9] However, the comment is too broad a generalization to be of much use; there is, furthermore, another perspective which suggests that after people have radios, they will want television sets all the more. Karl Marx fathered a theory of social change related to the first of these ideas. He believed that the continued impoverishment of the working class would create in them an ultimate despair which

[9] Murray Gruber, "Discussion," in John B. Turner, ed., *Neighborhood Organization for Community Action* (New York: National Association of Social Workers, 1968), p. 72.

would be the basis of an inevitable revolution. Other social theorists, and even Marx himself, suggest that the reverse proposition may also hold. As stated by Davies, this Marxian proposition is as follows:

A precondition of widespread unrest [is] not progressive degradation of the proletariat, but rather an improvement in the workers' economic condition which [does] not keep pace with the growing welfare of capitalists and therefore [produces] social tensions.[10]

That is, according to this view, the improvement of economic conditions along with an increased expectation of what society can and should provide is a more potent seedbed for radical social change than is continuous deprivation.

Whether these theories are accurate or not, they cast too wide a net to serve as a basis for evaluating sponsor objectives and activities. Other variables intervene which must be taken into account.

Although services may be offered to promote social control, peoples' needs require that they receive medical attention, legal help, housing, sanitation services, and the like, whether or not these serve long-range objectives. As Kenneth Clark observes, "The . . . approach of opportunity-power theory to the predicament of the poor will have to recognize . . . that social services cannot be ignored." [11] The issue at this level of abstraction is not whether the sponsor is pursuing a social control function, but whether the services are meeting needs, whether the people in most need are receiving them, and what the quality of the services is. Whatever one's opinion about the necessity for radical realignments, it can hardly be maintained that organizations should not provide significant and quality services, or that community workers should not be employed to "reach out" to encourage their use.

The Problems and Prospects of Sociotherapeutic Goals. Integrative goals are suspect because they serve to "coopt" and "cool out." But sociotherapeutic goals have their hazards as well. Community work-

---

[10] James C. Davies, "Toward a Theory of Revolution," *American Sociological Review,* Vol. 27, No. 1 (February 1962), p. 5.

[11] Kenneth B. Clark et al., *A Relevant War against Poverty: A Study of Community Action Programs and Observable Social Change* (New York: Harper and Row, 1969), p. 68.

ers who object to sociotherapeutic goals attack them for being inherently conservative, offering psychological solutions to political and systemic problems. The implication of community work that is oriented to changing people is, obviously enough, that people need changing—and by extension, that the cause of problems such as poverty is the inadequacy of the impoverished. Thus the victims of social problems bear the burden of blame for the problem.

The terms used in social work do, in fact, reflect a bias of this sort. Thus persons who avoid or take minimal advantage of institutional services are designated as "hard to reach," "multiproblem," and "dropout." Each suggests that the cause of service failure lies in some defect of the client. The presumably eager agency cannot serve a client who is "hard to reach;" "dropping out" of school is a manifestation of youngsters' rebelliousness rather than of school pressures or inadequacies; a client who does not take advantage of available services does not wish to improve his situation. The terms do not suggest that there is a reciprocal relationship between client "defects" and institutional "defects". Were agencies to be viewed as "hard to reach" or "apathetic," modes of intervention would be suggested which not many agencies would welcome. Community work which emphasizes client deficiencies and ignores the deficiencies of agencies, or the deprivation and discrimination of American society, may be said to have its priorities askew.

Critics of organizations which pursue sociotherapeutic goals argue from an institutional or structuralist perspective. In the structuralist view, social behavior is not the result of internal or psychological processes or of past social experiences, but primarily a response to present social arrangements, for example, the distribution of resources and power. Thus, an adolescent's lack of motivation to seek employment is not due to intrapsychic factors (e.g., poor identification with the father figure). Nor can it be accounted for purely in sociopsychological or cultural terms (e.g., as the product of cultural strain resulting from poverty or particular group patterns). Rather, it reflects current social facts and arrangements—such as welfare policies which reduce the income of families on welfare when youngsters in these families are working, or the lack of employment opportunities in any but "dead end" jobs.

What is required, the argument goes, is not an improved sense of self, but improved social circumstances. According to Rustin:

. . . the breast-beating white makes the same error as the Negro who swears that "black is beautiful." Both are seeking refuge in psychological solutions to social questions. And both are reluctant to confront the real cause of racial injustice, which is not bad attitudes but bad social conditions.[12]

But to dismiss the quest for community competence, for group selfhood, or even for psychological assistance, on the grounds that it is bad social conditions and not bad attitudes which cause the problems of blacks or the poor obscures the complexity of events. In so arguing, we do not reject the structuralist view. Rather, we would maintain that to automatically ascribe a negative evaluation to sociotherapeutic goals requires making too broad a leap. A structuralist perspective speaks to the needs of society but may say little about the immediate needs of individuals. To define individual or social problems as *either* exclusively individual *or* societal may distort both. And one may even agree with structural analysis as a high-level abstraction, as we do, without ignoring the fact that as a behavioral prescription it is at once too sweeping and too restrictive. The diagnosis of a cause does not lead directly to the prescription of a cure.

Even if bad social conditions and not bad attitudes are the cause of social injustice, as Rustin argues, the attempt to enlist blacks and the poor in the struggle to change those conditions may require heightened consciousness about themselves and their circumstances. One way in which powerless people adjust to wretched life circumstances is to identify with the powerful. In so doing, they accept and incorporate definitions of themselves which they perceive to be desired by the powerful. They see themselves—and become—inferior and unworthy. To break that cycle—for example, to maintain that "black is beautiful"—may not be so much a psychological solution to a social problem as a prelude to action to change social conditions.

Nor is it appropriate to downgrade the importance of changing the role image clients have of themselves and the image the larger community has of clients. When, for example, the welfare department

[12] Bayard Rustin, "The Failure of Black Separatism," *Harpers,* Vol. 240, No. 1436 (January 1970), p. 31.

views the client not as someone to be taken care of and trained to be a good client, but rather as someone in the system who has well-defined rights, who is to be consulted and negotiated with, a role change has been effected which allows for a healthier juxtaposition between institution and client.

Furthermore, to locate the source of social dissonance in institutions rather than in individuals ought not to lead to underestimating the importance of remedying individual pathology. Strategies aimed solely at basic causation cannot ignore the vast reservoir of human misery and injustice already created. People who are hurting, even though the hurt is societally induced, need relief from their pain. Nor could we, in good conscience, deny mobility programs to individuals which do no more than help them escape from their impoverished circumstances, whatever their genesis.

The Problems and Prospects of Environmental Change Goals. Environmental change objectives have, in their turn, been the subject of critical comment. One critic terms a single-minded focus on system change as a "new utopianism"—in which there is "much talk about 'destroying systems' and 'power and income redistribution'—all naively set within the existing economic structures." [13] Although the utopianism may be new, one aspect of the commentary is as old as the old left—namely, that social change attempts which do not take the profit motive and the economic system of the society as their central target will fail, at best, and, at worst, they will deflect attention from primary causes. For some critics, an attack on social welfare institutions serving the poor is misdirected because these institutions are among the least influential in the hierarchy of societal institutions and at the same time the most immediately needed by the poor.[14] For

[13] William Schwartz, "Private Troubles and Public Issues: One Job or Two?" *Social Welfare Forum* (New York, Columbia University Press, 1969), p. 29.

[14] The latter point is made eloquently, if mystically, by Schwartz. He says, ". . . the basic relationship between an institution and its people is symbiotic; each needs the other for his own survival. . . . What [the peer group] can do is strengthen its members and heighten their sense of poise and security in the processes through which they reach out to fulfill the terms of the symbiotic relationship. The institutions are theirs; they do not belong to anyone else. . . . And the move is toward the agency, not against it. . . ." *Ibid.,* pp. 38–39.

others, a challenge to welfare institutions is reformist tinkering.[15]

One need not be a revolutionary to recognize the need for basic alterations in the American economic and political system. As we implied in chapter 1, solutions to current social problems requires radical reformation over a wide ambit of entrenched institutions. In this context, the efforts of community work organizations to promote environmental change must be acknowledged as limited and stumbling. With minor exception, the sponsors of community work are too world accepting; they have too much of a stake in their society; their prerogatives are too circumscribed to permit them to play a consistent or significant role in the basic changes that are required.

Furthermore, the neighborhood locus of much community work constitutes an impediment to significant change. The local orientation of Americans of all income levels springs from values deeply rooted in the American ethos. The movements of low-income residents toward community control of institutions, and the sentiments of conservative groups against state and federal intervention in local affairs, are motivated by the same desires for autonomy and self-determination. Local government is more visible and accessible, and therefore the constituents of community work turn to it for redress.

But the problems which engage the consumers of services in neighborhoods are thereby limited, since the local residential community is many steps removed from the actual centers of decision making and power—from state and national government—in short, from many of the institutional structures which are determining forces in regard to the foremost problems experienced by residents in a local community. Generally, the closer a desired change is to a local level of functioning, the more illusory and ambiguous it is.

This does not mean, however, that nothing can be done at all. Nor, in our view, has the case been made for withdrawal from the fray because results are inadequate to the need. Activity which is generated on a local level, whether through a neighborhood council, a school parents' group, or a coalition of local groups, serves as a device for

[15] The latter was debated extensively by Left theoreticians in the 1930's—i.e., whether reformist efforts advanced or impeded the revolution. The communists of the 1930's resolved the issue in favor of supporting reformist efforts.

bringing residents into new organizational relationships with one another and the broader community. If the community work program then moves to questioning the larger institutional arrangements which give rise to community problems, it has the potential for achieving modest, though not insignificant, change.

An analysis of the efforts of forty-eight citizen organizations reports successful accomplishment in a number of circumscribed areas, among them: the improvement of local agency operations, the development and implementation of new community programs, and the acceptance by some public agencies of conformity to, or the reinterpretation of, regulations of import to constituents.[16] (These, it might be noted, are within the parameters of the purposes which we have suggested as professional goals).

Claims of this sort are modest, and purposely so. Even if they were all that community work could accomplish, the effort would, in our judgment, be worth making. In their own terms, limited gains, such as a better heated apartment, a larger welfare check, or an increase in parental dignity, are salutory gains for the people who win them. People who participate to achieve these gains do so, not for their own edification or education, but because such results may be won. The work thus constitutes self-determination in action, and from the perspective of the participants, represents success.

Moreover, we believe that modest achievements have, in accumulation, the potential for contributing to larger-scale change. They raise expectations, thus generating pressure for further activity and contributing to a social climate in which alterations in policy and program become possible. It can be hypothesized, for example, that the educational activities of the NAACP laid the groundwork for the protest movement in civil rights. The civil rights movement, in its turn, led to changes involving education, public accommodations, voting practices, and employment policies on national and local levels. It also constituted the motive force in the development of the poverty program which, for all its shams and shortcomings, influenced the democratization of social welfare. The poverty program also provided the arena and the channels of communication by which

[16] John Turner, ed. *Neighborhood Organization for Community Action* (New York: National Association of Social Workers, 1968), p. 181.

the leaders of the poor could engage established authority, and in that engagement, contributed to their politicization. We suspect too that the Economic Opportunity Act's concept of participation of the poor, in justifying their claim for attention and influence, also provided—inadvertently, to be sure—considerable impetus for the later press to achieve community control of education and health services, as well as the organization of the Welfare Rights Movement.

Factors beyond the purview of planning are responsible for major institutional changes.[17] A dramatic case in point is provided by an analysis of the size of peace demonstrations from 1965 to 1968. The number of demonstrators varied directly with the popular opposition to the war, as measured by the Gallup Poll, and this, in turn, was determined by the military situation in Vietnam. The authors conclude that the demonstrations were typically the *outcome* of larger social forces, rather than their determinants.[18] In effect, then, broad-scale social change cannot be planned, although planners can take advantage of social circumstances when opportunities occur.

In this context, the contribution of community groups which are unable to achieve community control of their educational system may nevertheless be contributing to a climate of opinion, or unrest, which will impel improvements in the system. And although welfare rights groups may have been able to obtain only modest increases in entitlements for their members, the movement has played a role, along with others, in advancing the idea of a guaranteed annual income.

All of which, we agree, is inadequate to the need of impoverished citizens. To the charge that it is reformist tinkering, however, we have no answer, for we know of no other acceptable way to proceed

[17] Warren observes, for example, that most purposive change at the community level is of a secondary, rather than basic nature. It is, he says, "a response to the uncontrolled aggregate of decisions to do one thing or another by individual actors in the community, or a response to the behavior of various adaptive organizations which have been set up to cope with these basic changes, or a response to changes occurring in the community as part of a national trend and not separable from it." Roland L. Warren, "Types of Purposive Change at the Community Level," in Kramer and Specht, *Readings in Community Organization Practice,* p. 207.

[18] Jerome H. Skolnick, *The Politics of Protest:* A Report to the National Commission on the Causes and Prevention of Violence (New York: Ballantine Books, 1969), pp. 31-33.

to obtain the required changes than through a determined, dramatic, sometimes militant working for major reform. Those who counsel revolution—not as rhetoric, but as policy, and who understand the meaning of the word—tend, we believe, to be romantics.

We would endorse the contrary opinion of Eugene Genovese, a radical historian and long-time advocate of revolutionary causes, who says, "Those who continue to prate about a present or foreseeable revolutionary situation in America are in danger of committing the one sin for which no radical may ever be forgiven: that of completely misunderstanding the country in which they live and therefore of becoming tiresome." [19] Che Guevera, one of the estimable revolutionaries of our time, has spoken of the proper assessment of the preconditions for revolution:

It must always be kept in mind that there is a necessary minimum without which the establishment and consolidation of the first center . . . [of guerrilla warfare] is not practicable. People must see clearly the futility of maintaining the fight for social goals within the framework of civil debate. . . . Where a government has come into power through some form of popular vote, fraudulent or not, and maintains at least an appearance of constitutional legality, the guerrilla outbreak cannot be promoted, since the possibilities of peaceful struggle have not yet been exhausted.[20]

The fact is too that a country as affluent as the United States can afford to buy off dissidence, assuming that its decision makers are rational enough and smart enough to take the step. (Buying off dissidence, it may be noted, is one source of social progress—or what Grosser has called "significant tokenism.") [21]

To espouse revolution through the organization of the poor and near-poor ignores other realities.[22] Planned change of a fundamental and long-range nature is close to impossible—at least through com-

---

[19] Eugene Genovese, "Letters," *New York Review of Books,* Vol. XV, No. 3 (August 13, 1970), p. 36.

[20] Che Guevera, *Guerrilla Warfare* (New York: Monthly Review Press, 1961), pp. 15–16.

[21] Charles Grosser, *New Directions in Community Organization: From Enabling to Advocacy in Community Organization* (New York: Praeger, forthcoming).

[22] For a discussion of some differences in revolutionary potential between urban United States and other societies, see Martin Oppenheimer, *The Urban Guerrilla* (Chicago: Quadrangle Books, 1969).

munity organizing. Unless issues can be transformed into concrete and personal terms, a series of immediately achievable ends articulated, some victories won, and some compromises accepted as forwarding one's objective rather than "selling it out," people are unlikely to rally to the cause. Revolutionary ideology and the structure of revolutionary groups (e.g., the prohibition against deviations from the "correct" position and the requirements of personal sacrifice), operate against the acceptance of these realities in practice.

In concluding this chapter, we wish to refer to the relationship of professionals to these institutional goal sets, although it is difficult, perhaps impossible, to define an appropriate professional stance in light of the diversity of practice, the uncertain state of the art, and the controversies among those who practice community organization.

The institutional goal sets are both exclusive of, and overlap, what we consider to be appropriate professional goals. If, for example, the integrative objective of a welfare department is to organize welfare clients to win client cooperation without the promise of more client pay-off than that they feel good about participating, a professional ought not to lend himself to the effort. Unless the assignment provides the opportunity to move beyond client-agency cooperativeness, it ought be avoided. Or community work programs whose focus is to train tenement dwellers to be better tenants (a sociotherapeutic objective), without attention to the improvement of housing, are, in our view, professionally indefensible. Nor do we believe that professionals, *as professionals,* can make revolutions. When institutional goals are not congruent with professional purposes, it is the task of the worker, along with his constituents, to shape them to his, and their, ends.

On the other hand, there are integrative, sociotherapeutic, and environmental change goals which are clearly harmonious with the professional objectives with which we began this chapter. The task, then, is to order them in some priority, taking account of the views of constituents and sponsors. In view of current social needs, our priorities would be as follows: (1) modifications in institutional programs and policies to meet the needs and protect the interests of the consumers of service—these modifications to be large scale, if the social climate permits, or modest, as is more usually the case; (2) assisting organized groups of recipients to become integrated into the institutional life of the community; and (3) increasing the sophistication and "know-how" of service users in their dealings with service institutions. It might be noted that, in reverse order, these suggest the steps in a process of influencing; that is, as constituent capacity is enhanced, community groups achieve cohesiveness and are recognized as "contenders" by officialdom. As this occurs, their ability to change organizational policy in their own interests increases as well. In the real world of practice, of course, priorities are set by community conditions—and opportunities must be hewn from fertile (or fallow) circumstances and the professional's skill.

Part II

ORGANIZING A CONSTITUENCY:
THE PROCESS OF COMMUNITY WORK

CHAPTER FOUR

ABOUT THE PROCESS OF
COMMUNITY WORK

THE IMPORTANCE OF THEORY in community organization practice is self-evident. Without a systematic approach—an understanding of "the specific conditions under which specific behavior will change in specific directions" [1] —practice efforts must necessarily be halting. It has been noted that "all practitioners formulate hypotheses about the nature and origin of problems and the institutionalized procedures for bringing about change." [2] Ordinarily, however, these are intuitive, implicit, or untested. Unfortunately, a body of theory which would allow the ordering of the vast array of discrete data about community characteristics, community problems, and methods of intervention is unavailable. There is, at present, no "theory" of community organization as such, nor is such a theory imminent.

We discuss process and method in this chapter as a mechanism for ordering many of the elements which must be considered as one practices community work. Our objective is not a "theory" of community organization, but rather to suggest the critical nature of certain variables in the organizing enterprise, as well as to provide some coherence as they are examined. We draw on some of the knowledge

[1] Robert Pruger and Harry Specht, "Assessing Theoretical Models of Community Organization Practice: Alinsky as a Case in Point," *Social Service Review,* Vol. 43, No. 2 (June 1969), p. 123.

[2] *Ibid.,* p. 123.

and theory of the social sciences in this and other chapters, in the same way that medical practitioners utilize knowledge and theory from physiology, biology, and chemistry in their practice. But while the application of social science theory to practice may result (hopefully) in new configurations, it is not itself community work theory. The schema which follows in this chapter is a device to order material, but it does not constitute, as would well-developed theory, a series of interrelated propositions from which outcomes might be predicted.

STAGES OF THE COMMUNITY
WORK PROCESS

Practice consists of method and process, that is, what workers do (method) in response to particular behaviors (process). Process is a term which connotes naturalness, an unfolding, as when reference is made to the "birth process." Method, on the other hand, implies a set of artificially created procedures. The terms go together because conceptions of processes are necessary to design methods to intervene in them—to encourage, guide, stop, or redirect the processes. Thus it is the physicians' understanding of the birth process which allows them to devise methods to prevent conception or foster it, to prescribe a regimen for a pregnant woman or to assist her in delivery.

Process, in community organization, is not a *natural* process, however, but a *social* one. Social processes are intellectual projections of how people are expected to behave in response to problems viewed within a specific framework of values and goals. Given a particular set of goals, the process of community organization is a statement about how we expect a group of people to act as they engage in activities to achieve their ends. In effect, then, the description of a social process is a series of questions or hypotheses about how people will behave.

Method is also a series of questions and hypotheses about behavior, but it refers to the behavior of one particular actor, that is, the worker. Essentially, these are hypotheses that say, "If the worker behaves in a prescribed manner, he will affect the process in a particular way." Thus the role behavior of the worker is the methodology of community organization practice (and of any social intervention for that matter).

The major elements of the process, and the tasks of the worker as he sets about influencing it, are summarized in the table below. The table includes a projection of stages in the behavior of an action system [3] which is derived from group functions: socialization; developing affective relationships; organization building; and, finally, the achievement of institutional change. It notes the "interactional" and "technical" tasks which may concern the worker at each stage of the process (the methodology of the worker is employed as he engages in these tasks) and indicates their order of importance in community organizing. Discussion of the stages of the process requires reference to a community's "social network," since the process is drawn from a community work perspective of the functions and types of groups in community life.

FUNCTIONS AND TYPES OF GROUPS

In constructing a model of process in community organization, we begin with the assumption that all groups fulfill basic social functions for participants, and that these functions are circumscribed and given importance by one's conception of community work, particularly its goals. (In our framework, the ways in which people can influence institutional decision making.)

Four functions are of particular interest to us: socialization, developing affective relationships, organization building, and mediating relationships between people and institutions. Each of these is represented in community life by group types for which the function constitutes its primary purpose (although *all* groups in community work fulfill these functions as they go through the process). The four types,

[3] An "action system" comprises those who participate in the change effort. There are three major sets of actors, in addition to the community worker: the funders, the sponsors, and the constituency or client population. The funders are those individuals or groups who provide financial support for the program; the sponsors receive the funds and are accountable for their use. The constituency or client population are the recipients of the benefits of the action, or their representatives.

PROCESS AND TASKS IN COMMUNITY ORGANIZATION

STAGES OF PROCESS	WORKER TASKS		PRIMACY OF TASKS
	TECHNICAL TASKS	INTERACTIONAL TASKS	
Socialization Groups: socialization	Identify and define problems	Identify potential members; motivate and recruit members; educate constituency	Secondary
Primary Groups: develop affective relations	Link problem identification to goal development	Cultivate social bonds and build group cohesion	Secondary
Organization-Development Groups: build organizations	Develop program objectives and organization structures	Broaden constituency; build a coalition; develop leadership	Secondary to primary
Institutional Relations Organizations: mediate the relations between individuals and institutions	Implement strategy (administration and planning)	Participate in organizational enrichment and change through use of tactics: education, persuasion, bargaining, and pressure	Primary

which constitute a "social network" in urban industrial societies, are: (1) socialization groups, (2) primary groups, (3) organization-development groups, and (4) institutional-relations organizations. "Pure" group types do not, of course, exist; the typology is a theoretical device, a screen, against which to examine groups and their functions.

Socialization Groups. The primary function of socialization groups is to teach individuals the values, expectations, and behaviors which the community (i.e., family, friends, teachers, government) considers important for them to learn. Family groups, play groups, and school groups are typical examples, each of which may perform some specialized assignment such as the family inculcating cultural and religious values and the school instructing in specific skills.

Although socialization groups are often associated with children below their teens, the function of these groups does not cease with adolescence. The graduate student enters socialization group experiences as he is taught the culture of the university by peers and faculty; the new factory employee is "socialized into" his job by co-workers and employers; and the welfare recipient learns the "score" about welfare from friends, recipients, and his social worker. Institutions frequently provide what might be called "re-socialization" experiences, through "treatment" or "sensitivity" groups, in which the function is re-education or correcting the individual's social functioning.

The structure of socialization groups may be either informal or formal. The latter are likely to be organized for some specialized and well-defined purpose, such as a class for housing authority tenants on housekeeping practices. By and large, the groups are transitory, and involve a broad cross-section of people in a time-limited experience. In community work, socialization groups, *as ends in themselves,* are most closely associated with the sociotherapeutic goals of organizations which were discussed in the preceding chapter. That is, their focus is *to bring about some change in the participants.* Their commitment to institutional development and change is weaker than any other type of group, and as such their usefulness in our model of community work must be qualified.

This point is often ignored in practice. Both socialization groups and primary groups, which we discuss below, may be seen as the mainstay of an organizing effort. Although it may seem naive in retrospect, in 1962, as Mobilization for Youth (and later, the other Community Action Programs which followed in its wake) began to organize the low-income community, it contributed resources to such groups as a parent-education club, a sewing circle, and even a teenage baseball league. These groups did, of course, perform important socialization and primary group functions for their members, and enriched the group life of the community, an important and even necessary task. But they did not advance the community work goal of the agency which was to influence organizations to better serve consumer needs. As a consequence, misguided relationships between the members and the agency, misunderstanding, and disappointment followed. The function of such groups militates against their use as a mechanism for modifying institutions, and there is also the danger of violating their integrity in seeking to use them in that way.

Many organizers count on social maturation taking place—that is, they believe that successful experience in a socialization or primary group leads to a willingness to experiment with other forms of group life. There is logic in the assumption, since one might expect that experience in a cooperative attempt would lead to learning how to meet other, perhaps higher level or more abstract needs, through group processes. Unfortunately, however, there is little evidence to demonstrate that an inevitable evolution of group life takes place, or that there is necessarily any transferability of social experience. On the contrary, as has been noted in the community work experience of Mobilization for Youth:

Many of the informal groups succeeded in gaining greater access to agencies, and the resources made available to them did "pyramid" as predicted. For example, when the mothers in a condemned building became involved in a controversy with city agencies, other organizations offered assistance, and some local activists and politicians entered the fray on the side of the mothers. By and large, however, the informal groups did not move from the immediate solution of shared individual problems to a common concern with larger social issues and action. It appears that, rather than small groups creating issues for institutions, issues created by institutions are imposed on small groups. Formal groups and organizations, leaders, and politicians select the salient problems and seek out small groups with grievances that present opportunities for confronting the underlying issues.[4]

In community work, then, socialization groups are of secondary importance. This is not to say that they are insignificant, only that their goals are instrumental to achieving other ends. Viewed in this context, they make a positive contribution to the community work process. Since, programmatically, socialization groups require less in energy, commitment, and other resources from participants, they serve effectively in the initial efforts of organizing. For example, a physician who wished to involve the Indians in her health district in planning a local health council found them unresponsive to her invitations. However, when she organized a tour of the health center for them, which included meetings with local officials, demonstrations of techniques used in the health programs, and refreshments, she met with an enthusiastic response and an expression of a desire to learn more about the services.

For participants of socialization groups to move into community action, another type of group must be formed. Either the socialization group must itself develop a membership and structure which will allow it to function differently, or some of its members must be recruited into already existing groups which are more community work-oriented. In effect, from a community work perspective, the major objective of socialization groups or programs is to *reach out* to the community. That is, in building community organizations, group experiences are required by which potential participants can be identified, motivated, recruited, and educated—or, in other words, socialized into these organizations. Identifying, motivating, recruiting, and educating potential participants thus becomes a major task of the community worker in the early stages of the organizing process.

Primary Groups. Primary (or "peer") groups are those in which more enduring affective relationships are formed. Their function is to satisfy people's needs for social and emotional connections with oth-

[4] George A. Brager and Harry Specht, "Social Action by the Poor," in George A. Brager and Francis P. Purcell, eds., *Community Action against Poverty* (New Haven: College and University Press, 1967), p. 146.

ers. Mutual affinity, comradeship, personal loyalty, and feelings of love are the forces that bind the members of the group together. Examples are the nuclear family, extended kinship groups, the neighborhood gang, friendship cliques, couples clubs, fraternal groups, the men who hang out at a particular saloon, and so forth. Primary groups may be found on the street corner, the work place, in coffee klatches at home, the mental hospital, the home for the aged, the prison—indeed, everywhere. Contrary to earlier speculation, Greer and Kube have demonstrated that as a neighborhood grows more characteristically urban, friendship and kinship relationships come to constitute a *larger* proportion of all social interactions. They suggest that ". . . the more 'urban' an area, the less important are formal voluntary organizations and the more important are informal face-to-face primary relationships." [5]

Primary groups are always informally structured, though they may be created by formal organizations or even shaped by them. Unlike socialization groups, informal peer groups *may* have an orientation to changing institutions, though this interest, if it exists, is secondary to its social-emotional function. Or primary groups may be involved in social action on an ad hoc basis. It is not atypical, for example, for a mother's club which comes together for social ends to become concerned about community problems relating to their children. Thus one such group took dramatic action and successfully obtained more police protection for the children of the neighborhood. The worker, however, was perturbed to find that the members were disinterested in moving on to other community projects, but, as often occurs, they apparently valued their group as a social group. Although the experience served to develop the leadership abilities of several of the women in the group (and one or two of them participated in later efforts), from a community work perspective, these were secondary gains. The primary group's function to meet the expressive needs of its members draws it inevitably back to activities which serve this function rather than an instrumental purpose.

Primary groups require more personal involvement and commit-

[5] Scott Greer and Ella Kube, "Urbanism and Social Structure: A Los Angeles Study," in Marvin B. Sussman, ed., *Community Structure and Analysis* (New York: Thomas Y. Crowell, 1959), p. 110.

ment of energy than the participants of socialization groups may be willing to give, and are also more useful contributors to the community work process. Nonetheless, they are also secondary in our perspective. (They may, of course, properly be the major focus of concern of other professionals, for example, group workers). Their primary purpose, which is *to bring about some change in the relationships among participants,* closely associates them with institutional goals which are integrative and sociotherapeutic. And like socialization groups, they provide an important source of recruitment for community action efforts. This is all the more significant, in light of the previously noted fact that formal voluntary associations tend to by-pass low-income participants. It is through acquaintanceship with the pattern of primary group relations within a community (or within a social agency or other formal organization, for that matter) that an organizer gets his bearings and seeks a constituency.

It is the function of primary groups rather than the groups per se which is most salient to the community worker, however (i.e., the development of affective relationships). Thus, in building a community organization, an important subgoal is *the development of a sense of belonging.* This requires activities which maintain a fine balance between those which build and strengthen relationships among members and those which support its organizational change ends. Organizers, because they are predisposed to emphasize substantive accomplishment, often tend to overlook the fact that high among the motives for individual participation in groups of all kinds is the search for stimulation, connection, and approbation from others. Experiences which enable participants to enjoy and appreciate one another—whether formal programs, such as family outings and folk festivals, or informal "gab" fests—are therefore necessary. On the other hand, such experiences may strain against other goals, that is, deflect members from the necessary "scut work" which is a concommitant of "getting down to business" in community work.

Organization-Development Groups. The major function of the organization-development group is to introduce people to others who share their personal, professional, political, or philosophical interests; it incorporates a wide range of circulation-enabling and horizon-expanding functions. We have chosen the designation "organization-development group" to underscore the function this type of collectivity can play in community work, however. Although organization-development groups may be almost purely social in their purposes, they frequently have political, ideological, and action commitments as well, and sometimes, these commitments are primary. Examples of organization-development groups are the numerous young adult social clubs which are organized by community centers and churches to meet the specialized needs of young adults: courtship, new friendships, career contacts. More directly germane to community organizing are groups such as the Western Student Movement, SNCC, SDS, and some of the local affiliates of national organizations like CORE, which are organized along political and ideological lines. Ad hoc coalitions and community forums are also relevant examples, since they serve the same functions and have similar structures.

For groups of their ordinarily large size, organization-development groups have an uncharacteristically loose structure. Membership is fluid, and the attachment of participants to the group is often peripheral. Commitments, although they may be vigorous, are not likely to be enduring. Activities are mass-based (e.g., dances, rallies, demonstrations, teach-ins), and have the potential for providing excitement, stimulation, and the image of massive public support.

Organization-development groups, as distinct from socialization and primary groups, may serve directly as a mechanism for achieving community work ends, rather than secondarily as an instrument to accomplish subobjectives. Thus, an ad hoc coalition of community groups may be brought together to dramatize an issue or solve a community problem, and in so doing, influence change in the program or policy of some target system.[6]

They are particularly useful in serving these ends with a constituency of the poor. That is, organization-development groups provide an especially suitable ambience and structure for the participation of a low-income clientele. Their problem focus can be specific, clearly

---

[6] We use the terms "target" and "target systems" throughout this volume to refer to those groups, organizations, or institutions that are strategic to a change attempt and that need to be modified if the objective of the process is to be attained.

defined, and time-limited. Their activities generate excitement, and tend to the expressive and informal. A structure which permits the conduct of business even though members may come and go is particularly apt for persons who, like the poor, have limited time and energy to expend in an organizational effort. Nor do the members (or at any rate, all except a small executive group) need concern themselves unduly with organizational "housekeeping." The accouterments of formal organization (by-laws, elections, procedures) which can become, for inexperienced participants, ends in themselves, are deemphasized.

Although community workers are often aware of the danger, their interest in democratic process and their concern for permanence sometimes leads to an overconcern with the trappings of formal structure to the detriment of ultimate purposes. A contrary view has been expressed by the worker who successfully organized one of the early welfare clients groups:

At that early time . . . we were not sure that we were heading for an organization of clients as such, and we handled much of what happened on a very pragmatic week-to-week basis. . . . For example, one of the decisions, which I said to myself is up for grabs, is do we have an organization, do we really need meetings, and if so what kinds of meetings. . . .

[Ultimately] it was necessary to evolve a concept of membership where people can come and go, where you don't preach or berate people for coming in and getting what they need and walking out and not coming back. . . . The need for a great number of people in campaigns led to the evolution of the relationship of member to organization as one of extreme looseness. What we came up with was the concept of membership participation whereby I concentrated on a relatively small number of people . . . whom I tried to educate as leaders to entice them toward participation at a high level.[7]

In effect, the welfare client worker started with mass meetings and the formation of an organization-development group. As time went on, however, the desire for a more enduring impact on the welfare system led to greater formalization (at least, at the group's core) and, ultimately, the development of an institutional-relations organization.

[7] Mary Rabagliati and Ezra Birnbaum, "Organizations of Welfare Clients," in Harold H. Weissman, ed., *Community Development in the Mobilization for Youth Experience* (New York: Association Press, 1969), pp. 107 and 120.

From a long-range perspective, although organization-development groups may serve a primary community work objective, they most often provide a step in the process to primary goals. Their main function, then, and the task of the worker, is to *expand the constituency,* to search out a new operating base, make contacts, broaden support, and develop new coalitions or new organizations.

Institutional-Relations Organizations. We have already indicated the major function of institutional-relations organizations, (to mediate the relations between institutions and individuals, as do trade unions, civil rights groups, and social planning councils), and also suggested that the primary goal of community work practice, in our perspective, is to help the consumers of service to use and influence institutional-relations organizations to better meet their needs and protect their interests.[8] As such, these organizations play a primary role in community work.

The goals of institutional-relations organizations are instrumental in the sense that their activities are geared to transacting "business" for their members—to achieve some substantive outcome—and only secondarily to serve their expressive or affective needs. It should be noted that the term "groups" was used to refer to all of the other collectivities of community life, but the term "organization" has been reserved for this one. This is because institutional-relations organizations are characterized by a stable structure, rules and procedures, and specialization—the qualities that define a group as an organization—and also, the qualities of groups which are necessary for citizens to deal with institutions in an on-going way.

Not all institutional-relations organizations are committed to social change, of course; many of them guard the portals of the *status quo.* Their primary function, from a community work perspective, however, is to *change organizations* in the interests of the constituents of community efforts. This change may range on a continuum from a concern with institutional attitudes and behavior, to institutional systems of service delivery, the redistribution of institutional resources, and the reorganization of authority and control within the institutional system.

In order for an institutional-relations organization to be developed

[8] Part I, chapter 2.

and sustained, it must maintain a delicate equilibrium of all of the functions represented by the other three group types. That is, the functions of socialization groups, primary groups, and organization-development groups are useful in building such an organization, but they must also be incorporated *within* an institutional-relations organization. Some ethnic associations contain all group types (e.g., the Sokols of American-Czechoslovakian communities and the Black Muslims) and may be viewed as subsocieties which parallel the institutions of the larger society. Institutional-relations organizations with more finite objectives are also strengthened by the inclusion of these functions. For example, Lipset found that a major factor accounting for the International Typographical Union's unusual history of democratic leadership and political vitality was the existence within the organization of a network of small groups of all types. The proliferation of these groups, allowing the continual development of new leadership, resulted in the union's ability to adjust to, and deal with, political and social developments with a degree of flexibility not found in many formal organizations.[9]

To summarize the discussion to this point, we have said that descriptions of process are models of how groups will behave in response to a particular framework of values and goals. In identifying the stages of the process—from socialization to developing affective relations, organization building, and achieving institutional change —we have suggested that *all* groups fulfill these functions as they go through the process *in community work*. Practitioners interested in the use of groups primarily for educational or therapeutic purposes will operate with different goals from those of community organization, and will therefore bring a different perspective and emphasize different aspects of group functions in their work. Thus Schutz, concerned with how groups fulfill interpersonal needs, postulates that all groups move through three phases of development: inclusion, control, and affection.[10] It should be clear that, although his perspective is different, his formulation is based, like our own, on the notion of a

[9] Seymour Martin Lipset, Martin A. Trow and James S. Coleman, *Union Democracy* (New York: Doubleday, Anchor Books, 1962).

[10] William C. Schutz, *FIRO: A Three-Dimensional Theory of Interpersonal Behavior* (New York: Rinehart, 1958), pp. 169–71.

sequential process in the development of groups. The word "sequential" connotes a more orderly progression of phases than occurs in reality, and in the following section, we will qualify its meaning in relation to community work. We shall then conclude the chapter with a discussion of the interactional and technical tasks of the worker and a word about his role.

SEQUENCE AND TIMING

The ideal model of a sequential process is the factory assembly line. Yet although that process deals with inert matter, even factory operators cannot achieve total predictability in their products because they cannot control all factors that affect the assembly line operation: raw materials may not be obtainable; distributors may not sell finished products; unions may demand changed working conditions, and so forth.[11] Compared to the assembly line, organizations that offer social provisions have infinitely less ability to predict the outcomes of their efforts.

Human service organizations, like factory management, try to deal with their inability to exercise "quality control" over their "products"—although they would hardly define their efforts in these terms. As Goffman has noted, "total institutions" (mental hospitals, prisons, etc.) attempt to control the behavior of inmates by stripping them of their individuality, that is, treating them in some measure like the inert matter on the factory assembly line.[12] Community organizations make the attempt as well, although not as dramatically or effectively as total institutions. For example, when organizations try, subtly or otherwise, to dictate the primary group relationships of their members with "outsiders," they are attempting to exert this kind of control.

How, or even whether, community efforts move through the stages of the community work process constitutes an attempt to shape the outcome in one or another direction. Much depends on the goals of

[11] James D. Thompson, *Organizations in Action* (New York: McGraw-Hill, 1967).

[12] Erving Goffman, "The Characteristics of Total Institutions," *Symposium on Preventive and Social Psychiatry* (Washington, D.C.: Walter Reed Army Institute of Research, April 1957), pp. 25–59.

the effort, the "world-view" of the worker or sponsor, and the previous experience (separately and together) of the constituents. Some examples will illustrate what we mean.

The *Girard Street Project* is a report of a two-year organizing experience which follows the classical sequential order.[13] The worker describes how she began by getting to know individuals in the community, offering friendship and short-term services. She brings small groups of neighbors together to discuss their interests and problems, at the same time that she tells them about herself and her agency's goals. Essentially, she has been "socializing" the residents.

She then begins to form interest groups (e.g., a mother's sewing club), which meet on an informal basis, and for several months devotes her energies to what we have referred to as "primary group development." She notes, however, that these activities remain primary group experiences, with only tangential interest in community affairs. With her newly acquired knowledge of community relationships and problems, she turns to organization-development programming, and begins to form an association, which sponsors a forum for considering community problems, and which serves as a vehicle for attracting community leadership. The worker completes the process with the establishment of an institutional-relations organization, a community council which, through specialization of function and a degree of structure, is able to draw on the expertise and resources of a wide range of individuals and organizations.

Although the *Girard Street Project* seeks the community work objective of helping people to use and influence institutional-relations organizations, it also reflects the worker's (or agency's) "maturational view" of group life—that is, that successful experiences in socialization or primary groups will lead to the development of more complex group efforts. Consequently, the process in Girard Street is protracted, and, significantly, there is considerable turnover of membership as it moves from one to another form of group life. Had the worker's conception of the process been different, she might have turned more quickly to organization-development activities (in which case, of course, other aspects of the project would have turned

[13] Dagmar Horna Perman, *The Girard Street Project* (Washington, D.C.: All Souls Church Unitarian, 1964).

out differently as well, i.e., membership composition and organizational structure).

When a more specific objective is sought, for example, to influence planning for housing rehabilitation in a community, the time frame of the process is likely to be encapsulated. Thus two student organizers, attempting to establish a tenants' council on the site of a city rehabilitation program, were faced with the same absence of organization as the Girard Street worker. They knew, however, that "they would be confronting a situation where rumors had been circulated for many months, and a great deal of misinformation was prevalent. . . . Extended personal interviews were certainly called for. And yet . . . too many families had to be seen; time was limited; and the necessary manpower was not available." [14] Instead, the organizers scheduled a series of small socialization meetings, leading to several large community-wide mass get-togethers.

The sequence and timing of the process are, of course, influenced by the extent to which constituents have previously shared group experiences. (Only rarely do workers recruit members who have not had prior involvement with one another.) Even in such instances, however, or when a worker enters an ongoing organization, there will be need for socialization, primary group, and organization-development experiences. An organizer, assigned to challenge tenement code enforcement by the leadership of a militant organization which had operated programs successfully for many years, reports that he had to: attract the interest of a large enough group of members; persuade them of the significance of the effort; assist in the selection and recruitment of leaders (chairman, speakers, organizers); contact other organizations; and jointly develop a program strategy.[15] Although the sequence of actions and their timing were not "well-ordered," the case exemplifies the socialization, primary group development and organization-development work which must take place even within a well-established institutional-relations organization.

[14] Fred Barbaro, *The Struggle to Provide Low-Income Housing in Coney Island* (New York: Columbia University School of Social Work, 1970), p. 26. (Mimeographed)

[15] *Developing a Housing Program in a Grass-Roots Organization* (New York: Columbia University School of Social Work, 1968). (Mimeographed)

Groups may begin at any phase of the process, or operate at all stages at once. This is the case because the phases represent social functions with which all groups must be concerned. The timing, then, is influenced by the particular values and prior experience of the actors, as well as by the exigencies of the social climate and the ways in which the external environment impinges on their efforts. We believe that groups generally, as groups, must fulfill these functions sequentially (socialization precedes developing affective relations, developing affective relations precedes organization building, etc.). But our interest in sequence is as much to order our discussion of worker tasks in the succeeding chapters as because we anticipate regularity in any process of human interaction. No matter how fervently it might be wished, it cannot be expected that groups composed of widely diverse individuals functioning in a complex social setting will go through the stages of the community work process in a sequential manner.

INTERACTIONAL AND TECHNICAL TASKS AND
THE ROLE OF THE WORKER

Interactional tasks involve communicating with and relating to others; these are the tasks most typically associated with social work practitioners of all methods. In our discussion of groups and their functions, we suggested some of the interactional tasks which are germane at each step of the community work process (e.g., recruiting a constituency, building social bonds, developing leadership, promoting changes in institutional attitudes). Technical tasks, on the other hand, are concerned with the analytic and substantive aspects of community problem solving, and are indicated in the table on page 70. These include problem assessment, a specification of objectives and goals, the structural, budgetary, and other resource requirements of the program, and an evaluation of the undertaking. Technical tasks require substantive knowledge of the particular problem area (e.g., housing, education, mental health) which is the focus of the community effort, and although such specific expertise is critical to effective community work, it is necessarily outside the purview of this volume.

Interactional and technical tasks are interrelated, and the worker deals with them simultaneously. Thus, in the socialization stage, while the organizer is identifying and recruiting participants (interactional tasks), he is also attempting to help the developing constituency define the problems about which they may eventually take action (technical tasks).

The issue of whether community organization is concerned with process or product, developing interpersonal relations or solving substantive problems, has concerned practitioners over the years. It is true that one or another of these aspects of practice may be primary within a particular setting at a specific moment relating to an explicit goal. In Rothman's typology, for example, locality development would appear to emphasize the interactional; social planning, the technical; and social action might stress either. Nevertheless, the issue is, at least in part, diversionary, since it avoids a major problem in describing practice, which is to integrate the methods by which interactional and technical tasks are accomplished. The art of community organization—and it is an art, not a science—is in the worker's use of knowledge and skill to enable constituents to organize to solve problems, that is, to deal with process *and* product simultaneously.

Bales, reporting on small group experimentation, describes this tension between interactional and technical tasks, although in somewhat different theoretical terms. All social systems, he notes, swing back and forth between two theoretical poles: task requirements and emotional needs. On one extreme, there is optimum adaptation to the outer situation of the group at the cost of internal malintegration, and at the other pole, optimum internal integration at the cost of maladaptation to the outer situation.[16]

Bales found empirically that there were identifiable changes in the quality of activity of groups as they attempted to solve their problems. An increase in task-oriented activities constitutes a disturbance of equilibrium in affective relationships which is then redressed by an increase in social-emotional activities. Task accomplishment requires that the roles of participants be differentiated, both as to func-

[16] Robert F. Bales, "The Equilibrium Problem in Small Groups," in A. Paul Hare, Edgar F. Borgatta, and Robert F. Bales, eds., *Small Groups: Studies in Social Interaction* (New York: Knopf, 1965), p. 453.

tion and amount of participation. This differentiation leads, in turn, to the disruption of relationships, for leadership which is instrumental and focused on "production" impairs the group's basic solidarity. This state of affairs is characteristically resolved by the emergence of an expressive leader, or best-liked man, who restores the equilibrium. (Some groups, of course, never manage to arrive at a stable differentiation of roles, and antagonism builds from meeting to meeting). Although ultimately the test of satisfaction for the members of a task-oriented group is the accomplishment of its objective, some balance between these two forces is necessary. An ideal solution, Bales concludes, is a coalition between instrumental and expressive leadership in which each acts to support the other.[17]

Paradoxically, the community worker must attempt to fill either role—or however inconsistent it may seem, both at once—depending on the state of equilibrium (or lack of it) which exists within his group at a particular time.

The above is suggestive of a basic concept of worker role and "professional function." Community organization is a social process in which each participant is likely to consider himself something of an expert, whether a professional or not. Community organizers are thus (sometimes implicitly) challenged with the query, "Why should you be paid a salary when I'm doing the same thing for nothing?" The answer is not simple, because in fact there may be no task or role which can be said to be a solely professional one. The professional's unique function lies in his *knowledge of the requisite roles to be filled and his skill in helping constituencies to fill them.* Sometimes this means filling the role himself, sometimes helping participants to fill the required roles, at other times, training new community leadership for them, or helping a group acquire the resources whereby they can command the skills of others.

The technical skills necessary for some roles are often unavailable in an action system, particularly in new groups and groups of the poor. Skills in problem analysis, goal development, administration, evaluation, and so forth, are likely to be in short supply. And knowledge about substantive problem areas—for example, the institutional systems which control these areas, the range of programs available

[17] *Ibid.,* pp. 470–75.

for improving them, the interest groups which impinge on them—
may need to be provided to improve technical performance, even
when technical skills are at hand. Roles requiring interactional competence, such as chairman, negotiator, and agitator, are usually more
readily available. But even so, professionals may contribute to their
improved performance. Indeed, apart from his knowledge and skill,
the fact that a worker can devote full time to his efforts is important
in helping constituents fill the requisite roles. This is particularly the
case with a constituency of the poor for, as Zald has noted, "The
lower the socioeconomic status of the constituency, the more difficult
it is likely to be to maintain their interest and participation." [18] Organizational (and worker) energies will thus be disproportionately
devoted to motivating participation and sustaining relationships
whatever interactional skills may be available in the community.

There are times when the organizer must fill the "missing role."
He may do so in order that constituents may learn through observing
him in action, as takes place in student teaching. Or he may feel it
beneficial to them to identify with him in a particular way as a role
model. He may also fill the missing role in order that the group may
achieve its objectives—in the recognition that the emotional rewards
of a successful effort can sustain a group, and encourage its movement to further activity. Whatever the reason, however, he must
make the choice because it is in the best interests of the group, and
not because he happens to be good at performing one or another
role.

There are differences in the personalities of organizers, of course,
and workers do have particular "styles," that is, they have a penchant
for enacting one or another role. Not infrequently, workers are dis-
couraged because they themselves cannot fill a particular role, such
as the "public speaker," addressing large audiences, the "negotiator,"
driving the hard bargain, or the "agitator," mobilizing the troops.
The essential question is not whether the organizer's personal style
allows him to perform in any specific role. Although his preferences

[18] Mayer N. Zald, "Organizations as Polities: An Analysis of Community
Organization Agencies," in Ralph M. Kramer and Harry Specht, eds., *Read-
ings in Community Organization Practice* (Englewood Cliffs, N.J.: Prentice-
Hall, 1969), p. 149.

and predilections should we weighed before he decides to take on one type of organizing assignment as opposed to another (and there is a sufficient variety of agencies, constituents, and problems to occupy the energies of all), the important question is not whether the worker is a "good" organizer in a particular situation at a particular point in the career of a community action group. It is, rather, whether he can assess the needs of groups in different developmental states at different stages of the community work process and help them deal with *their* needs, thereby increasing their competence or aiding them to achieve their goals.

CHAPTER FIVE

COMMUNITY WORK PROCESS: SOCIALIZATION

THE FIRST STEPS of the community work process contain elements of every other. Even the briefest encounter can contain conceptually distinct elements as, for example, when a worker is explaining his role to a constituent (socialization) and simultaneously engaging in an empathetic interchange (developing affective relations). To separate them for analytic purposes, as we do in this and chapters 6 and 7 is to wrench them from their "natural habitat," and thus, unavoidably to distort.

The distinction we have made between the interactional and technical tasks of the worker is similarly distorting. In this chapter, for example, we discuss socialization, a phase in which the worker, sponsor, and potential constituency each learns what may be expected of the others, and how all of them fit into the scheme of things. The major interactional task is the identification, recruitment, and induction of a constituency; the major technical task the identification and definition of a substantive problem area.

After some comments on preorganizing, we organize this chapter on socialization (and chapters 6 and 7 on developing affective relations and organization building) by beginning with the interactional tasks of the worker, rather than the technical ones, since the emphasis of this volume is "people work." In so doing, however, we do not intend to diminish the technical aspects of practice. On the contrary, we wish to emphasize at the outset that the major focus of interaction in community work is *on the tasks community groups must undertake to achieve the goals of the process.*

PREORGANIZING

No organizing starts from scratch. Someone (e.g., a foundation, an agency, a community group) sponsors the effort, and engages the worker to carry out the organizing task. The sponsor might be a constituent group that has not yet evolved its structure or program; or it might be an agency that is primarily service oriented but desires a community work component. In effect, organizers begin with varying degrees of structure. At one end of the continuum is the established agency, providing the support of an on-going program and formal structure, in which the assignment is to an existent group with its own history and tradition. At the other end is the newly formed organization in an unfamiliar community, in which the worker's charge is to get a program or group underway.

However amorphous the situation may be, the worker carries the sponsor's "baggage" (or lack of it) around with him. If it has developed an image in the community, the image is something he will either have to use—or overcome. If it has not yet made its mark, it will nevertheless have ideas, plans, and purposes which he must embrace—or contend with. The worker too will bring notions about organizing and some vision of the end state he hopes to bring about. Indeed, it is a necessity, for *before* he starts, the worker must have some idea about *why* he is there.

Focus is required as an organizer identifies, recruits, and inducts a constituency, even under the most ambiguous, open-ended, and unstructured community circumstances. In deciding what information to seek (he cannot learn everything), which people to talk to (he cannot speak to everyone), or how to explain himself (he cannot say everything), the worker must have purposes and direction. The content and source of his information, and how his role and goals are defined, will in itself shape the outcome. To define his purpose as vaguely as "bringing people together to solve their problems"—which is sometimes adjudged "democratic"—is to allow accident to determine outcome. He may thus end up with a constituency because they sought his help first, rather than because they needed it most, or were most amenable to community work intervention.

Many factors influence the preorganizing orientation of the sponsor and worker. We wish, however, to indicate only one, which we consider to be major: the long-range or institutional purposes which underpin the worker's activity.

Institutional Goals and Constituency Recruitment. Earlier, we referred to the fact that sponsor/worker interest in a problem area influences which constituents will become involved in the effort. The point is important enough to emphasize, since we believe that institutional objectives effectively determine who in the community will or will not participate. For example, the Columbia University School of Social Work placed community work students in a welfare center organizing clients to improve welfare services, and simultaneously assigned students to a militant chapter of the Congress of Racial Equality (CORE), which was organizing recipients of welfare for the same purposes in the same center. When the latter group leafleted the welfare center, its officials registered a complaint with the school on the ostensible grounds that there was confusion and lack of coordination in two student groups performing the same functions with the same clients, although under different auspices. The school, in its review of the situation, noted that although the immediate goals of the two programs were similar, their purposes institutionally were quite different, and that consequently, the clients drawn to the two organizing efforts were not at all the same persons. Clients organized within the welfare department were courting approval from welfare staff, and were participating, at least in part, to please their "benefactors." They were recipients whose timidity made it unlikely that they would challenge welfare staff. The CORE group, on the other hand, consisted of angry clients whose militance reflected the social change goals of CORE.

Sponsors and workers serving integrative goals will seek and recruit the least alienated among the poor as participants, those who can be counted on to legitimate the program without seriously challenging its policies or premises. Although they may not be conscious of the dynamic, they will tend to admire those consumers of service who prefer cooperative rather than contentious relations with authority figures. A study of citizen self-help organizations has observed that those which are service-oriented, as opposed to change-oriented "attract members who are less alienated and more hopeful that [change will occur] through community education and organizational demonstrations, that is, neighborhood clean-up activities." [1]

When the objective of a community work program is institutional change, particular problems are faced in the recruitment of a constituency. It has been noted that social change is least likely to be generated by the lower strata of society:

Those who have nothing to lose but their chains are too closely chained, psychologically, to the desperation of their lot to generalize their predicament, face the consequences of a malcontent position, or otherwise add to their suffering by striving for social change.[2]

This contention is supported by a study comparing the attitudes and perceptions of community residents and professional social workers in New York's Lower East Side. The residents, who were overwhelmingly low income, expressed less dissatisfaction with community conditions than the professionals had anticipated, yet were more pessimistic about the possibility of changing these conditions than was the social work staff.[3] The community reaction—relatively uncomplaining acceptance of depressed conditions coupled with a lack of faith that they could be improved—may be interpreted as a realistic adjustment to the facts of low-income status.

The problem may be conceived in cost-benefit terms. The realities of lower-class life—that is, the necessary preoccupation with the day-to-day problems of survival—suggests that there is a significant cost in time and energy to the poor who engage in community ac-

---

[1] Project staff, "Citizen Self-Help Organizations: An Analysis," in John B. Turner, ed., *Neighborhood Organization for Community Action* (New York: National Association of Social Workers, 1968), p. 17.

[2] Seymour M. Lipset and Juan J. Linz, "The Social Bases of Political Diversity," reported in Bernard Berelson and Gary Steiner, eds., *Human Behavior* (New York: Harcourt, Brace and World, 1964), p. 617.

[3] Charles F. Grosser, *Perceptions of Professionals, Indigenous Workers and Lower Class Clients,* unpublished doctoral dissertation, Columbia University School of Social Work, 1965.

tions. The cost is increased when their lack of verbal or literary requisites, necessary for organizational accomplishment, becomes obvious, and causes discomfort. A further price is the risk of retaliation. Conversely, the benefits of participating are often not readily apparent. A concrete benefit in the present, or even in the immediate future, is hardly assured. Even so specific an aim as obtaining a clothing grant from a department of welfare may seem too difficult of achievement to make it worth the hard work and risk to a low-income person.

The cost-benefit equation is also influenced by the potential participant's lack of centrality to the effort. A British political scientist has noted that even established pressure groups, which consist of persons with higher participation quotients than low-income people, may not be as voluntaristic as has been assumed.

The origins of large groups (such as unions and trade associations) is essentially non-voluntaristic. . . . What is the point of an individual employer expending his resources in participating in group action to obtain favorable government legislation when his own contribution is marginal and the group will be successful without him, so providing him with the desired benefit at no cost to himself. . . . Only by coercion and offering other specific rewards can such a group mobilize support.[4]

The effort to promote community change requires capital, and workers with environmental change goals will seek to recruit those poor people who have the capital to expend—that is, those who have not succumbed to self-defeating pessimism or who are not so apathetic that they may not be aroused, or who have not been depleted of energy. The clientele who are sought—or are attracted to—institutional change efforts are those whose resources are small enough to incur resentment at their insufficiency, but large enough to permit their expenditure in community activity. We expect, in short, that it is the angry poor (since anger generates surplus energy) and the upper-lower and lower-middle class who will engage in institutional change activity. To the extent that the trade union movement is comparable, our expectation is confirmed. Workers who are most

[4] Francis G. Castles, *Pressure Groups and Political Culture* (New York: Humanities Press, 1967), p. 76.

active in organizing and participating in unions are not the poorest workers, who need unions most, but those with higher incomes, who have greater resources.[5]

INTERACTIONAL TASKS

In identifying, recruiting, and developing a constituency, a worker engages in three major steps. He must gather information, elicit interest in collective effort, and suggest what he and potential constituents may expect of the other.

Workers often feel great pressure to establish a "base" in the community, even before they have found their own moorings. Sponsors, in their interest to get a program underway, may be the source of the pressure. Or a worker's anxiety in beginning may be sufficient cause. Questions regarding who he is or what he's there for are difficult to answer when a worker is merely "gathering information." If, however, he hastens to establish himself before he knows his way in the community, he may find himself committed to the wrong group, the wrong leaders, and the wrong issue. One might expect, for example, that a community effort—unless fired by a volatile issue or dramatic conflict—would initially attract persons seeking social contact. Experience confirms, as a matter of fact, that when a worker attempts to organize, at random, a group of unaffiliated neighbors to do something as general as "to improve the community," it is the lonely and isolated (i.e., the "nonrepresentative") who generally volunteer first.

In starting, therefore, a worker must "hedge his bets" and mitigate the risk of precipitous commitment. As he studies the community, motivates interest in collective activity, and defines expectations, he employs three techniques. These techniques entail an increasing intensity of relationship and greater commitment on his part to particular courses of action, in the following order: (1) use of public information and meetings, (2) private contacts, and (3) group beginnings.

[5] William Spinrad, "Correlates of Trade Union Participation: A Summary of the Literature," *American Sociological Review,* Vol. 25, No. 2 (April 1960), pp. 237–44.

PUBLIC INFORMATION AND MEETINGS

There are many ways one can explore a community that require a minimum of explanation or commitment. Documents available to the public may be studied, meetings of public bodies and agencies attended, and community gathering spots visited.[6] Each requires a somewhat greater degree of worker involvement, and apart from examining the printed word, each can be used to get to know and get known by other people.

The census is an important source of secondary data.[7] So too is the demographic data collected by Planning Departments (of cities and counties), Relocation and Urban Renewal Agencies, and other service-giving organizations. Community studies conducted by universities and institutes dealing with research on a wide range of social problems may also be useful. There is, finally, the communications media, the big-city or hometown newspaper, the neighborhood, "ethnic," or "underground" press. Organizers should not be without their daily paper, no matter how poor the coverage or how onerous its editorial policy, since it provides a significant source of information about the thinking of some segment of the community.

A second source of public information is the meetings and hearings which take place in every community and deal with issues of concern to the organizer's potential constituency. Even agencies whose regular meetings are closed to scrutiny conduct programmatic "events," such as annual meetings, fund-raising affairs, educational

[6] For specific direction on studying a community, see Roland L. Warren, *Studying Your Community* (New York: Free Press, 1965) and *Where It's At* (San Francisco: Movement Press, circa. 1967).

[7] Census data provides such demographic information as population size, racial composition, family size, income, condition of housing, employment status, and the like. It is organized according to the size of the unit, from block to enumeration district to tract. The block unit contains least data, though it has material on race, condition of housing, marital status, population by age, etc. Enumeration districts cover approximately 820 people, are one-fourth to one-fifth of a tract, and contain all tract information. Block data and enumeration district material, which are available only on tape, may have to be ordered from the U.S. Bureau of the Census, although much census information is available in local libraries.

conferences, and the like, which offer observational opportunities. In addition, there is a continuous stream of demonstrations, protests, and rallies to aid the community participant-observer.

By and large, these meetings, hearings, events, and rallies are community ceremonies. Although at this stage of the process, organizers only observe community ceremonies (they plan them later on), it might be useful to digress somewhat to distinguish between "ceremonial" and "informal" activities.

"Ceremonies" are formal public encounters during which the relationships among actors are clarified and confirmed *for others*. Formal exchange of resources are made, contracts signed, appointments and sentences announced. Allegiances and beliefs are also formally proclaimed at these ceremonies (e.g., oaths are sworn, testimonials read, and position papers delivered).

"Informal work" refers to activities which prepare for ceremonies, somewhat like the work that precedes the presentation of a stage scenario. Their purpose is to increase the actors' ability to direct or control what takes place in the ceremony. The participants in informal work are the key persons in the decision-making process: group leaders, professionals, politicians, influentials.

Although it is important for community workers to distinguish between ceremonial functions and informal work during their observation of the community, it becomes even more crucial later on that workers understand that ceremonies have usually been worked out "behind the scenes." By the time the curtain goes up, the different actors have—or should have—a good enough idea of the script so that they can come in on cue.

Thus conceptualized, one problem of service recipients may be viewed as their exclusion from the informal work at which agreements get made. When there is no way for them to engage in preceremonial activities, aggrieved parties may choose to "bust up the ceremony." That is, they try, through confrontation, to make it impossible for the formal system to function until changes are made in the informal system. Although we discuss tactics extensively in Part IV of this volume, it may be noted here that the use of personal encounters at ceremonies *as a tactic to induce change* is not a substitute for ceremonies themselves.

Immediately before and after public meetings are times when the dress rehearsals and *post mortems* of important community ceremonies take place. As such, there is a high degree of "leakage" of the informal work which has gone into them. In searching for the bent coins in the local currency, therefore, organizers ought to arrive a little earlier and stay a little later than the planned public presentation. In that way, they may begin to assess which issues are being openly discussed and which kept beneath the surface. In addition, these moments provide the opportunity to begin making "connections," especially useful since they allow for only brief encounters in which contacts, explanations, and commitments are necessarily limited.

In addition to observing public events and organizations, wandering about the community and visiting the places people congregate are useful in gathering information for a preliminary analysis. Wandering gives a "feel" for the place (e.g., the mix of industrial and residential use, the tone and attitude about home and surroundings, etc.). There are also places in a community which serve as communication centers for particular subgroups, such as teenage hangouts, "street people" areas, "junkie" turfs. In one city a luncheon bar serves as a place where politicians gather to see, be seen, and find out what's happening. Patterns of territoriality reveal the networks of social relationships in a community and may be indicative of community boundaries, geographic and pyschological. The receptivity or suspicion with which new people and ideas are accorded may be revealed. Workers who spend time at these gathering places develop a familiarity with the community system and have access to information which becomes increasingly useful as their goals become more focused.

Visiting community gathering spots puts the worker into a more familiar position with a potential constituency. He becomes less of an outsider simply because he's there. He learns his way around, discovers who's who, and becomes more of a known quantity himself. One worker has observed, for example, that his community action project achieved legitimacy within the first year of operation in the community, "just because we had been there for a year. We became part of the scene, and people expected us to show up at Council meetings and have something to say about what was done."

Up to now, we have discussed *where* the participant-observer may obtain information but have only implied *what* information may be necessary. All public bodies cannot be observed, nor all hangouts visited—and even if they could, the cost in time and energy would be inordinate. With whatever level of information an organizer starts, he must increasingly direct attention from the general to the specific, pinpointing relevant information and ignoring the rest. As problems are identified, goals specified, and programs developed, he will not only need to "zero in" on a particular network of organizations and groups but he will also have to sharpen the focus of the information he attempts to elicit.

Since a primary goal of community organization is to influence change in institutional-relations organizations, community groups must develop a problem focus. A primary informational task is to get the sense and feel of potential problem areas. If the nature of the problem has been decided before he has started, either because it is the sponsor's function (e.g., a housing agency, drug program) or because a spontaneous issue has exploded on the community scene, his primary task is to explore its many ramifications. Particularly, he must relate himself to how potential constituencies perceive the problem, to *how it feels to them.*

Another important category of information as the worker searches for a constituency has to do with the individuals and groups who might compose it. The organizer must assess the propensity for community work of potential constituents, their level of sophistication about community action, and their degree of compatability with his own or his agency's goals. Do they believe, for example, that the problem is individually determined or a consequence of the social structure? Do they see it subject to citizen influence? Are they persons for whom benefits will exceed costs? Do they have the resources in time and energy to devote to a community effort? Do they have community or organizational "know-how?" Do they have leadership abilities or a ready following? Are they responsive to the worker's vision of possibilities? When potential constituents are ultimately brought together to form a group, it is necessary that there be affirmative answers to *some* of these questions. At the very least, the worker will have had to find some community legitimators, persons trusted by local residents who are willing to sanction his efforts.

The third major category of information is related to the network of officials, groups, and organizations for whom the problem has particular salience, whether as potential allies or targets. The worker has to assess whom he might count on, and for what, as well as the resources and resistances of possible target institutions. But we shall have more to say about this.

PRIVATE CONTACTS

A second technique in beginning the process is the use of private contacts, that is, seeking specific people with a particular contribution to make. They may be the victims of social problems, apparent community leaders, relevant agency officials, and/or groups with an interest in the problem. The types of information mentioned above are obtained in private contacts as well as through public sources. An important difference, however, is that in private contacts, the worker must explain who he is and what he hopes to do. The process thereby moves a step forward toward eliciting potential interest and defining mutual expectations.

Private contacts are primarily, though not exclusively, individual ones. Since there is considerable material on the uses and techniques of interviewing in the literature, we shall make only brief reference to this aspect of worker skill.[8] We wish, however, to indicate that interviewing may be distinguished from conversation on three important grounds: (1) it is *goal-oriented,* that is, the worker has a purpose, something he wishes to come out of the contact; (2) it is *self-conscious* in that he is thoughtful about the interaction and his own role in it; and (3) it is *focused,* that is, the worker selects his questions and responses in the context of his purposes. Although the above may sound imposing or overformal, experienced interviewers

[8] For some examples, see Robert L. Kahn and Charles F. Cannell, *The Dynamics of Interviewing* (New York: Wiley, 1957); Raymond L. Gordon, *Interviewing, Strategies, Techniques, and Tactics* (Homewood, Ill.: Dorsey Press, 1969); Lewis Anthony Dexter, *Elite and Specialized Interviewing* (Evanston: Northwestern University Press, 1970); Stephen A. Richardson et al., *Interviewing, Its Forms and Functions* (New York: Basic Books, 1965). Dated, but still relevant, are: Annette Garrett, *Interviewing: Its Principles and Methods* (New York: Family Service Association of America, 1942); Alice Voiland et al., *Developing Insight in Initial Interviews* (New York: Family Service Association of America, 1947).

can be friendly and warm, if required, without violating these strictures.

There are a number of matters which must be covered at the beginning of the contact. The worker must introduce himself and identify his agency. How the agency is perceived by community residents
or others becomes an important consideration. The introduction must
either use the agency's image, counteract its stereotype, or separate
the worker from its onus. He must give an early indication of his
purposes, since the person will want (and has the right) to know why
the worker is talking to him. He will also want to know why he was
chosen to be interviewed, and the worker ought to use whatever positive connections he has, for example, "Mrs. X said that you're an
important person to discuss school issues with." He should, finally, in
the introductory portion of the interview suggest what is expected of
the interviewee; for example, how long it will take and what facts or
attitudes the worker wishes to elicit. All of this ought to be no more
elaborate than is necessary (which is *less* elaborate than inexperienced or uncomfortable interviewers often believe).

In the following excerpt from a record from the South Bronx Mental Hygiene Clinic of the Jewish Guild, the worker indicates her
thinking about the difficulties in making a private contact, and how
she coped with them.

One of the stickiest problems related to my interviewing has been the
presentation to the tenant of who I am. The first order of business is to
establish that I am *not* an investigator, so I quickly give my name and
where I'm from. Because Jewishness is not a pass key into black homes, I
omit the name of the agency. Because "Mental Health" may conjure up a
what-do-you-think-I'm-crazy reaction, I reserve the name of the clinic.
Because service is the main point I'm trying to get across, I mention the
Block Service Program first: I'm from the Block Service Program of the
South Bronx Mental Health Service. That's quite a mouthful and the latter part tends to get lost in the shuffle, which is O.K. for initial interview
purposes. The point is not to deceive, but to avoid alienating people with
titles that are not necessarily relevant at that moment.

The next problem is to explain what I'm there for. This, too, is difficult since I'm not offering a specific service. What I'm offering is help in
determining what services are needed and how to gain access to those
services. But that's rather abstract and wordy. I've found that a more ca-
sual and easily comprehensible way of getting the same idea across is to

say that my agency is concerned about the problems of housing, health, education, employment, and welfare on the block. Since I'm still dealing in the abstract, I go on to say that my co-workers and I have been talking to people on the block, trying to find out what kinds of problems are bothering people. Unless I get some reaction at that point, I mention a few more specific and personalized problems the neighbors have complained about: lack of heat, closed schools, infrequent garbage collection, etc. I mention problems clearly related to an outside agency (landlord, teachers, City) and avoid mentioning problems that the tenant may construe as being his fault, or may construe as my judging to be his fault (garbage-filled lots, purse snatching in the street, vermin). I try to mention a full gamut of problems in order to reach the tenant where he's "at."

Once some discussion of a tenant's own problems has been elicited, I try to direct the discussion toward the idea of forming a group. I remind the tenant that some of his neighbors have expressed similar concerns and doesn't it make sense that when people with similar concerns get together they might be able to make their will known with more force than a single person? I believe this, and that's why I'm doing the kind of work I'm doing. I don't think it's too imposing to make that clear. I don't pretend that the idea of organization just struck me while talking to that tenant. The tenant is simply not that naive, and I think he welcomes knowing something about me, where I stand, what's my angle. Until I assert my faith in organizing, or the strength of numbers, he has very little to go on if he's to put some faith in me. If I feel that the tenant is still suspicious about me, and what my angle is, I explain that I'm a student whose interest in c.o. led me to a placement in the Block Service Program.

Then I give more information about the program: My agency felt that it wasn't making its services available to a large part of the community that had no way of knowing of its services. The Block Service Program was seen as a way of reaching the community, and so such a program was funded. I think it's important to mention that it is funded because that implies that we might be able to do something, that we're legitimate, that we're not simply students taking another survey for our own use. I also described our storefront and assure the tenant that he will be welcome there at any time if he has questions, or problems, or suggestions about ways of dealing with problems on the block.

Now that hopefully my being there makes sense to the tenant, I encourage the tenant to talk about himself, his ideas, his problems, or if he seems preoccupied, or to have said enough for now, I leave, saying that I'd like to come back to discuss further the idea of a tenant group, and that I hope he is interested and will feel free to share his thoughts on the matter with me.[9]

The South Bronx worker reveals her awareness that low-income people may be suspicious of organizer-strangers, who might turn out to be social investigators in "sheep's clothing," bill collectors, process servers, or agents of some feared bureaucratic oppressor. She appears to understand that poor people expect, with some justification, that they will be patronized, manipulated, and exploited, and one ought not to be judgmental that they, in their turn, will manipulate and use workers or other helping persons—for the latter may appear to them as surrogates of an oppressive system.

The worker's explanation of her "angle" also carries her empathy with the life circumstances of the poor. In discussing problem areas, she avoids abstraction and asks nonthreatening questions. In mentioning the full gamut of community problems, she provides direction but also encourages choice. Finally, she risks putting forth her own stake in the process. Constituents often wonder, though they may never ask, "What's-in-it-for-the-worker?" One aspect of community work skill is to "tune in" to questions such as these and deal with them appropriately and with grace (neither too heavy nor too light a touch for the circumstance). Although such questions may not surface, they will not go away until they are dealt with. It takes some courage to indicate one's feelings and admit one's self-interest, particularly when such expression can be avoided easily.

The South Bronx worker pushes toward group formation perhaps too quickly in an initial encounter. She appears not to leave options open regarding who might or might not become a constituent. More important, we do not get the sense that she has or will explore the social network of the block to learn who speaks to whom, who is listened to on what kinds of matters, and the like. She makes a common mistake in separating the potential constituent from the social life which teems outside the interview place.

Things are often not what they seem, of course, and individuals

[9] *An Interview in the South Bronx,* a student paper prepared at the Columbia University School of Social Work, 1968. (Mimeographed)

may readily agree with the worker when in fact they may be reluctant to express real disagreement, or their lack of understanding. Later, then, they will "vote with their feet." Strong disagreement may also not necessarily be taken at face value, since it sometimes reflects the mood of a moment, a reaction unrelated to the substantive issue, or the need for more time to consider ideas. Misjudging the intentions and interests of others is particularly problematic for low-income leaders, since, as has been suggested, there may be a match between an isolated constituency and marginal leaders (i.e., marginality is associated with difficulty in maintaining and visualizing reciprocal relations with others).[10] For the worker, what is required is that he pick up on nonverbal expression and behavioral cues, understand and use overt and covert responses, discover "hidden agendas" when they exist, and know when they do not. It is, in the long run, more useful for a worker to encourage individual and group expression, even when these expressions do not support his own values and goals, than to avoid noticing them.

In concluding this discussion of private contacts, we note a dilemma of the worker. As soon as he presents himself as trying to help a community solve its problems, he may be besieged with concrete requests for assistance. He will, on the one hand, want to proffer help because the need is great and he identifies with a constituent's plight; because he wishes to establish his own credibility as a helping person; and because tangible and immediate benefits provide an incentive for participation (in much the same way that politicians trade favors for votes). On the other hand, providing services draws the worker into relationships and casts him in a role which can commit him to the wrong constituency and role relationship; or, what is worse, it depletes him of resources which deflect him from his community work objectives.

This dilemma confronted the two organizers in the *Bay and Park Street* effort, to which we referred in chapter 4. Fortunately, they were able to resolve it more responsibly than is often possible.

It was painfully clear that some of these tenants were so overwhelmed by their own struggle for survival that they would never be able to become

[10] Frank Pinner, Philip Selznick, and Paul Jacobs, *Old Age and Political Behavior* (Berkeley: University of California Press, 1959), p. 272.

involved in any ongoing or concerted effort to gain participation in a tenant's council. Nevertheless, Margie and Carlos found themselves spending extra hours with this group of tenants rather than devoting the time to those who would be instrumental in organizing the council. . . .

(The organizers) were troubled by their inability to properly service the residents. They did provide some direct help, such as notarizing forms for rent reduction, having several meetings with social investigators, and making appropriate referrals. Cognizant of the inadequacies of this approach and their need to get on with the main task, they decided to put pressure on the (local settlement) to provide social services to the tenants. Carlos also wrote a proposal for a social service component to the rehabilitation program and submitted it to the [various funding sources].[11]

GROUP BEGINNINGS

As the worker begins to bring people together to form a group or take some action, he must be ready to commit himself to a particular constituency. He must be prepared to discuss one or many problem areas, elicit and incorporate constituent reaction, as well as develop and express his own positions. And he must be ready to define his role and explore mutual expectations.

How the worker goes about starting a group (or beginning his work with one already started) is influenced by his own goals and orientation, as well as by the circumstances of sponsorship and community condition. If the orientation is *individual,* for example, he will call together some of his private contacts and their friends (or some of the sponsor's clients) to discuss group formation. Informal "house meetings" has been suggested as a mechanism, at which the worker begins "discussion by briefly describing his work to a small group of neighbors, friends, or relatives of the hosts, using illustrations of the accomplishments of the organized poor in other places." [12]

The community work effort may, instead, follow the organized *group* life of the slum community itself. In that instance, the worker

[11] Fred Barbaro. *The Struggle to Provide Low-Income Housing in Coney Island* (New York: Columbia University School of Social Work, 1970), pp. 27–28. (Mimeographed)

[12] Warren Haggstrom, "Can the Poor Transform the World?" in Ralph M. Kramer and Harry Specht, eds., *Readings in Community Organization Practice* (Englewood Cliffs, N.J.: Prentice-Hall, 1969), p. 311.

will begin this phase of his work by offering his services to one or more indigenous groups, such as storefront churches, hometown clubs, and fraternities.[13] Or, in what is a somewhat similar case, the worker may be assigned by his agency to an existent group. In that instance, of course, the constituency and group are predetermined; what is most new to the situation is the worker.

One may also start with an *issue* orientation: the worker's primary concern is with influencing a particular issue rather than organizing a group. On an individual basis, this may be done through leafleting or by drawing on those private contacts whose interests and proclivities lend themselves to issue impact. On a group basis, the worker would begin by calling together (or having others call) existent groups in an attempt to form an ad hoc or permanent coalition (not, however, before having engaged in considerable preliminary work).

There are two aspects of group beginnings which we wish to note: The first relates to the worker's introduction of himself, and the second to his attempt to elicit interest in collective action.

Introducing Oneself. Introducing oneself is an on-going process; it starts at the first meeting and continues on throughout the worker's interaction with the group. It takes place through words, nonverbal communication, and through what the worker in fact does. Too often, we are afraid, community groups are unsure about what they can expect from their organizer.

The following are two reports of how a worker introduced himself; both were second-year students in community organization.

Worker A was assigned to work with a tenant organization in Beau Monde, a public housing project, which had a declining membership and a history of failure in trying to influence the Housing Authority. Its constituency was ethnically mixed, heavily burdened by poverty, and the worker culled from her two individual interviews prior to the first meeting that it was likely to resent Caucasians and outsiders. She reports:

[13] Many of these groups are invisible to the "established" community. In a study of a small neighborhood in Manhattan, for example, Hurley Doddy found 218 small informal groups, most of which were unknown to the established community agencies. Hurley H. Doddy, *Informal Groups and the Community* (New York: Columbia University Press, 1952).

The worker was introduced before the meeting began. She briefly introduced herself as a graduate student in community organization who had learned about the efforts of the Beau Monde tenant organization through the service center. The worker expressed the desire to attend the group's meetings and to work with the tenants in any way they might find useful. The tenants were asked if they had any objection. Although their facial expressions conveyed to the worker that the tenants were hesitant, puzzled, and suspicious, no one opposed her offer. During the rest of the meeting, the worker assumed the role of "observer" rather than participant and remained as unobtrusive as possible. The tenants had not invited the organizer to join the group, and thus it would not be possible for the worker to assume a more active role in the group until the members began to accept her presence.[14]

Although the Beau Monde worker was able, over an extended period of time, to gain the confidence of the group, she had hardly made an auspicious beginning. There is little wonder that they were hesitant or puzzled, since how were they to know what species "a graduate student in community organization" was? Her introduction hardly tells them what she does, much less what kind of help "they might find useful." Nor does it tell them why this stranger would want to help, assuming they knew what kind of help to ask for. The explanation is, in short, too general and abstract to be meaningful.

One may feel compassion for the Beau Monde worker, facing a suspicious and possibly hostile audience. But her question about whether there were any objections to her helping is a cheat since she knew there *were* objections which they were fearful of putting forth. She was aware in advance of the meeting that the members of the group felt exploited by officialdom, but she did nothing to dispel their concern that she might be in league with their "exploiters." Indeed, how were they to think otherwise? One way out of the dilemma would have been to raise the issue directly and to face with them that they might have grounds for suspicion. Another would have been to recognize that they might not wish to decide yet about her helping, or would prefer to discuss the matter when she was not present. In so doing, her sensitivity to their feelings would, at the least, have been manifest.

[14] Patricia A. Conley, "The Student Community Organizer in a Tenant's Organization," *New Perspectives*, Vol. 1, No. 1 (Spring 1967), p. 70.

Worker B was assigned to organize a ward of a hospital as part of an in-hospital community development project for the chronically ill. The patients were poor, old, and crippled; their years in the hospital had effectively deprived them of their individuality, sense of self, and assertiveness. Following pre-meeting interviews of the patients, the worker appoints Frank to serve as chairman, and although he and Frank plan the agenda and discuss group purpose, it does not work out quite as the worker had planned.

Frank opened the meeting with seven patients present. He made a statement, the gist of which was that we should talk about what we could do to get more activities on the ward. He said, then, "I think we ought to get more games going. What do you think?" Clara said, "We could have a party on the ward." Others were prepared to put forth suggestions when I said that before we considered activities, perhaps we ought to talk about the functions of this group and how I saw my role in it. Some of them might be interested in what they could gain from it, and curious about what I had to gain. I then mentioned that I was a community organization student, and gave examples of the types of activities c.o. people engage in, i.e., assisting in trying to influence change around community-wide problems, housing, etc. I pointed out that I had completed one year of study, and felt that I had something to offer in the nature of advice and suggestions about how things could be changed. I stressed Frank's role as chairman, and asked that discussion be directed to him. My relation to the group was that of an additional resource, which I said I hoped they would use, while together we investigated the resources, both physical and mental, which lay within our patients. I said that the group was not a therapy group, but I hoped they would enjoy being a part of it. I defined them as the most active and concerned patients, who would get things started. The goal of the group, as I saw it, was to make a beginning at breaking the chains of apathy that bind so many of the patients to the ward. I suggested that my self-interest in having that effort succeed would not conflict with their interest in improving the climate of the home in which they live. I asked how this idea struck them. Noises of agreement met this, followed by a comment from Mac that he liked what I said about the group.[15]

It should be noted that worker B had a significantly different relation to his constituents from that of worker A. In bringing together a collection of individuals, none of whom had shared a group experi-

[15] First Meeting of the Ward C Planning Committee, student record, Columbia University School of Social Work, 1969. (Mimeographed)

ence, he did not face the feeling that he was an interloper in a potentially unsympathetic group. He could, therefore, be freer. Once this has been said, however, it still remains that worker B explained what a "community organizer" was in a way that made it clearer. His explanation also supported the direction of his goals for the group and provided the patients of the ward with some notion of *how* he was prepared to help. His introduction established, in effect, a beginning "contract" between himself and the group which defined mutual interests and expectations.

Eliciting Constituent Interest. The orientation of the Ward C effort was *individual,* that is, the calling together of a collection of individuals with common interests. Beau Monde, on the other hand, although it was not related to the *group* life of the community per se, began with the offering of service to an existent group. Neither was specifically *issue* oriented.

An issue-oriented beginning would be directed to eliciting interest in the issue, as opposed to an emphasis on group function or worker role. Sometimes this takes the form—appropriately, we believe—of "rubbing raw the wounds of discontent." (Organizers, we note parenthetically, cannot make satisfied people angry; they can only help to make latent anger manifest, or to direct the anger in appropriate directions, for example, away from self and toward systems.) In the welfare rights organizing to which we referred in the prior chapter, for example, the intention was to start a cause, not a group (though group organization followed). Socialization, therefore, focused on welfare injustice. It is reported that:

A certain style of procedure soon developed in the Committee of Welfare Families. The first step the organizer took was in the direction of instilling confidence in those who attended the . . . meetings—confidence that they were capable of standing up for their rights. . . . At each meeting people were encouraged to stand up and bear witness to their feelings. Although those who spoke knew that everyone in the room was suffering from the same problems, yet they persisted in describing their common experience: how they had been addressed rudely by their investigators, how their homes had been searched . . . how they had been refused help without explanation.[16]

[16] Mary Rabagliati and Ezra Birnbaum, "Organizations of Welfare Clients," in Harold H. Weissman, ed., *Community Development in the Mobilization for Youth Experience* (New York: Association Press, 1969), p. 107.

An emphasis on clients' rights and the injustice of an institutional system is a potent means of eliciting constituent interest and support. This is particularly the case when, as above, persons bear witness, much as they might at a gospel meeting, thus energizing group feeling.

In addition to an agitational stance, another means by which workers elicit interest is by correctly identifying and dealing with constituent needs and problems. Often, these must be inferred, for example, by who they are (welfare clients are likely to be troubled by welfare systems), where they are (as in communities beset by racial conflict), what is behind what they say (in Beau Monde, the tenants felt "put down" by outsiders), and by how they act. The worker observes, listens, and identifies with the problems of group members. He clarifies problems, agrees with constituents, and disagrees with them. Throughout, he is seeking points of *goal convergence* between himself and them, points of commonality and common interest. He looks to find those issues and activities which will provide sufficient satisfaction to the group to sustain their interest, while at the same time the issues and activities advance his own community work objectives. Often, time is required for members to discuss their experiences and express their feelings before they are ready to consider taking action.

TECHNICAL TASKS

The technical or analytic task of the worker in the socialization phase of the process is to identify and explore a problem focus. Ultimately, goals must be set, programs devised to achieve those goals, and the resources garnered and structures developed by which to implement the programs.

Problems, goals, programs, and resources are often conceptually confused. People (organizers among them) tend sometimes to define problems in terms of programs, for example, "what this community needs is a neighborhood service center." What the problem really is, or what the goals of the center should be, is thus obscured.

Problems are defined differently, depending on the perspectives of the definer. Each brings a diverse set of interests and value system to his consideration of the problems needing attention, or their causes and solutions. This is as true for workers as it is for community influentials who tend to make up the community agenda. Although problem identification and formulation take place within a political framework among actors with varying degrees of power, we discuss it here from an analytic perspective. For in meeting the challenge of varying definitions of problems, or operating in a political arena, it is well for the worker to "have his head together."

We conclude this chapter with a discussion of two aspects of problem exploration. The first considers those questions which must be addressed in problem analysis. The second concerns those qualities of a problem or issue which make them amenable for collective action.

PROBLEM ANALYSIS

Essentially, problem analysis calls for answers to a series of subqueries to one overriding question: "What is the state of affairs to be altered? [17] Four may be cited as of particular importance: Who is it that is suffering? What are the characteristics of the victims? What is it that they suffer from? And what other work has been done on the problem?

Who—and how many—are suffering is an important aspect of problem analysis. The order of problem is different, for example, if a few clients are not receiving medicare benefits than if dozens are not. And the situation of dozens who have been deprived is different than when hundreds have been victimized.

As well as the dimension of the problem, analysts must know the characteristics of the victims, such as age, income, ethnicity, and location in the community. Are the victims clients in the Aid to Dependent Children Program or all welfare recipients? Is agency mistreatment directed only against black clients or all clients? Does this occur in one local office or in all agency offices?

A third question relates to the exact nature of the complaint. What, in fact, are the victims suffering from? Constituents may be

[17] Franklin M. Zweig and Robert Morris, "The Social Planning Design Guide: Process and Proposal," *Social Work,* Vol. II, No. 2 (April 1966).

deprived of services because of their ignorance about entitlements and proper procedures; or because of staff officiousness; or because an administrator may be trying to cut costs. The action implications in each case are different. Knowing the who, what, when, and where of the complaint is essential if wasted energies, or worse, are to be avoided. An example is the community action group which spent considerable effort in successfully pressuring a city government to establish a child care program. When the program was implemented, however, there were few users. In preliminary exploration, the organizers had found many people who had said that they would *like* to have a child care program. They did not inquire, however, how many people *needed* a child care program, the reasons why it was required, and how many would *use* it.

Finally, community groups need to ask who else is concerned with, or has worked on, the problem. Apart from saving needless effort, this information indicates sources of support, or what kind of barriers may have to be confronted.

The importance of these four questions is illustrated by the experience of a community group which chose to bring pressure on a department of welfare to provide recipients with medical care benefits. The clients believed that benefits to which they were entitled were being intentionally withheld. They decided to demonstrate at the welfare department, hoping to pressure the administrator. Instead, the demonstration resulted in a demoralizing failure for the group, which subsequently dissolved. Many factors may have been involved in their ignominious defeat, but one, surely, was their lack of information. How many people were affected, for example? As it turned out, they knew of only a few. (There may have been more, but the group had not found them). What were the characteristics of the people affected? The organizers had brought together people from diverse types of groups, whose interests in and views about welfare were disparate. What was the exact nature of the problem? This was unclear. One client had been promised medical funds by a worker which she had not received. Another had been given funds, but they were insufficient. And a third person could have received funds but had not let the welfare worker know of her needs. What kind of work had been done on the problem? As it turned out, unknown to the group, an

OEO legal services program was active on welfare issues in the same community. What might have been an excellent technical resource for the clients and the group thus went unused. Whether or not this group would have continued had there been a more adequate problem analysis is unknown, but a group's decision to act or not to act which is based on an informed assessment of the problem gives them a greater command of the field.

GUIDELINES FOR SELECTING "GOOD" PROBLEMS

Problems are sometimes thrust upon groups by community conditions, unusual events, and stirrings within the wider social scene. Often, however, a problem will be selected by a group, and in such case, problem analysis is insufficient to indicate whether the issue is necessarily a "good" one for community action. Other considerations, beyond technical analysis, must be brought to bear on problem selection. An issue may or may not excite the interest of potential constituents, may or may not increase group solidarity, encourage leadership development, or win public support. In short, it can contribute to, or hinder, the attainment of the goals of the different stages of the community work process.

Degree of Concreteness and Immediacy. One important characteristic of problems is the degree to which they are abstract or concrete. Concrete problems are felt directly, whereas abstract problems are more intellectual, indirectly experienced, and their solutions ordinarily longer range. Failure to receive a medical benefit to which a client is entitled is concrete, as is insufficient police surveillance of a neighborhood. At the other extreme, the "lack of a family policy" to direct federal welfare programs, or the absence of a centralized planning mechanism by which to allocate the resources of a city are abstract. The latter are more significant in that they have a greater impact on the lives of more people. However, they are also many steps removed from the immediate felt needs of people. People engaged in the struggle to subsist, as are the poor, are unlikely to make the required intellectual leap from the pressing problems of survival to those of greater significance that are not directly felt.

The more (organizationally) unsophisticated the group, and the less experienced the members and leaders, the "guttsier" the problem must be. No heat in the building, children expelled from school, the evicted family, an incident of police brutality—these are problems that people can feel, see, and understand. The genius of the great leaders of reform and revolution, like King, Chavez, Gandhi, and Guevera, is their ability to forge links in the minds of men between what they feel and see, and the somewhat more abstract "forces" that are at work in the society. On a more modest level, it is an organizer's task to locate concrete problems which stir interest or passion, and relate them to issues of wider moment.

Potential Rewards and Benefits. Since the organizer is competing for a precious commodity (i.e., the time and energy of participants), the question of *why* people participate is paramount. Will the rewards and benefits of participation be sufficient, for example, to induce the cost in commitment which is required to build an organization?

The organizer has to assess whether specific rewards flow from action on particular problems. Problems that are concrete and immediate do not always offer direct benefits to participants. And, of course, some problems have greater potential for providing benefits than others. For example, given a choice, pressing physical needs— heat, food, shelter—will produce visible benefits more readily than obtaining an ethnic studies program in a school or increasing police coverage in a neighborhood. The importance of making a cost-benefit analysis is indicated in the reactions of experienced community leaders. When asked to join in community action, they are likely to ask directly and unabashedly, "What's in it for me or my organization?" And whether "what's in it for me?" is verbalized or not, the organizer had best be ready with an answer.

Potential for a Successful Outcome. "Does it work?" "Does it help?" The acid test of any intervention is whether it can provide what people are seeking. As groups select problems with which to deal, an important consideration is whether success can be achieved and an immediate victory won. This is particularly the case with fledgling organizations, since the flush of victory is energizing and, conversely, members are unlikely to return to groups which fail to produce. It is for this reason that unions are typically sensitive to the importance of making or appearing to make gains—even if it requires celebrating as success what in reality was much less than the organizers had bargained for.

There are times, it is true, when an organization may need to maintain a "low profile." For example, in an effort to bring together a wide range of community leaders and groups, an organization might choose to remain out of the spotlight in order to avoid competition or to protect a fragile coalition. Generally, however, dealing with problems that give a group visibility and win the admiration of members and others for "getting things done" are organizationally enhancing.

The potential for success depends on the resources which are required to take action on the particular problem. This, in turn, is related to the particular stage of a group's development. In newly formed groups of inexperienced people, problems that require little organization and time are clearly advantageous. Launching a rent strike, for example, requires a high degree of planning, trust, commitment, and endurance. On the other hand, a group may be organized to press a health department to act on tenant complaints with little difficulty, particularly if the organizer has had experience in that area. The latter action may well produce a more modest result but, compared to the former, it is quicker and surer. The less experienced and well-organized the group, the more important that the problem lend itself to an early victory.

The Accessibility and Vulnerability of the Target. In addition to a group's resources, the potential for winning is determined by the target. Problems which direct attention outside of the community (e.g., the state legislature) rather than within it (e.g., the city council) present more formidable, because they are less accessible, targets. Similarly, when problems require changes in the law, rather than changes in its administration, or when group decisions are necessary for change rather than being within the purview of a single person, greater resources are required and victory more difficult to achieve.

Large bureaucratic organizations are well-provided with devices to insulate against change. Making appointments (often through a whole chain of command), requiring that forms be sent in quadruplicate, obtaining a place on a meeting agenda, reporting to committees, following the "proper" guidelines—all of these may or may not be nec-

essary procedures for operating complex agencies. Malevolent or benign, however, they can slow the hardiest of groups to a debilitating
snail's pace. Other targets may be more accessible and vulnerable.
The official on the scene in the local agency, the landlord (assuming
one can establish who he is for a slum tenement), and the supermar-
ket manager may be readier targets, particularly for the newly
formed group with limited resources.

Just as problems themselves must be concretized, so too is there
value in personalizing the targets associated with the problem. One
may not completely agree with the following admonition of one organizer, but there is assuredly practical wisdom in his words:

In dealing with low-income people who rarely have the experience or education of thinking in conceptual terms, in terms of where the system is
at fault, it's the immediate thing like the . . . landlord, the . . . cop on
the beat . . . the grocery-store owner, the lousy teachers, or the welfare
investigators, and it's important to maintain this immediate close-at-hand
target and let the chips fall where they may, even though this might in
the long run harm certain other things that you might want to be doing.
But if you try to tone this down at the very beginning, you're running
the danger . . . of alienating yourself from the people you want to organize . . . People will yes you to death about the system, it sounds very
nice, but it's the immediate target that has the real emotional force.[18]

Some estimation of how the target will respond is also necessary
as one considers problem areas. Later in this volume we discuss the
dialectic of community action and reaction. For the present, however, it should be noted that a target's response to community action
may be a more important determinant of success or failure than anything the action system might do. Sophisticated public officials are
likely to bend over backwards to give *something* to protesting citizens, even if it is only a sympathetic reception and the promise to
consider the matter. This can be useful to an inexperienced and
unstable group, although it may be unhelpful at some later stage. On
the other hand, a tense public official can be provoked into defensive
and insulting behavior which could be a shattering experience
for a timid or unstable group, but exactly the provocation needed to
get a developing group to close ranks.

[18] Rabagliati and Birnbaum, "Organizations of Welfare Clients," p. 106.

Potential for Public Support. The support or resistance of significant reference groups is an important tactical consideration in selecting a problem. Two characteristics are important in this regard; one has to do with the dramatic content of the problem, the other with its moral nature.

Drama for its own sake is useless and may, indeed, deflect from essential matters. On the other hand, the dramatic content of a problem is often a dynamic which gets it placed on a community agenda, which is a prerequisite for its solution. People are not likely to be aroused by safety legislation, for example, but multitudes are moved watching the rescue of a child who has fallen into an abandoned well. The ludicrousness of New York City's having to house one needy family at the Waldorf Astoria Hotel created more attention than the well-documented scarcity of low income housing in that city. Problems can excite fear, outrage, sympathy, hatred, and other emotions. Unfortunately, they can also generate disinterest and ennui.

Similarly, the moral nature of the problem is a significant factor. It has been observed, for example, that welfare recipients react more angrily to disrespectful treatment and threats to their dignity than to the inadequacies of the welfare grant.[19] Their response, we suspect, is in part due to the fact that their value system is in accord with the larger society, that is, that they have more *right* to humane treatment than to additional money.

The interest and support of a wider public, often required for community work success, requires consideration of the moral nature of the problem as well. Problems which highlight the failures of society to conform to its own values are particulalarly effective in generating sympathy for the victims of social problems. The "work ethic" is a powerful norm of the American value system. Thus, pointing up the failure of the system to provide men an opportunity to work will gain the support of many, whereas guaranteeing income (without a work incentive) finds lesser acceptability. This is not to say that only problems which support existing values are suitable; but rather, that the values underpinning a particular problem must, at the least, be assessed, since societal norms constitute a base from which groups encounter support or resistance.

[19] *Ibid.*

Potential for Collective Solutions. The analysis of problems in community work is in effect a search for collective solutions to social ills. Even problems affecting large numbers of people, however, may be more or less amenable to collective solution. When the victims are not naturally in interaction with one another or interaction is hard to manage (e.g., consumers of commercial products), collective action is more difficult. This is true too when the targets of the problem are many and dispersed. Thus inadequate housing in an entire neighborhood is hardly subject to solution through tenant organizing (unless a single target can be found, such as the city building department or the urban renewal agency). Finally, some problems are less amenable to collective action because of the requirements of their solution. Thus, although unemployment is a major issue in the low-income community, its potential for solution by community action is more limited than the problems of welfare and education.

In sum, the worker who has amassed the appropriate information, accurately analyzed community problems, elicited potential constituent interest, selected the "best" issue with his constituents and, together with them, has defined mutual expectations, has "concluded" the socialization phase of the process.

CHAPTER SIX

THE PRIMARY GROUP PHASE: "BELONGING"

THE FUNCTION OF THE PRIMARY GROUP PHASE of the community work process is the development of affective relationships and a sense of belonging among the participants. It is here that individuals develop an identification with the emerging group and a commitment to its purposes.

The interactional task of the worker during this stage is to aid constituents to cultivate social bonds and foster group cohesiveness (while remaining focused on the instrumental ends of the process). The technical task is part ideological and part intellectual. The worker is concerned with the ideology of the community action, the core of values and beliefs which constitute its rationale, as well as with goal development, and the theory which links problem identification to particular solutions.

INTERACTIONAL TASKS

Relationships are established through the *content* of the interaction between people. It is obvious, for example, that in the course of obtaining information in the socialization stage, the worker does (or does not) develop rapport with others, and helps (or impedes) constituents in fashioning connections among themselves. In seeking information, in fact, workers have to weigh their need for the data against what it may cost in the development of relationships with informants. Too great curiosity too early, for example, may provide data but cause irritation or suspicion. Similarly, relationships do not remain static, but constantly shape, and are shaped by the content of experience. Developing affective relationships is a continuous process; and the primary group phase of community work takes place at the same time as socialization and organization-development activities.

The worker has two major concerns regarding social-emotional relations. The primary one is the constituents' relationships with one another and the development of group solidarity. The second concern is his own relationship to his constituency. We shall discuss them in reverse order.

WORKER-CONSTITUENT RELATIONSHIPS

Three aspects of the worker-constituent relationship are of interest to us here: (1) elements which must be considered by the organizer in establishing rapport with his constituents; (2) the respective contributions of workers and constituents in decision making; and (3) the issue of worker passion or neutrality.

Establishing Rapport. Since the literature of the helping professions deals amply with worker-client relations,[1] we shall touch on only a few salient elements. It should be understood, however, that relational skills are critical to success in organizing-planning. The point is particularly relevant in work with constituents, pertinent but somewhat less so in dealings with action systems, and least applicable in regard to targets. Even in the last case, however, where relationship per se is an insufficient source of influence, relational skills are important.

Persons who share values and beliefs become socially attractive to one another. However, although workers must find areas of common

---

[1] For some examples, see Ronald Lippett et al., *The Dynamics of Planned Change* (New York: Harcourt-Brace, 1958); William Schwartz et al., ed., *The Practice of Group Work,* (New York: Columbia University Press, 1971); Lee J. Cary, ed., *Community Development as a Process* (Columbia: University of Missouri Press, 1970); Nicholas Van Hoffman, "Reorganization in the Casbah," *Social Progress,* Vol. 52, No. 6 (April 1962).

beliefs and shared feelings with their constituents, the test of their relationship is not agreeability or "nice guy-ness," but rather its effectiveness in promoting the joint enterprise. In being agreeable, the worker must also be authentic.

Acceptance of another requires the ability to appreciate the person without necessarily accepting his ideas and attitudes. (This is a difficult distinction, but it can be made.) Workers sometimes confuse acceptance with giving social approval or support; and although approval (a smile, a compliment, an indication of agreement) acts as a social reward and reinforces the response which called it forth, it is behavior which is subject to a law of diminishing returns. Approval by a person who is always ready with approbation is less valuable—in part because it is less believable—than approval by someone whose support is more frugally and thoughtfully granted.

Empathy is the ability to take the role of the other,[2] to answer the question "How would I react in his place?" with some degree of accuracy. It has been demonstrated that empathy is furthered by commonality. That is, persons who have experienced similar events (e.g., a life joy or crisis), who share cultural backrounds, or who fill similar roles (e.g., client, worker, student, teacher) are more likely to assess accurately the feelings and reactions of others with similar experience, culture, or role.[3] The point suggests that the demand for black workers to work with blacks, or low-income nonprofessionals to provide social services to the poor, is not just a nationalistic aberration or a political ploy, but has some basis in the greater empathy among people in like circumstances. This is not to say, of course, that empathy is the only (or even major) worker characteristic of import, that similarity of life circumstance insures similarity of perspective, or that empathy among the unlike does not exist or cannot be cultivated.

To see life from the perspective of another is simple enough as a concept, but exceedingly difficult to translate into actual practice. It requires hard work: listening (which is not merely attentive silence),

[2] *The Social Psychology of George Herbert Mead*, edited by Anselm Strauss (Chicago: University of Chicago Press, 1956).

[3] Raymond L. Gorden, *Interviewing, Strategies, Techniques, and Tactics*, (Homewood, Ill.: Dorsey Press, 1969), pp. 18–28.

a self-conscious "tuning in" to the other's words, and the ability and willingness to explore the inferences in those words.

A related, though distinct, point concerns the worker's willingness to encourage feedback. Norbert Wiener has remarked, "I never know what I said until I hear the response to it." [4] The term "feedback" is a shorthand word for the process of obtaining reactions to ourselves, our words, and our actions; its skillful encouragement is the only way in which workers can be assured of correctly assessing constituent reactions. To *really* do so (in contrast with *appearing* to encourage it) is anxiety-producing, particularly since the feedback is personal to what the worker has said or done. The authors of this volume, both of whom teach in a university, can attest to their own inner tension when they explore their students' reactions to the classroom and professor. It is a tension, however, which teachers—and organizers—must learn to bear.

The acceptant and empathetic worker will also encourage free expression of socially unacceptable and/or worker-unacceptable attitudes, apart from those relating to the worker himself. Thus the black who hates "whitey" must be free to say so to the worker; the white who excoriates black welfare mothers, and the older person put off by long-haired young activists must similarly be able to express their prejudices. The task of the worker in such instance, although difficult, is to make clear that these values differ from his own, while at the same time responding permissively to their expression. In the long run, workers cannot deal with intergroup problems unless people sense their permissiveness and acceptance.

To establish rapport, a worker must also be able to "speak the language" of his constituents. We do not mean this literally, though it applies literally as well. That is, organizers who work with a Spanish-speaking population must struggle to learn and speak Spanish, even if their constituents can manage in English, since the struggle alone evidences respect for the constituents' culture. The point is perhaps obvious, although a reputed professional social agency served a population of 100,000 people, 60 per cent of whom were Puerto Rican, without a single Spanish-speaking social worker on staff!

[4] Edgar H. Schein and Warren G. Bennis, *Personal and Organizational Change through Group Methods: The Laboratory Approach* (New York: Wiley, 1966), p. 41.

By "speaking the language," we mean learning the customs and culture of the constituent group. Once again, a fine balance must be maintained between knowing and appreciating the culture, on the one hand, and adopting it, on the other. In Whyte's classic study of a neighborhood, *Street Corner Society,* Doc, who was Whyte's local friend and informant, wisely advises that it would hamper relationships for him to act like a "corner boy," since Whyte was a college student. Whyte, nevertheless, found himself making more gestures than was his wont, and speaking in a more animated fashion.[5] In effect, he avoided adopting the corner boy style, but moved in its direction. He may thus have had the best of both worlds by projecting a consistent picture of himself, while at the same time indicating his knowledge and acceptance of the Italian street scene. The organizer must do the same. Adopting the jargon of the streets will seem to be pandering or patronizing—though the worker must understand and accept the lingo.

Appropriate worker behavior in establishing rapport depends on the cultural expectations of the people whom he is organizing. One student organizer, confusing professionalism with formality, reports as follows on his initial interview with Mrs. G., a woman with middle-class aspirations:

I went through some mental gymnastics trying to figure out if I had to ask permission to remove my sport jacket as it was warm there, and decided to remove it without asking. As you can see, I am clearly uncomfortable in my role as "professional social worker."

. . . As I left she said something like, "It was real nice talking to you, Mr. Kline." I said "I'm Ted." I figure that even though I'm a student, I have a right to set my own professional style, and I much prefer informality.[6]

Ted was neither right nor wrong in removing his jacket, nor in suggesting a first name basis to Mrs. G. He was wrong, however, to be guided *solely* by his own preference. The "professional" act had nothing to do with formality in this instance, but much to do with Mrs. G.'s expectations. If he had assessed her possible reactions, and

[5] William F. Whyte, "The Slum: On the Evolution of Street Corner Society," in Arthur J. Vidich et al., eds., *Reflections on Community Studies,* (New York: Wiley, 1964), pp. 3–69.

[6] Malcolm Tenant Council, student record, Columbia University School of Social Work, pp. 1 and 5. (Mimeographed)

correctly felt that she would appreciate his apparent ease, his decision could be commended. As it was, she might have been puzzled or insulted by what appeared to her to be "unseemly" behavior.

Decision Making: Who Decides? Few issues are as heatedly debated within community organization, or are as complex, as the question of who decides on choice of problem, goal, program—or indeed, the multitude of minor matters along the way. Points made in the preceding chapter illustrate the complexity: an agency which embarks on a housing program has, in effect, determined the problem area; a worker who recruits a particular type of constituency has predetermined goal directions. Yet prescriptions in the field suggest that it is the client who controls group destiny. Thus, according to Ross, the worker "cannot be 'the leader' or make the decision or recommend the 'right' course of action." [7]

Proponents of participatory democracy have identified another contradiction of "self-determination." On the basis of their "movement-oriented" organizing, Fruchter and Kramer note that:

. . . the attempt to proceed as a group without leaders and to achieve decisions by consensus often masks the more pernicious force exerted by powerful personalities whose decisions are unchecked, because their leadership, denied by the project, is not required to be responsible.[8]

There is, unfortunately, no *right* answer regarding the respective contributions of the three actors (that is, sponsor, worker, constituents) to the decision-making process. Even if there were, the actors are not free agents, but operate within a field of forces which circumscribes "right" and "wrong." The sponsor is likely to be the most powerful of the three partners. The sponsor can, therefore, unduly influence the most significant of the decisions, and it takes professional blinders to ignore the sponsor's omnipresence. We shall develop this point in Part III of this volume. For now, we note only that how agency and worker play out their decision-making prerogatives is less morally ambiguous than worker-constituent relations in this

[7] Murray G. Ross, *Community Organization: Theory and Principles* (New York: Harper and Row, 1955), pp. 210–11.

[8] Norman Fruchter and Robert Kramer, "An Approach to Community Organizing Projects," in Ralph M. Kramer and Harry Specht, eds., *Readings in Community Organization Practice* (Englewood Cliffs, N.J.: Prentice-Hall, 1969), p. 236.

regard. We omit reference to the sponsor in the discussion which follows, concentrating instead on the contribution of the other two participants to decision making.

Clearly, the goal of the community effort constitutes an influential determinant of the respective roles of workers and constituents in decision making. It is one thing when the goal is a specific policy change and group action is the means to achieve it, and quite another when the goal itself is the development of an institutional-relations organization to exert on-going impact on policy and program. Both, we believe, are relevant professional community work objectives. In the former instance (the policy change goal), workers will attempt to influence decision making more vigorously than in the latter case (the group development goal).[9] In neither instance, however, do we believe that professional ethics permit the *use* of constituents without their knowledge and compliance.

One of the major tenets of community work, as we have defined it, is to increase the participation of service recipients in affecting their own destinies. In what may seem an apparent contradiction, we also believe that community workers must provide direction and leadership to community groups. In practice, the contradiction is resolved in the attempt by each to influence the other. There is nothing untoward, for example, in these comments of the welfare client organizer:

I accept the fact that . . . I have to initiate ideas, point out directions, whether asked for or not. I make it very clear to members that, because I state my opinions, that doesn't mean they have to accept them. When they want to head in a direction that I think is wrong, I'll force them to show me why they're right and I'm wrong. I'll stand by my guns, but if it comes down to a complete confrontation where they won't budge, then I will give in.[10]

The only question in the above is whether the constituents can, in fact, stand by *their* guns. With an excessively timid or dependent community group, the task of the worker would be to encourage the expression of opposition to himself as well as to others.

[9] We discuss the reasons why we believe this to be so in chapter 8.

[10] Mary Rabagliati and Ezra Birnbaum, "Organizations of Welfare Clients," in Harold H. Weissman, ed., *Community Development in the Mobilization for Youth Experience*, (New York: Association Press, 1969), p. 132.

An obvious point, regularly overlooked, is the difference between democratic form and democratic reality. The test of democratic decision making in community groups is not whether its officers are elected, by-laws adopted, votes taken, or the other trappings of democracy observed. The test is whether the decisions result from a process in which many participate and which reflect, in fact, what the group wants to do. The *Beau Monde* tenants' council (see chapter 5) "democratically" decided to accept the organizer, although the members neither understood her role nor wanted her help. Later in the life of the council, the *Beau Monde* organizer, discussing the goals which had been adopted, notes that; "Two objectives were selected from the tenants' lengthy list. Choices were made on the basis of personal preference [of the chairman and the delegate faction]. . . . The other tenants responded to this dilemma by decreasing their participation in the meetings and by failing to involve themselves with either objective." [11] A vote, in such an instance, is irrelevant. Professional responsibility requires that the worker attempt to intervene to prevent undemocratic decisions democratically arrived at.

A typical mistake made by inexperienced organizers is to press for elections before group members hardly know one another, or before the worker can assess leadership patterns. Elections may be, in part, a search for program activity; often it is sheer ritualism; or it may reflect the desire of the worker to avoid responsibility. On the other hand, a worker who fills the role of central figure with inordinate relish may be loathe to relinquish it. Elections, votes, and by-laws will not prevent an over dominant worker from imposing his will, however.

Worker imposition and worker directiveness are sometimes confused. The welfare client organizer, quoted above, was active and direct, but he did not (necessarily) impose his position on the group. How directive or how much of a "doer" a worker must be is implied by our previously noted concept of the professional as one who fills the requisite (or "missing") roles. He directs or does to the degree it

[11] Patricia A. Conley, "The Student Community Organizer in a Tenants' Organization," *New Perspectives*, Vol. 1, No. 1 (Spring 1967), p. 75.

is necessary to increase constituent competence and/or the achievement of their goals.

There are some guidelines in this regard. The stage of the process of a group's development is one salient factor. New, impermanent, ad hoc, and informal groups have more missing roles to fill; the corollary to this point is that, as time goes on and structure develops, a worker's role becomes more circumscribed and clearly defined. Thus it is during the socialization phase that the worker's initiative and autonomy is greatest. This shifts as the process moves forward, and in a later stage—organization-building—his autonomy is likely to be considerably diminished.

Another factor is the organizational experience of the participants. Indigenous leaders are not necessarily those who observe middle-class niceties, and some new groups, including those composed of the poor, contain organizationally sophisticated participants. The organizer of a newly formed Ad Hoc Committee on School Suspensions indicates his perception of this fact in the following characterization of the Committee:

The members of the Ad Hoc Committee did not come as individuals. They generally came as members of other groups. Most centered around nuclear leaders. . . . (Mrs. T., for example, is a large attractive woman who speaks with a West Indian accent, and is a veteran parent leader.) The nuclear leaders are constantly shifting about to new bases of power. They come from three main axes: churches, parent associations, and block associations. . . . This group and its members could not easily be . . . coopted. When manipulation was done, it was done with their collusion, either overt or covert.[12]

There are two other guidelines affecting worker activity which ought to be noted. One has to do with the organizer's need to establish his expertise; the other, with the expectations of the constituents.

Workers sometimes try to impress constituents with their modesty and lesser status in the group with statements like "I'll try to help, but only the group is competent to make decisions." Apart from the un-

[12] *A Conference on School Suspensions: The Bedford-Stuyvesant Neighborhood Association,* student record, Columbia University School of Social Work, p. 11. (Mimeographed)

reality of such a position, the statement overlooks the fact that modesty strengthens regard only for persons whose outstanding qualities are already appreciated. If social attraction has not yet been established, modesty can be discomforting, since it is a claim for acceptance which others may or may not wish to honor.[13] More important than modesty is the organizer's ability to demonstrate his knowledge and skill to constituents. This entails a risk, however, for to act the expert, one must give signs of task competence, and one's advice must be effective.

In large measure, worker activity and directiveness ought also to be influenced by constituent expectations. A community group's satisfaction with an organizer's performance depends not only on their need for help, but also on how much activity it believes workers *should* engage in. Of course, the worker's definition of his role in the socialization phase influences what constituents may anticipate. Groups may also expect too much—more than it is helpful for them to get, or more than can be given. Nevertheless, organizers should look to constituent cues regarding how active or directive they should be.

The Worker: Neutrality or Passion? It is undoubtedly clear by now that we believe an organizer's primary commitment is to his constituents. The issue of worker partisanship, however, is another of those community work dilemmas in which the choice of one value may entail sacrifice of another.

Workers who assist the poor to participate in community activities cannot, with equanimity, proclaim neutrality when contentious issues are confronted. To help service users challenge institutional conditions without at the same time putting himself "on the line" is a contradiction which will not be lost on constituents. In the face of constituency passion, worker (or agency) neutrality seems like timidity. Workers cannot, in any case, remain unmoved by the social injustice they observe, nor help the victims of social problems without also strongly identifying with them in their plight. Groups have the right to expect that organizers will be partisan in any social conflict.

On the other hand, there are some advantages to professional dis-

[13] Peter M. Blau, *Exchange and Power in Social Life* (New York: Wiley, 1964), p. 48.

tance. Worker objectivity allows for more accurate, and therefore more useful, appraisals of conflict and other situations. An impartial stance sometimes permits the worker to perform a critical bridging role, linking the contending group with target institutions, to the former's advantage. Indeed, research suggests that whereas the task of leaders of *formal* associations is to engender follower loyalty, some social distance is advantageous for leaders of *informal* groups.[14] A study by Fiedler, for example, showed that the performance of informal groups was more effective under leaders who manifested some separateness from members than under leaders who did not.[15] In some measure, the issue is related to the tension between the task and expressive functions of groups and the necessity to fill both types of leadership role. In addition, the appropriate worker response varies with his role. Organizers engaged in social planning are counted on to be rational and impartial whereas "grass roots" organizers are expected to express passionate concern.[16] Nevertheless, the dilemma persists, and the worker must seek the best of both worlds. Haggstrom summarizes our view when he calls for this tall order from the organizer;

He [must] be able to identify with the poor and view the world as they view it, without losing his identity as an organizer nor his ability to understand the powerful. He [must] not instinctively rebel against nor instinctively identify with authority . . . [but] be able to channel his anger and emotions into ending injustice, and not merely bearing witness to it.[17]

DEVELOPING GROUP SOLIDARITY

During socialization, a sorting-out process takes place among those initially involved. Some drop out because they are indifferent to the goals or believe them to be unachievable, others because they are disinterested in the work, and some because they dislike the other

[14] *Ibid.,* p. 210.

[15] Fred E. Fiedler, *Leader Attitudes and Group Effectiveness* (Urbana: University of Illinois Press, 1958), chapter iii. As cited in Blau, *ibid.,* pp. 210–11.

[16] This point is made in John B. Turner, ed., *Neighborhood Organization for Community Action* (New York: National Association of Social Workers, 1968), p. 147.

[17] Warren C. Haggstrom, "Can the Poor Transform the World?" in Kramer and Specht, *Readings in Community Organization Practice,* p. 313.

participants. In the primary group stage of the community work process, participants must decide whether to commit themselves, and the task of the worker is to encourage identification with the group and its purposes.

Social bonds are more easily developed among persons who have similar characteristics and beliefs. Groups composed of people of the same ethnicity, color, class, sex, age, and so forth, will be more cohesive than those in which membership characteristics are disparate. Homogeneous work groups, for example, participate more in union activities than do heterogeneous ones,[18] and the same principle undoubtedly operates among community action groups. Thus, there may be no alternative in ethnically mixed communities but to organize ethnically homogeneous groups which later come together to pursue superordinate goals. Often, such structure is more effective in encouraging harmonious intergroup relations than attempting to organize integrated, but weak and floundering, small groups.

Similarity of belief, or a common ideology, is also a potent force for solidarity. Ideology functions as a "rallying point (and) a symbol of group identity." [19] Groups pressing for social change are often composed of people whose values, behavior, and characteristics have been invidiously defined. Participation in group action requires that they identify as members of the larger group to overcome the stigma associated with their role category, as did welfare recipients in welfare rights organizing. An improved self-image is not only an important step in victims acting in their own behalf, but contributes to modifying the image the larger society has of them as well. A task of the organizer, then, is "to arouse the poor from their bad dream (which includes an underlying fear of their own weakness and inferiority) . . . [and] create an alternative and more accurate view of their world and of their position in it. . . ." [20] Ideologies which focus on the denial of citizen rights and place responsibility for social injustice on systems rather than individuals contribute importantly in this regard.

[18] Peter M. Blau and W. Richard Scott, *Formal Organizations* (San Francisco: Chandler, 1962), p. 47.

[19] Blau, *Exchange and Power in Social Life,* p. 233.

[20] Haggstrom, "Can the Poor Transform the World?" p. 310.

In addition to identification with a broader movement, constituents must identify with the participants and purposes of their community group. Commitment to a group, of course, varies with the needs and proclivities of individuals and groups. The task is to find the right fit between individual needs and group requirements. There are two aspects of this match which are important in developing a cohesive and effective group: (1) the uses of group structure; and (2) accommodating the task and expressive functions of the group.

Group Structure. Structure may aid or impede membership commitment and group identification. The roles which must be filled by a group as it develops organizationally is one important element of its structure.

Four types of participants contribute variously to group life: executives, actives, occasionals, and supporting participants. *Executive participants* are the group's "oligarchy," or central decision makers. As groups increase in their complexity, they require a small number of people who make decisions regarding such matters as agenda, programs, and administrative business. The existence of an "oligarchy" does not indicate a lack of democratic functioning. The test is, rather, whether the executive group is broadly representative of the diversity among constituents, and the extent to which the executives are open to direction by the larger membership. *Active participants* (who may also be executive members) are those who take part in most of the group's activities, and can be counted on to do much of its "scut work," for example, telephoning, attending meetings, mailing letters, etc. *Occasional participants,* as their name suggests, only show occasionally, usually when there is an interesting or crucial meeting or demonstration. This type of membership makes an important contribution to the group's image as "representative" of the community. They are the members who affirm that there are voters or potentially disruptive adherents who can be called upon by the group, and that it has the community's support. *Supporting participants* are the least involved, and their physical presence is rarely available. They do support the group, however, by "joining," thus swelling its ranks and adding to the image of group potency. They may "participate" in nonactive efforts, such as an economic boycott, and may also make financial contributions.

Thus not all members need to be similarly committed or involved, though groups need all types of participants in sufficient numbers to function effectively. The point is important, since organizers tend to ignore the inevitability of different levels and degrees of participation in community groups, and frequently try to induce the fullest participation of all members. The effort is not only wasteful of energy, and impossible of achievement, but it leads to self-defeating sermonizing and the (sometimes subtle) chiding of members for not giving their "all." Instead, the worker's attention should be devoted to the roles which must be filled; or, in other words, searching out persons to fit the requisite roles, rather than dunning or manipulating people to fill participant categories in which they are disinterested. It also means that activities which develop a small group of leaders (the executives) and enhance their prestige, marking them as different from the rank and file, ought to be sought rather than avoided.

Structure can be used to expand involvement and to train people for leadership positions (e.g., from actives to executives). A formal training program is one such device. Structure which extends the number of tasks to be done is another. For example, at the *Beau Monde* housing project, two delegate councils were organized, one consisting of parents and children, the other of a representative from each of the buildings in the housing project who functioned as individual "complaint bureaus." [21] Thus tasks which interested, challenged, but did not overtax participants were devised. Program content which permits diversification of work is also useful, since it provides people with a choice of activity and, therefore, greater incentive for involvement.

Structure ought also to support affective relationships. Committees, when possible, should consist of people who find one another socially attractive. Participant enjoyment is thus increased, and interpersonal attraction creates cohesion.[22] In addition, when friends share labors, performance is improved, and acts which are difficult or discomfiting become less so. Thus a petition campaign, even leafleting, conducted in teams rather than by solitary individuals, is more eagerly undertaken.

[21] Conley, "The Student Community Organizer," p. 74.

[22] Barry E. Collins and Harold Guetzkow, *A Social Psychology of Group Processes for Decision-Making* (New York: Wiley, 1964), p. 197.

Accommodating Task and Expressive Functions. According to Lee Rainwater, voluntary associations "probably function more as entertainment and leisure-time activities than as serious mechanisms for attaining one's central life goals." [23] Because organizers believe that group action will contribute to solving problems, they are frustrated by a lack of progress which members, viewing the group as an avenue for expressive gratification, accept with greater equanimity.[24] Though perhaps overstated, this difference calls attention to the tension between the instrumental and expressive functions of groups to which we alluded earlier.

Groups organized to achieve tasks which transcend the immediate gratification of their members must take steps toward the achievement of their purposes, or they will fail to survive. Experimental studies indicate that, at a minimum, high task effectiveness is associated with high participant satisfaction.[25] On the other hand, task accomplishment may be "vague, undifferentiated, late in coming, and relatively unimportant to the momentary satisfactions of the group members." [26] Thus expressive activities are needed to spice the group stew. Though conceptually distinct, task achievement and expressive gratification are interdependent.

What is required, then, is that the organizer consider both instrumental and expressive needs as he assists a community group. The group must always be helped to accomplish what it sets out to do, whether it is involved in short-range activity (e.g., conducting a community meeting), or even if task achievement requires the organizer's doing some of the work which is ordinarily the group's responsibility. Simultaneously, the worker must see that members are involved in pleasurable activities, from which they may derive immediate rewards.

Community groups often expend considerable time in discussing what they should do, and leave hanging at a meeting's end the "who's" and "how's" of getting it done. Indeed, many groups flounder because they decide on actions without giving thought to the subtasks required by the action, or who will do them. At all stages in a

[23] Lee Rainwater, "Neighborhood Action and Lower-Class Life-Styles," in Turner, *Neighborhood Organization*, p. 31.

[24] *Ibid.*, p. 33.

[25] Collins and Guetzkow, *Social Psychology of Group Processes*, p. 197.

[26] *Ibid.*, p. 222.

group's life, workers must see that assignments are concretized, and follow up on the members who take them, help them plan their work, and make sure that the plans are reported back to the group.

Studies of task-oriented and conference groups indicate that participants are more likely to reach consensus or express more satisfaction with meetings in which: (1) agendas are well prepared and completed; (2) discussions are orderly without backward reference to previously discussed issues; (3) matters are discussed one at a time; (4) give-and-take is allowed among the participants; (5) topics are finished with dispatch; and (6) decisions are made that members feel are good ones. Finally, shorter meetings are more satisfying than longer ones.[27]

Bales makes a series of recommendations regarding the task effectiveness of committees based on his work in analyzing the interaction process. He suggests, for example, that committees ought be no larger than seven members and that length of meeting time and seating arrangements should allow for adequate and direct communication. The discussion should start with facts, then move to values and opinions, or how people feel about the facts, and sufficient time taken to lay the groundwork for the final stage of soliciting specific suggestions for action. He admonishes the leader to listen when someone else is talking, to react actively, whether the reaction is positive or negative, to make sure his eyes are on the group as a whole when speaking, rather than on friends or supporters, and to search constantly for reactions to his words.[28]

The dull, difficult, or demanding day-to-day tasks which are part of all community action should be interspersed with program content which, to the extent possible, is colorful, instructive, or indicative of the importance of the effort. Symbols of group identification or individual accomplishment may also be used to serve expressive purposes. For example, one tenants' organization issued membership cards to provide a symbol of belonging. By-laws and constitutions are often as much a sign of group status and importance as they are a means of ordering the group's business. Awards and ceremonies

[27] *Ibid.*, chapters 5 and 10.
[28] Robert F. Bales, "The Committee Meeting," in William A. Glaser and David L. Sills, *The Government of Associations* (Totowa, N.J.: Bedminster Press, 1966), p. 133.

which honor contributors to the group are other such symbols. Organizers who are "all business" make a mistake when they perceive these as unnecessary frills. Thus, an agency-sponsored welfare rights group conducted an eight-session training program for leaders which resulted in conflict between staff and constituents regarding the granting of diplomas and a graduation ceremony.

Agency staff were appalled at the demands of the women for . . . funds for the graduation ceremony. The women for their part wanted more . . . recognition. The idea of doing something for the community or for others on welfare was not the only significant reward some of these women sought.[29]

TECHNICAL TASKS

Goal development is the link between problem analysis and program alternatives. Forging that link is the major technical task of the worker in the primary group phase of the community work process.

During the socialization stage, the worker has identified a relevant problem; he now takes the process a step further—to an analysis of its causes and cures. The worker, during this phase, is concerned with bringing the perspectives of theory, strategy, and ideology to bear on the group's efforts, thus providing it with purpose and direction. In this section we first discuss the worker's contribution to theoretical and ideological clarity, after which we shall conclude the chapter with some suggestions about how goal differences are adjusted.

THEORETICAL AND IDEOLOGICAL CLARITY

What people choose to do about a problem is based on what they perceive causes it and how it may be remedied. We have already discussed how intrapsychic, sociocultural, and structural theories of behavior lead to the acceptance or rejection of alternative goals (e.g., integrative, sociotherapeutic, and environmental-change objectives). Many new careers programs, for example, are based on the implicit assumption that institutional arrangements are more effective if low-

[29] Rabagliati and Birnbaum, "Organizations of Welfare Clients," p. 114.

income people, acting as staff members, serve as integrative links between the institution and the community it serves; or, in other words, that poor communications cause problems. Many self-help programs are based on theoretical notions that problems occur because internal social development is lacking in the low-income community.

The examples are limitless, since *all* programmatic solutions to social problems are based on some theory of cause and effect, even though the theory may not be explicit. We do not intend to discuss particular theories at this time, but wish, rather, to underscore the importance of theory per se—a necessary point in view of the anti-intellectualism by which community work is marked.

We use the word "strategy" to define the *long range* goals of groups, or the way in which groups and organizations link problems and solutions. For example, in chapter 5 we described a community group that was concerned about the withholding of medical benefits from welfare clients. The group's problem analysis was inadequate, but had it been otherwise, it might then have gone on to explore a wide range of possible goals which, implicitly or explicitly, would have been based on some theory about the problem. If the withheld benefits were thought to be caused by inadequate or punitive workers, the programmatic strategy might be concerned with worker training, supervision, or accountability. If the problem had been caused by an administrator hoping to win political support through repressive policies, then litigation, political pressure, or social action would follow. On the other hand, if the allowances as mandated were insufficient, or budgetary allocations inadequate, legislative action might be the strategy of choice. Had the welfare clients been uninformed about their rights, or too apathetic to claim them, the goal might be winning client representation or re-educating them to assert themselves in their use of the welfare agency.

In fact, in this particular community, transportation *to* medical facilities was a problem for clients. Most were forced to live in a remote and isolated section of the city due to a critical limitation of housing for low-income people. It was also unclear as to whether adequate medical facilities were available (even if the welfare agency had granted the necessary funds and the people were able to travel to the facilities). Lack of transportation, availability of housing, and adequacy of medical services as "causes" of the problem suggest different strategies.

Which of all the possible "theories" about the problem is right? Any or all of them may be relevant. If, as is most often the case, there is multi-causality, "a one-variable approach is likely to be as ineffective as a quarterback who knows only one play." [30] But groups cannot take action on every front. Some causes are less remediable than others; some have less potential for offering immediate benefits; and some are less useful in the development of organizations. In effect, worker and group must develop a theory which relates cause and cure, and choose a strategy based on that theory, as well as on the resources and development of the particular group.

The terms "strategy" and "tactics" are often used interchangeably. The latter is more appropriately applied to the short-range and specific behaviors of groups, however. Groups having widely different long-range goals (strategies) will engage in the same kinds of behaviors (tactics). And a specific group may utilize a wide range of tactics in pursuit of their goals. In Part IV we discuss a spectrum of tactics from the consensual to the conflictual, and when and how they may be used by community workers. It should be clear now, however, that tactics and strategies are not the same.

The confusion of the terms is based on complex reality, for there are times when the strategies of groups consist only of tactics. For example, a group's plan for dealing with a problem may be continuously to assault an institutional target until there is change. The expected change is undefined; only the tactics are specified. Similarly, the proponents of community development in underdeveloped areas tout the "process" (i.e., a set of tactics) as their essential strategy.

Both of these "tactical" models of practice have been criticized as atheoretical and "ideological." In truth, however, though their theories may be inadequately developed—or even not readily apparent— both are based on some notion of remediation. In the first instance (assault on an institutional target), community power theory is the point of reference, and it is held that by continuous struggle between "the people" and "the establishment," a reallocation of power will be

[30] J. Milton Yinger, *A Minority Group in American Society* (New York: McGraw-Hill, 1965), p. 98.

brought about. In the second instance (community development) educational theory is relied on, and it is thought that increased interaction between subsegments of a community will produce change.

"Ideology" is a type of theory. The word has a somewhat pejorative
cast, since it usually refers to theory which is strongly held and nar-
rowly applied. For some, it refers to the *only* permissible explanation
of problems; for others, it refers to the other man's theories, that is,
those which are abjured. Like it or not, however, an ideology is a
theory that has been turned into a social lever. This occurs when large
numbers become strongly committed to an idea and insist that all
behavior and beliefs be explained by it. Ideologies are shorthand
descriptions of complex phenomena. "Racism," *"liebensraum,"* "nonviolence," "community control," "Christian temperance," "black
power," "the Jewish conspiracy," and "the domino theory" are examples of ideologies which have exerted great impact in this century.
Ideology is, by definition, neither good nor bad; it merely represents
an idea which has captured the imagination. The evaluation of an
ideology must rest on the intrinsic worth of the idea and the effect
which it has on other values.

We have already suggested the importance of ideology in reshap-
ing the self-image of a social group and forging cohesive bonds among
the members of community collectivities. If the poor and others are to
be immunized against diversionary tactics or helped to resist coercive
pressures, they must develop a value system and set of beliefs which
inform their efforts. To the extent that this is possible, it is a priority
task of the community worker. Organizers who rejoice in their constituents' "rebirth through doing," while problems remain unrelated to
their sources in the institutional structure, are failing in the more difficult and important task. It is only as the worker helps the community
organization develop a theory about the institutional system with
which it is dealing that people can move beyond meeting individual
needs to addressing institutional causes.

Theory, strategy, and ideology can be the regulating features of
all the other aspects of organization, since they provide purpose and
direction. Uninteresting work is more sufferable when the long-range
goal is highly desirable. The interpersonal demands members make
of one another can be both limited and justified, as the case may be,

in view of the more important long-range purposes. The values of activities and tactics can be weighed in light of their potential for achieving desired long-range objectives.

Theory, strategy, and ideology come from the intellectual leadership of the community. Intellectual and ideological leaders elucidate the historical, legal, and political relationships which underlie community problems, and in so doing, enable organizations to maintain vigor as they move toward goals. Examples of such leaders within the past decade are numerous: Martin Luther King Jr., shaping the ideas of Thoreau and Gandhi for contemporary American use, provided the civil rights movement with the power of moral suasion; Stokely Carmichael, following the direction of Malcolm X and using Milton Gordon's theories of assimilation in American life, articulated a powerful political argument for the internal development of black communities; Cesar Chavez absorbed tactical principles from an Alinsky organizer and then went on to develop his own analysis of the Mexican-American community vis-à-vis the Southern California landowners.

We do not, of course, expect the neighborhood organizer to be a King, Carmichael, or Chavez, although such leaders could develop from among organizer ranks. Indeed, we do not ask even that the organizer *be* the intellectual or ideological leader on a more modest scale or in a more derivative way. He must, rather, be aware of the importance of the role. These leaders may reside in the community, or they may come from elsewhere. The organizer helps constituents by introducing them to the ideas by such activities as inviting speakers, visiting other groups, making films and writings available, and conducting discussions. Unfortunately, the anti-intellectualism of much community work, as well as the pragmatism inherent in the practice, supports avoiding the development of institutional theory and long-range strategy. The equalitarian values of organizers and the day-to-day requirements of organizing lead to the rejection of any view of the process which suggests an *un*equal relationship between worker and community. In place of theoretical analysis and clarity of goal, we are sometimes offered assertions that faith, hope, love, heart, righteous indignation, and "power from the point of a gun" will solve problems. Sometimes there is even a latent desire to keep constituents isolated from the larger community, to create a "counter-community." The implicit rationale underlying this vision is that of protecting the simple members of the folk society from the temptation of corruption by the world "out there." But in elevating the socialization and primary group phases of the organizing process to a primary goal, the organizer short-changes his group and denies the nature of his leadership.

ADJUSTING GOAL DIFFERENCES

Goal development is an on-going process, and community groups discard, reaffirm, or modify their objectives in the light of ongoing experience. A group's objectives, or its subgoals, may be compatible or incompatible; and in holding two or more goals simultaneously, acting on one may support or endanger the other. The process is all the more complicated by the fact that there are three actors (i.e., constituents, workers, and sponsors) attempting to influence the outcome—each of which may disagree with the others, or among themselves.

A major task of the worker, we have already noted, is to clarify and articulate goals. He may also have to order them in some priority—or leave them ambiguous, as the circumstances warrant. This requires an understanding of how groups and organizations adjust disparate goals, and we conclude this chapter by considering this matter.

Broadly speaking, organizations deal with differences among goals in three ways: (1) when the objectives are viewed by participants as compatible, compromise is possible, and two goals may be sought at once; (2) a second form of compromise is accomplished by "planned ambiguity," a form of adjustment which occurs when an action system's objectives seem to conflict; (3) the third method is to achieve clarity by choosing one goal as primary from among conflicting claims, discarding others, or assigning them a lower priority. Which of the three is chosen depends on organizational conditions; and each method carries its own advantages and disadvantages.

Compromise is effected in two ways when goals are compatible. One is through their merger: different goals can be pursued through mutually supporting actions. Workers must search for this convergence; the welfare rights movement constitutes an example of its successful accomplishment. Movement leaders saw constituent action as a way of exerting pressure to induce changes in income maintenance arrangements. Welfare clients, on the other hand, sought more modest and short-range ends, such as an increase in emergency assistance. The actions necessary to effect both ends were similar, and their merger was therefore possible.

Compromise is also effected by pursuing different, though compatible, goals in sequence. A third form of compromise—when goal compatibility is less—is to insulate one goal from another, so that contradictions are rendered obscure. In such an instance, one portion of the action system pursues one goal, while another seeks a second end deflecting of the first. This adjustment is common within large organizations which may point firmly in two directions at once.

Examples abound in the public bureaucracies. Thus, in the mid-1960's, the Department of Labor, which traditionally offered employment services to the stable working force and employer groups, was enjoined to shift some of its attention to the needs of the chronically disadvantaged worker. Providing services to all three groups entailed, in some measure at least, contradictions in policy. Although these might have been resolved theoretically, the Department made the political (but rationally problematic) decision to insulate its services to the disadvantaged in a new and separate manpower program. Strains between the latter and other bureaus did occur, but had the Department done otherwise, internecine warfare between old- and new-line staff would have been inevitable. What is more significant, however, is that, in the conflict, the political potency of the old-line bureaus would have forced the submergence of the new direction.

Conditions for compromise also result from the nature of the relations among constituent groups. Compromise is a potential solution when relative parity of influence exists, that is, neither party to the conflict may feel sufficiently confident of a successful result to chance a struggle. Compromise may be sought as well when the more powerful members (e.g., the sponsor elite) wish to grant a concession to gain equity with lower participants (e.g., the community group or staff), or the price of strained relations is not deemed worth the cost of legislating a particular end. Whenever getting together is more important to the participants than ends which might be contentious, peace through accommodation is sought. In such cases, the more "hard-nosed" rather than more formally powerful members of the coalition win the day.

Goal clarity is important in the development of a practice focus, for without clarity participants are required to create their own operational definitions and, if they wish, can interpret the goals in any way they want; or, in other words, "go into business for themselves." The result is often confusion, actions which are at cross-purposes, and even the pursuit of "wrong" ends. Minimally, should an action system choose, like Gertrude the Governess, to "ride off in all directions," it should be aware of the potential cost.

Planned ambiguity is a means of dealing with goal incompatibilities. It allows participants with diverse values to share participation in an action system with an assumption of commonality, whereas goal clarity might reveal conflicting interests and strain the coalition. Ordinarily, planned ambiguity takes the form of defining a mission in such global terms that it satisfies all factions (e.g., "To help people help themselves").

The function of organizational ambiguity is illustrated by the political system in the United States. Downs has observed that "political rationality leads parties in a two-party system to becloud their policies in a fog of ambiguity." [31] The incentive to design overlapping policies and obscure issues stems from their interest in increasing the number of persons who will vote for the party. The ambiguity is not absolute, however, since, as Downs also notes, the parties must develop an ideology to economize in the process of building coalitions.

The applicability of the analysis to community action systems is clear. There are three conditions which would appear to suggest goal ambiguity: (1) when the community effort is composed of differing interests; (2) when there is a need to attract widespread outside support; and (3) when the purposes of the action effort tend to be unpopular or controversial, particularly to those whose support is necessary for a successful outcome.

All other things being equal, ambiguity is more advantageous to

[31] Anthony Downs, *An Economic Theory of Democracy,* (New York: Harpers, 1957), p. 135.

the *least* powerful members of the coalition. Certainty decreases individual license, so that options are fewer when an organization's values are well defined. Since the least influential members of an organization have the fewest options, they benefit disproportionately from permissiveness. The point may be illustrated by considering the outcome of a struggle over values within any organization. The losers (by definition, the less influential) are ordinarily worse off for the conflict, since the new-found clarity forecloses their position with a finality which could not have existed before the conflict began. In effect, the precise goals of organizations represent the clarity of their most powerful members.

The practice implications of this point are considerable, and much of our later discussion regarding sponsorship and community work tactics bears on it. We wish to conclude this chapter, however, only by calling attention to the paradoxical nature of our argument. We have, on the one hand, indicated that workers must offer or seek an intellectual and ideological inspiration to inform the community work effort. This, in effect, requires clarity and definitiveness. We have now argued that ambiguity is advantageous to the less powerful members of a coalition (e.g., ordinarily the worker and community group). Thus must the worker's art be finely calibrated to the nuances of particular circumstances.

CHAPTER SEVEN

ORGANIZATION BUILDING IN
THE COMMUNITY WORK PROCESS

ALTHOUGH THERE IS TRUTH in the maxim that "In unity there is strength," strength is unlikely to be realized without a structural framework. "The slumbering lions" are, indeed, the "many," but the "few" are well organized. Organization, in the classic sense, is a mechanism for achieving economy of energy in community action, creating solidarity among people with shared goals, coordinating complex tasks, and focusing numerical strength. Without organization, masses are mobs, or collections of individuals, or socialization and primary groups, and thus they are less able to use and influence institutional-relations organizations.

Organization building, then, is the next phase of the community work process. A worker's success in fulfilling the tasks of organization building is a test of what has gone before. The effective development of a community organization depends, in effect, on how solid a foundation was established in the earlier stages of the process.

The interactional tasks of the worker, at this time, are broadening (and maintaining) the constituency, building "outside" support (or a coalition), and developing leadership. The technical tasks of the worker assume greater importance as an organization develops. Decisions must be weighed on the basis of the mileage which can be achieved organizationally, and the worker's concern is with the manifold aspects of organizational program and structure.

INTERACTIONAL TASKS

For organization development to take place, there must be an outward expansion of the primary group—to reach those in the community who will constitute its major body of supporters. Expanding the group's membership base requires defining the population of potential organizational supporters, that is, *who* will be reached and how many. An organization will not ordinarily settle for having *some* welfare clients as members, but rather will attempt to speak for *the* welfare clients of the community. While no organization ever succeeds in engaging its total potential constituency (Alinsky has suggested that the active involvement of 4 to 5 per cent of a neighborhood is the epitome of success), a sufficient base is required to present an image of representativeness. This is what is meant by broadening the constituency.

The organizer's second interactional task is to assist in "building a coalition," by which we mean helping a group make the contacts and establish the arrangements, both formal and informal, with other leaders and organizations whose input might be significant to the achievement of group purpose. For example, the welfare rights movement, in winning the backing of professionals, both individually and through groups (e.g., "Social Workers for Welfare Rights"), was able to obtain necessary funds, technical assistance, and public support.

The third interactional task, developing leadership, takes place within the framework of the other two. That is, broadening the constituency and building coalitions provide the content through which leaders are developed.

BROADENING THE CONSTITUENCY

The major purpose of broadening the constituency is to establish an organization as the legitimate spokesman for a particular interest group. Legitimacy, as well as numbers of people, is the focus of worker concern. To some degree the matter is circular: as organizations establish an image of representativeness, they are more likely to win benefits for their interest group; and as they win benefits, they attract additional adherents. The task, to begin with, is to *seem* to control the sentiments of large numbers. So, for example, a group of ten Parent Association presidents, in polling their chapters, discovered that they were unlikely to get an attendance of more than 100 of their 4000 members in a planned confrontation with a public official. Instead, they set up a meeting with the official to consist only of chapter officers, figuring that the 40 attendees who were the elected representatives of 4000 members would present a more potent appearance than a "mass" meeting of only 100 members. In part, the success of such a stratagem depends on the content of the organization's demands. The *appearance* of membership support is ineffective when there is strong target resistance, because the bluff is likely to be called and the organization's impotence exposed.

It was to establish the legitimacy of representation by the poor that Community Action agencies of the anti-poverty program conducted public elections for board positions. The device proved to be ineffectual, since turnouts were slight and expectations were high. Had Alinsky's figure of 5 per cent been the touchstone, success would have been heralded. But comparisons were made with other, more general elections. The outcome should not have caused surprise, since the anti-poverty elections were largely "popularity" contests and issues were usually either absent or unclear. While many elections in this country similarly attest to the popularity of the candidate rather than to support for his platform, they at least have the advantage of widespread publicity in the mass media. In his research on this subject, Hawley concluded that nonpartisan elections "generally enhance the electability of Republicans, and . . . this advantage . . . increases as the size of the city and the proportion of low socioeconomic status citizens increases." [1] Since more poor tend to be Democrats, one may infer that it is partisanship (or a volatile issue) which induces them to the polls. The anti-poverty elections offered neither.

Nevertheless, the electoral device did become more effective over

[1] Willis D. Hawley, "The Partisan Consequences of Nonpartisan Elections," *Public Affairs Report, Bulletin of the Institute of Governmental Studies*, Vol. 12, No. 3 (June 1971), p. 3.

time. For example, although voter turnouts in Model Cities elections were also generally "low," they were higher than in the earlier OEO experience. Thus nearly 30 per cent of eligible voters participated in the Model Cities election in Trenton in 1968.[2]

Although the electoral device was a "failure" in the anti-poverty program, it does offer some lessons regarding the broadening of a constituency. For one thing, it demonstrates that when a device to affirm someone's legitimacy to speak for a community is defined as a failure, the consequence may be considerably worse than if it had not been tried. The OEO elections, used to prove the torpor of the poor, made the poverty program more vulnerable to its enemies. Second, candidates who were elected were generally the poor who had established organizations behind them. In effect, elections do not necessarily serve to recruit or expand a constituency. From the point of view of organization development, the process is quite the other way around—organization must precede elections if the poor are to participate.

To win adherents requires both "inspiration" and attention to administrative detail. Sometimes, an explosive issue provides the tinder for kindling community interest. Ideology may also fill the void when leadership and effective organization have not yet developed. The militance of a small leadership cadre can stimulate the enthusiasm of a larger group as well. However, militancy can be a double-edged sword, for, as Demerath and Thiessen observe, militant groups are subject to the pathology of overcommitment. They often suffer from:

a penchant for the spectacular rather than the efficient and a tendency to grapple with the first task at hand instead of considering other tasks with more delayed but important effects.[3]

Lacking an explosive issue, or the spur of a potent ideology, or the resource of a militant cadre, a group must educate, entertain, or persuade in order to provoke interest in a problem and its solution.[4] They must, in other words, contrive the necessary "inspiration."

[2] *Technical Bulletin,* National League of Cities, Vol. 1, No. 3 (January 1970).

[3] N.J. Demerath III and Victor Thiessen, "On Spitting against the Wind: Organizational Precariousness and Irreligion," *American Journal of Sociology,* Vol. LXXI, No. 6 (May 1966), p. 685.

[4] See chapter 14 for a discussion on the techniques of persuasion.

Detail work is also important and on an on-going basis there is no substitute for attention to the myriad number of tasks to be done to insure a successful effort. Members of the group must "fan out," recruiting others in a variety of ways. Face-to-face contact is most effective if manpower resources are available, and there is propinquity, for example, inviting friends and neighbors and door-to-door canvassing. Leafleting and the mass media may be used for increased scope (i.e., reaching larger numbers) although, as Litwak points out, the ability to "tune out" is greater with some mechanisms (the written word) than with others (the direct contact).[5] Not only must contacts be invited to the meeting, but they must be reminded to attend immediately prior to its date.

The meeting must be carefully planned—its setting, the convenience of the location, the size of the meeting room, seating arrangements and, of course, the program itself. After its "inspirational" portion, the means by which potential members can act must be spelled out. There might, for example, be sign-up sheets to take down pertinent information; a description of specific times and places where members can help or get helped; the next meeting date announced; and volunteers sought for specific jobs. (If there is a public request for volunteers, it is useful to have some "shills" in the audience who will start the ball rolling by volunteering themselves.) If social action is contemplated, it should be ready for immediate implementation. Thus a welfare rights organizer notes that one part of each meeting was devoted to helping clients express their rights by "signing a petition, sending in a request for winter clothing, composing a letter to a welfare administrator which would be sent in the name of the group." [6]

An excellent illustration of the detailed planning which goes into such an operation is provided by the student organizers in *Bay and Park Streets* in their attempt, referred to in preceding chapters, to organize a tenants' association for a city rehabilitation program.

[5] Eugene Litwak, "An Approach to Linkage in 'Grass Roots' Organization," in Fred M. Cox et al., eds., *Strategies of Community Organization* (Itasca, Ill.: Peacock Publishers, 1970), pp. 126–38.

[6] Mary Rabagliati and Ezra Birnbaum, "Organizations of Welfare Clients," in Harold H. Weissman, ed., *Community Development in the Mobilization for Youth Experience* (New York: Association Press, 1969), p. 108.

[The two student organizers] divided the two block area into eight sections and planned to have eight meetings to discuss the program and answer questions. A ninth meeting would be held to discuss the formation of a tenants' council (although it would also be mentioned at the other meetings), and a mass meeting would follow where the tenants would meet the sponsors, city officials, architects, and attorneys to bring the parties together to establish the machinery for an ongoing working relationship. In addition to the creation of a strong tenants' council that would ultimately control the project, the strategy called for an interim step of having tenants elected to the Board of Trustees of the Improvement Corporation.

The work was divided between the students and Vista Volunteers. Each apartment would be visited, the program would be briefly explained, "fact sheets" would be left with the tenants, and they would be urged to attend their "section" meeting. The community aides would circulate flyers during the week a section meeting was scheduled and two hours before the meeting, the organizers, volunteers, and aides would knock on each apartment door to remind the tenants of the meeting place and time.[7]

[From the students' notes:] "Whenever the tenants were not at home, the aides and volunteers were to slip a flyer under the door and ask a neighbor to please inform the tenant who was not at home. We also asked the aides and Volunteers to take down the name of the head of the household whenever they spoke to tenants. They were [also] to keep a record of vacant apartments."[8]

The date of the mass meeting (following the completion of the "section" meetings) . . . was nearing. Tension within the students began to increase as they realized that the success of their efforts over the past months might well ride on the results of this meeting. They felt that they had successfully organized a large number of tenants into a loose, nonstructured interest group who were beginning to identify with the two block area. . . . They decided to show a film of a City-sponsored rehabilitation project that was successfully completed, sensing that visual evidence was more . . . convincing than word from City officials. Every step in the presentation was planned. The speakers were chosen and the content of their speeches, and time duration, were strongly suggested. The students role-played their own presentations and practiced responses they would make if heckled from the floor.[9]

[7] Fred Barbaro, *The Struggle to Provide Low-Income Housing in Coney Island* (New York: Columbia University School of Social Work, 1970), pp. 26–27.

[8] *Ibid.*, pp. 28–30.   [9] *Ibid.*, p. 45.

It is to be expected that occasional and supporting participants will come and go. That is, they may participate in a particular activity or for a circumscribed period, only to drop out, possibly to reappear at some later time. This "circulation" of participants is sometimes viewed as a sign of group failure, when in fact the process is inevitable and, for many of the participants, appropriate as well. An organization which has a core of active members, and which can call forth the numbers of occasional and supporting members its program requires, may have considerable potency.

Nevertheless, the organization must be concerned with maintaining the interest and "connection" of this type of participant. In part, this is achieved through program activities which are discussed later in this chapter. Thus service programs may provide the inducement for participants to maintain contact; offering benefits through intercession with welfare bureaucracies constitutes a "quid" for some future "quo"; victory in social action brings prestige to the organization, pride to the participants, and encourages affiliation. Effective follow up—through the face-to-face contacts of the worker, influential members, and others—is another means of sustaining participant interest. Attractively done, organizational bulletins and newspapers also keep occasional participants informed and they serve an educational function as well.

BUILDING A COALITION AND DEVELOPING LEADERSHIP

Broadening a constituency primarily entails management of the ceremonial aspects of community work—the public encounters which create and affirm allegiance to the organization. Informal work is required for the preparation of these observances and is a major element in building leadership and a coalition as well. It is in the act of planning these ceremonies, in approaching, winning the support of, or negotiating with potential allies, and in handling target institutions that leadership develops. The techniques of winning allies and handling targets are discussed later on in the section on tactics. We wish now to explore the worker's role in leadership and coalition development.

Leadership carries two connotations of interest to us. One refers to the actor's ability, his skill in handling ceremonies and informal work in ways which advance the organization's purpose. The other relates to the accordance of leadership status by others. In regard to the latter point, Wilson points out that enterprise precedes leadership. "The existence of functioning, formal, civic organizations," he says, "is an important factor in creating civic leaders." [10] In other words, it is the existence of the social structure which makes for the attribution and reality of leadership. In the very act of contributing to organization building, the worker is developing leadership.

In some measure, this constitutes another dilemma for the worker. On the one hand, a potent organization spawns effective leaders, that is, they represent a constituency which must be respected. This suggests that a worker may have to cajole, argue, or press for particular positions that enhance organizational strength. In so doing, however, he risks taking some of the "play" away from the group's leadership, or depriving leaders of the experience of "learning by doing." To a large degree, what he will decide to do rests on an assessment of how critical the issue is and how damaging to the organization a mistaken judgment would be.

In the organization building stage of the process, the worker focuses more sharply on the development of executive and active participants. As a group begins to turn into an organization, new roles and structures are introduced and responsibilities are dispersed. A worker can no longer fill all the missing roles, nor should he. The worker's attention must partly shift from managing his own relationship with group members to helping members manage their relationship with each other and with third parties.

Differences among members emerge as an organization develops. Size is an important factor. Studies indicate, for example, that while some people typically do more talking than others in small group discussion, this tendency accelerates with group size, so that a relatively few persons dominate the interaction of larger bodies.[11] In the primary group phase, many could join in the group's work. But in organization development, greater differentiation takes place, and authority is distributed among executive committee members and

[10] James Q. Wilson, *Negro Politics* (New York: Free Press, 1960), p. 106.

[11] Barry E. Collins and Harold Guetzkow, *A Social Psychology of Group Processes for Decision-Making* (New York: Wiley, 1964), p. 170.

various committee chairmen. In the process, some may lose the authority they held as "best-liked" men; others are awarded ascendancy on the basis of their task competence.

In an informal group, influence is not a function of formal position. The chairman, for example, may be an active participant with little influence. This distinction is important in considering potential organizational leadership. High-power people may be identified as follows: they tend to talk more than other members; their communications include more influence attempts; and they more often win their way.[12] As organizations become more complex, influence more likely inheres in formal position, because formal position grants resources to the holder which can be traded for compliance.

Strong feelings are likely to be stirred as leadership shifts with the transition from the small informal group to a larger, more formal, one; and the competition for leadership is a shoal on which many community groups founder. Internal conflict is not necessarily undesirable, but it is beneficial only if there is a basic loyalty to the organization, and there are mechanisms through which the conflict can be mediated.

Workers help executive participants deal with *substantive* conflict through a review of the facts of the case. The worker may gather and organize information and prepare material for officers, which throws light on the issues and alternatives. He encourages the chairman to allow give-and-take in the discussion at meetings and to seek out data which have a bearing on the dispute. It has been found, for example, in a study of decision making in business and government that "chairmen of groups in high substantive conflict which ended in consensus did three times more seeking for information of an objective factual nature from members of their groups than did chairmen in groups which did not end in consensus." [13]

Socioemotional conflict, on the other hand, may need to be swept under the rug, in order for the organization to proceed with its business. But we suspect that this mechanism is overused by community workers, because the conflict will not stay submerged for any length of time. Playing the middleman is another device of organizers. They talk to both parties, trying to help each see the viewpoint of

[12] *Ibid.*, p. 154.   [13] *Ibid.*, p. 113.

the other, while emphasizing the commonalities and the need of all to work together. If the conflict is due to misunderstanding or inadequacies in communication, this may reduce the tension. In many instances, however, especially when disagreements are not irrevocable or based on sharply conflicting interests, the discord must be recognized and confronted by the respective parties themselves, and its causes and consequences fully explored. The presence of the worker during this exploration can provide the necessary ballast, so that communications remain open and are clearly understood by both parties.

In addition to helping leaders deal with internal interpersonal matters, the worker also explores the various alternatives open to groups in their search for external support. A coalition may be viewed as a system of organizational exchange,[14] in which resources are traded in order to pursue some shared objective. The shared goal may, however, be a short-range one, some immediate end which serves the interests of both groups. Too often, community organizations insist on the ideological purity of their partners, which may effectively limit cooperative action.

The basic questions to be asked in engaging in this organizational exchange are: Is external help required to achieve our goal? Are the resources of the other organization necessary? Do they complement our own, or provide resources which we have in short supply? What will we have to give up in the trade? If there are disparate groups in the coalition, will the resultant position represent a least common denominator, and if so, how compromising to our own objectives will such a position be? What are the devices for adjudicating differences among the partners, and are our interests protected by these mechanisms?

Planning meeting agendas is one occasion in which wide-ranging discussion between workers and officers can be devoted to these domestic and foreign affairs. For example, they might review the desirability of appointing a committee, what its charge should be, who might be asked to serve, and what possible reactions the group could

[14] Sol Levine and Paul E. White, "Exchange as a Conceptual Framework for the Study of Interorganizational Relationships," *Administrative Science Quarterly*, Vol. V, No. 4 (March 1961), pp. 583–601.

have to their proposal. The worker's knowledge of organizations and his special position as "staff" offer a valuable perspective. As a full-time participant, he has the time to do thorough "work ups." Because of his special status, he will be privy to confidences which are concealed even from executive members of the group. This is particularly the case if there are cliques or vying factions, and the worker has taken care to keep his channels of communication open. He will not, of course, share privileged information, though he may give counsel based on his knowledge of it. In addition, the worker is most likely to have contact with, access to, or information about both potential allies and target organizations.

Role playing is a useful device for helping officers prepare for occasions about which they feel insecure, the idea being to help leaders "walk through" the anticipated event. If an officer is concerned about trouble from an adversary at a meeting, a worker might recommend a number of possible responses, and then suggest that he act like the member while the chairman tries out the responses. A recommended technique for groups which are to meet with the public officials is for the delegation to first discuss what their position ought to be, then act it out to obtain comfort in their roles, and follow by considering the effectiveness of their approach.

In addition to helping officers think through their various tasks and organizational problems, the worker encourages review of how the tasks were performed, the meetings conducted, and the problems resolved. This requires special sensitivity since, while he must be authentic, he must guard against being either oversupportive or overcritical. Once an officer has acted (in distinction to preparing an action), he has developed a personal investment in his performance, and an evaluation inevitably constitutes a judgment.

A CAVEAT ON LEADERSHIP

When a constituent is cast in a leadership role, a series of changes take place which have important consequences for the community organization. Generally, the dynamic impact of a leadership experience is overlooked in community work or, when considered, it tends to be viewed optimistically. Because Mr. X became chairman of the group, the thinking goes, his view of himself undergoes dramatic change. He—and others—discover that he has hitherto unknown resources and capacities. All of which may be true.

But leadership resources are as scarce as all other resources in the low-income community. Thus it is also true that once Mr. X has attained power, he is not likely to relinquish it voluntarily. Not surprisingly, much of Mr. X's organizational energy may be devoted to preventing a return to his previously more obscure position. His leadership role will have enabled him to meet people and make contacts; it will have shaped his view of the organization, of other prestigious positions, and of available resources and political rewards. In his personal transformation he will, to some extent at least, see an equivalent transformation in the surrounding world, one which will support his organizational position regardless of its impact on the community group. He will, in short, be motivated by as high a degree of self-interest as any other leader of any other organization.

Struggles for internal power are generated by the interplay of self-interest, organizational goals, and the objectives of community work. For example, the controversy which ensued over "Black Power" cannot be attributed entirely to differences in philosophic orientation, though undoubtedly it was a factor. Although there are, of course, genuine strategic differences between those with nationalist and integrationist sentiments, one cannot dismiss the possibility that the conflict also represented an expedient means for some leaders to seize organizational control of the civil rights movement and to command the loyalties of a flagging membership.

Thus community organization programs will change the status of a certain strata in the newly organized community with both positive and negative effects on the leaders and, therefore, on community groups. The risk is high for constituents, since their resources to control leaders are as scarce as are low-income leadership resources to begin with. Community organizations which start as mechanisms for environmental change thus risk becoming ends in themselves for leadership.

We began this book by discussing the competing values of participation, leadership, and expertise which inhere in community work. With organization development, this competition in values begins to emerge in earnest. In broadening the constituency, groups embrace the value of participation. As they assert their right to speak for someone and can demonstrate that they have been awarded that position by an identifiable constituency, they can claim the voice which leaders are accorded in institutional decision making. If they speak only for themselves, or if the people they purport to represent disavow their leadership, they need not be listened to.

This second value—leadership—is most clearly embraced in building a coalition. The set of activities required for this engages leaders of the group in negotiating for the organization, making exchanges, awarding positions, promising support, and so forth. Organizations must produce results for members, as well as be responsive to their wishes, if they are to continue representing them. On the other hand, they must demonstrate to institutional representatives that they can discipline and control their membership—for otherwise they have nothing to trade off for the benefits they demand. It is as though the very act of developing the means by which to represent a constituency contains the seeds of unrepresentativeness. Leaders cannot lead unless they are able to form coalitions, nor can they lead if they do not represent a constituency. But as soon as they achieve the position of leadership they become vulnerable to the charge of "dealing with the enemy," or "selling out." Lipsky has noted this dilemma in the black community:

This phenomenon is in evidence when Negro leaders, recognized as such by public officials, find their support eroded in the Negro community because they have engaged in explicit bargaining situations with politicians. Negro leaders are thus faced with the dilemma that when they behave like other ethnic group representatives, they are faced with loss of support from those whose intense activism has been aroused in the Negro community, yet whose support is vital if they are to remain credible as leaders to public officials.[15]

Maintaining the delicate balance between the two values—particpation and leadership—is one of the arts of effective leaders.

Subsequently, when an institutional-relations organization has taken shape, one can be sure that the third value—expertise—will emerge. The professional, with his technical knowledge, will have to compete against the two other values which he fostered earlier. Rob-

15 Michael Lipsky, "Protest as a Political Resource," *The American Political Science Review*, Vol. LXII, No. 4 (December 1968), p. 1153.

ert Michels, in *Political Parties,* commented on the relentless emergence of these organizational characteristics. He compared the contending groups in these struggles to "groups of dancers executing a *chasse' croise'* in a quadrille." Michels saw no contradiction between the doctrine that history is a record of a continued series of such struggles and the doctrine that these struggles culminate in the creation of new oligarchies which eventually undergo fusion with the old.[16]

However, the view need not be pessimistic. We referred in an earlier chapter to *Union Democracy,* a study of the International Typographical Union. The findings of this study suggest that the development of undemocratic oligarchies in organizations is not necessarily inevitable. The delicate balance of different kinds of subgroups in the ITU provided a system by which there was a continuing renewal of leadership. Michels' view of communities may look somewhat more hopeful if we accept his view of organizations as a dialectic:

The democratic currents of history resemble successive waves. They break ever on the same shoal. . . . Now new accusers arise to denounce the traitors; after an era of glorious combats and inglorious power, they end by fusing with the old dominant class; whereupon once more they are in their turn attacked by fresh opponents who appeal to the name of democracy. It is probable that this cruel game will continue without end.[17]

TECHNICAL TASKS

Program planning and implementation and the development of organizational structure logically follow the identification of a problem area and the specification of goals (or strategy). Program design and the format of written program proposals tend to follow the same sequence: problem analysis, specification of goals, description of program elements, required resources (e.g., staff, structure, budget), plans for implementation and, ultimately, evaluation.[18] Devising programs

[16] Robert Michaels, *Political Parties* (New York: Dover Publishers, 1915), pp. 377 and 391.

[17] *Ibid.,* p. 408.

[18] For a useful guide for the design and planning of program proposals, see Tony Tripodi, Phillip Fellin, and Irwin Epstein, *Social Program Evaluation* (Itasca, Ill.: Peacock Publishers, 1971). Other useful materials are: Alfred J.

and developing organizational structure constitute the worker's technical tasks in the organization building phase of the community work process.

PROGRAM

We limit our discussion to three types of programs which community groups frequently undertake: (1) self-help, (2) advocacy-brokerage, and (3) social action programs. Our intention here is to discuss only what are theoretical types or models. In practice organizations may engage in any combination of programs simultaneously, and move from one to another over time. For example, a community group which hopes to influence the educational system to deal more effectively with school drop-outs might conduct any of these three kinds of programs. It could work directly with youngsters who have left school, to show the way it *should* be done, that is, conduct a self-help program. It might set up a consumer organization for the parents of school children, and act as advocates for youth who were poorly treated. Or finally, it might engage in actions to pressure the board of education to consider system change. The three program types call for different relationships between the action system and its constituents. In the first case, it provides services to them; in the second, it represents them; and in the last instance the action system may or may not have a direct relationship with constituents.

Self-help Programs. Self-help programs are those which are operated by clients or by their friends and neighbors. Services are offered

---

Kahn, "Social Work and the Control of Delinquency: Theory and Strategy," *Social Work,* Vol. 10, No. 2 (April 1965); June L. Shmelzer, ed., *Learning in Action* (Washington, D.C.: U.S. Dept. of Health, Education and Welfare, Welfare Administration, Office of Juvenile Delinquency and Youth Development, U.S. Govt. Printing Office, 1966); M.P. Brooks, "The Community Action Program as a Setting for Applied Research," *Journal of Social Issues,* Vol. 21, No. 1 (January 1965); Elizabeth Herzog, *Some Guide Lines for Evaluative Research* (Washington, D.C.: U.S. Dept. of Health, Education and Welfare, Social Security Administration, Children's Bureau, U.S. Govt. Printing Office, 1959); Sidney E. Zimbalist, "Research in the Service of a Cause: The Changing Context of Community Welfare Research," *Social Service Review,* Vol. 38, No. 2 (June 1964); Norman A. Polansky, ed., *Social Work Research* (Chicago: Chicago University Press, 1960); Franklin M. Zweig and Robert Morris, "The Social Planning Design Guide: Process and Proposal," *Social Work,* Vol. 11, No. 2 (April 1966).

outside the formal service structure. Some examples are the programs of Alcoholics Anonymous, Synanon, as well as neighborhood tutoring programs, "hot lines," and community clinics.

A major benefit of the self-help program in organization building is that the group can offer concrete services to its constituents. Its visibility in the community is increased, and it can demonstrate that it "cares" and "gets things done." For another, in providing services, the participants learn from the experience. They not only acquire knowledge in services management but also become "experts" on the consequences to people of institutional failure and on the programmatic and policy issues involved in the delivery of services. Finally, community groups which obtain support for a self-help program also acquire staff, facilities, and financial resources that provide them with an important source of community influence. (It was in the development of service institutions that Catholics, Protestants, and Jews established on-going and respected bodies which were attentive to the interests of these groups.) Kenneth Marshall may have had this point in mind when he recommended institution-building in the ghetto:

What should have been developed was a number of particular institutional structures that would get money from federal and foundation sources and set up private enterprises to trap some of the money going out of the community. . . . All the way from halfway houses to straight business enterprises, an attempt to develop viable institutional structures dominated by people who have a specific interest—vested in some instances, altruistic in others—would result in something more real than a general purpose action apparatus.[19]

There are disadvantages in self-help programs as well. Unrelated to long-range strategy, self-help programs can become a substitute for needed services, a substitute that is inferior because the resources ordinarily provided are inadequate to the need. Furthermore, the taxing tasks of service provision may so absorb the energies of a community group that it is diverted from any further action in regard to influencing the larger institutional system. It is thus hardly surprising that

[19] Kenneth Marshall, "Discussion," in John B. Turner, ed., *Neighborhood Organization for Community Action* (New York: National Association of Social Workers, 1968), p. 100.

the larger community is more willing to provide the financial largesse for self-help than the other types of program, or that established institutions often view the self-help program as highly desirable. At one and the same time, it gets the responsible institution "off the hook" of responsibility and, by deflecting group energies, gets service-recipients "off the back" of institutional personnel.

Organizations undergo similar processes and life cycles, whether their participants are poor, service recipients, professional staff, business men, or anyone else. They tend to move from their original goals to concentrating on maintenance and enhancement needs, which is a clear and present danger of self-help programs. The test, in the final analysis, is whether the maintenance needs overtake, or are in balance with, organizational goals—and whether the service-giving community group has been "bought off" at too low a sum.

Advocacy-Brokerage Programs. Advocacy-brokerage programs are those in which community groups represent constituents in their dealings with institutional-relations organizations, in much the same way that the lawyer represents his clients or the real estate broker acts as liaison between buyer and seller. Analogous to advocacy-brokerage programs is collective bargaining, in which labor unions act on behalf of their membership's interests with management. The program of the National Welfare Rights Organization is an example from the community work field.

The assumptions underlying advocacy programs range widely. We believe, as a matter of fact, that advocacy-brokerage provides some of the essential programmatic means for meeting the professional goals of community work, as these goals have been articulated in this volume. It may, for example, increase the competence of the service consumer (e.g., by providing an educational experience for constituents in utilizing service institutions); encourage the responsiveness of service organizations to consumer needs (e.g., by revising the service personnel's image of the client and his needs or through group pressure); and promote alterations in service policies and programs (e.g., by calling community attention to institutional inequities). Proponents of advocacy-brokerage programs range from those who believe such programs are educational to those who hold that forcing an institution to meet all legitimate demands will impel a radical rearrangement of its functioning or force it out of business.

From the perspective of organizational development, advocacy-brokerage programs offer some of the same concrete benefits and community visibility as self-help efforts. An added advantage, in our view, is that it prevents the institutional "escape valve" that self-help programs often afford. In advocacy-brokerage programs, the constituents, community group, and organizational personnel *must* engage with one another; and in such circumstances, it is less likely that an organizational change focus will be neglected. Moreover, lesser resources are required to operate advocacy programs, and the yield is clearer than in many self-help programs, the benefits of which (to the client) may be dubious. Advocacy-brokerage, quite clearly, is intended to provide what *the law* indicates clients are entitled to.

Some of the disadvantages of self-help programs are also applicable to advocacy programs. Here too, there may be too great an investment in providing client service as a permanent substitute for adequate services provided by the responsible institution. An example is the community group which, faced with the choice of taking a "class action" or of processing the grievances of individuals, chooses to provide ongoing visible services to individual constituents rather than invest its energies in a long-range court struggle, although the latter might benefit many more people.

The long-range prospects for advocacy-brokerage programs present potential pitfalls not unlike those faced by labor unions. Ultimately, the successful leader of such programs must be able to exert some degree of control over both his constituents and the adversary organization. He must win gains from "management" or his clients will leave; and if he cannot get his clients to accept the inevitable compromise settlement, organizational representatives will not deal with him.

The interests of the community leader and the organizational representative are, therefore, often confluent. The organizational representative will prefer the former's leadership if his views are more moderate than those of a challenger for the community group's support. Thus do militants strengthen moderate hands. The advocate-broker, on the other hand, may seek to maintain peace between constituents and the organization, in order to reduce the threat to his leadership. (Thus do "sweetheart contracts" develop.) The dynamic is similar to collective bargaining situations in which the shared interests of labor and employer representatives lead to understandings which supersede the common strivings of union members and their representatives.[20] In similar community work situations, the organizer can sometimes function as a "third party" and encourage or discourage a settlement. Which of these he does, however, ought not to depend on the motive of the community group leader—but what is gained or lost for constituents in settling.

Social Action Programs. Social action programs may or may not directly involve the victims of social problems themselves. A group (of victims and/or other interested people) engage in a wide range of tactics in order to influence a reorganization of institutional attitudes and behavior, a redistribution of resources, or a change in authority relatonships.

The advantages of social action programs to organization building are numerous. Such programs can be undertaken in a shorter period of time and with a less enduring organizational apparatus than is ordinarily required of self-help and advocacy programs. They are highly visible, and offer the potential for winning tangible benefits quickly. Social action programs also provide the opportunity to fill a large number of participant roles with minimal requirements. It takes little in training or understanding of organizational operations to sign a petition, join a picket line, or march to city hall. Similarly, the tactics used are communicated to, and learned by, others quickly so that the program can "spread" to involve a broad constituency more readily than with the other program types. Finally, there is least possibility, in social action programs, that people will be diverted from the view that the source of social problems lies in institutional systems.

Many of the characteristics of social action that yield its advantages give rise to its disadvantages. Planning for social action takes place in the informal work of groups, and the action involves large numbers only in its ceremonial aspects. (Self-help and advocacy programs, on the other hand, tend to involve larger numbers in informal activity, where significant decisions are made and organizational commitment and learning take place.)

Organizations whose *raison d'être* is social action must maintain a critical stance toward institutions almost regardless of the institu-

[20] This point was suggested to the authors by Simon Slavin.

tional response; they exist, so to speak, as the "party of permanent opposition." Politically, they derive minor benefit from an institution's becoming more humane and responsive, since this defuses constituent feeling. Although they must win victories, they must also, as Alinsky has put it, have "a fight in the bank." As a consequence, the incentive for institutional accommodation is lessened, and the wider public (indeed, even constituents) may dismiss the group as interested in "protest for its own sake."

Militant social action tends to bring forth leaders with agitational rather than administrative skills. While these may not be inherently incompatible abilities, they do set up conflicting role demands. Thus, as Lipsky notes, "When a protest leader exhausts time and energy conducting frequent press conferences, arranging for politicians . . . to speak at rallies, delivering speeches . . . , making contacts, he is unable to pursue the direction of office routine, clerical tasks, research and analysis, and other chores." [21] The pursuit of these administrative chores is, however, what makes continuance in the organizational arena possible.

Finally, the success of social action can be its undoing. In achieving a victory, and satisfying their needs, members may see little purpose in maintaining their group affiliation. Or they may fall away during the process, as the action moves from ceremonial activities such as massive confrontations at public meetings to engagement in the informal work of bargaining (as it must if it is to achieve success). From the streets to the back rooms, the interests of the masses dwindle.

Although organizers must be aware and wary of the powers and pitfalls of self-help, advocacy-brokerage, and social action programs, they are often unable, by circumstance, to shape a group's program direction. Often, the program is predetermined, and the organizer must provide coherence to what is essentially given.

DEVELOPING ORGANIZATIONAL STRUCTURE

The ways in which the ceremonial and informal work of an organization are patterned; its lines of communication and control; how the expectations and responsibilities of the participant roles are de-

[21] Lipsky, "Protest as a Political Resource," p. 1153.

fined; all of these and more constitute the formal structure of an organization. Developing organization structure to suit organizational purposes is a major technical task of the worker as a collectivity moves from group to organization.

One structural question which has absorbed the interest of community organizers relates to the base of participation, that is, a structure in which individual members compose the organization as compared to organizations consisting of representatives of other groups ("an organization of organizations").[22]

Membership organizations bring together like-minded people; they consist of persons who are more homogeneous in class, culture, and value system than representative groups. They tend, therefore, to be more cohesive, to engage in expressive activities to a greater degree, and to need less formality to conduct their business. They can, with less strain than a representative organization, deal with controversial issues and take quick action. Representative organizations, on the other hand, have larger and more varied constituencies, a wider set of interests, and a greater range of resources. They are constrained by the varied organizational interests to which they must respond for, essentially, the members of representative organizations (e.g., a welfare council) participate only insofar as the organization furthers the interests of the members' own groups. While each representative attempts to bend the council to his group's interests, the council (or more properly, its most powerful actors) attempts to bend the interests of the groups to those of the council.

The association between an organization's base of participation and its goals and strategies have been discussed in a trenchant article by Rein and Morris.[23] For example, because of the diversity of interests and allegiances of its members, a representative organization requires integrative rather than change-oriented goals. It tends to avoid

[22] Each of these types of organizations, membership and representative, have various subtypes which serve to amend the generalizations about them which follow. Our interest, however, is less in the specifics of the organizations than in the point that their base of membership importantly influence their goals and programs.

[23] Martin Rein and Robert Morris, "Goals, Structures, and Strategies for Community Change," in Ralph M. Kramer and Harry Specht, eds., *Readings in Community Organization Practice* (Englewood Cliffs, N.J.: Prentice-Hall, 1969), pp. 188–200.

specific and predetermined objectives, emphasizes the process by which decisions are made, and invests its energies in a search for common values.

The number of structural variables is countless, and they exist on many levels of abstraction. Since there is already an extensive literature on the theoretical aspects of organizational structure, however,[24] as well as on its practical elements,[25] we shall conclude this chapter by exploring one variable of particular interest in community work with the poor: *the degree of formality* which is required for effective and efficient organizational functioning.

It is sometimes erroneously assumed that low-income groups eschew formality. The assumption has some basis in the fact that the poor tend to be found in expressive rather than instrumental associations. But it ignores another fact; namely, that these expressive groups often incorporate a high degree of formality in their operations. The welfare women, referred to in the preceding chapter, who pressed for diplomas and a graduation ceremony following their completion of a training program were, after all, demanding a formal procedure.

More precisely, low-income groups (and others too) seek formal structure for expressive as well as instrumental purposes. Inexperienced people may also seek structure because they believe "this is the way organizations are supposed to be." Formality, in imitation of "successful" organizations, risks ritualism. In substituting form for substance, attention may be diverted from more significant group concerns.

There is, of course, nothing wrong with formality as entertainment (the entertainment may, in fact, be necessary); or with structure to produce status (the status may be group enhancing) as long as it does not impede the pursuit of more central objectives. Indeed, structure *should* serve these purposes.

[24] Every bibliography on organizational theory is replete with references to organizational structure. For just two representative samples, see James G. March, ed., *Handbook of Organizations* (Chicago: Rand McNally, 1965) and William W. Cooper et al., *New Perspectives in Organization Research* (New York: Wiley, 1964).

[25] See for example, Arthur Dunham, *The New Community Organization* (New York: Thomas Y. Crowell, 1970). Part Three, "Community Organization at Work" is particularly useful in regard to the practical aspects of structure.

Specific rules cannot be laid down. Thus Robert's Rules of Order may be a useful device for handling business or a nuisance which impedes progress. Much depends on how large, diverse, and potentially conflictual the organization's meetings are. The larger and more diverse the group, the more useful Robert's Rules.[26] Although parliamentary procedures evolved historically as a means of achieving consensus in conflict situations, there is some evidence to suggest that formal meeting procedures do not reduce the impact of interpersonal clashes any more than informal ones.[27] But they do provide a framework to permit the orderly conduct of argument. (And it might be noted parenthetically, they allow sophisticated users to score points for their position. So, for example, "negative" action may be forestalled by a less than majority vote when proponents are conversant with Robert's Rules. Or amendments which would not otherwise bring a majority may be tacked on to highly favored motions, thus insuring their passage. Political tacticians—and community organizers—do well to be familiar with these rules.)

A constitution or set of by-laws is an example of another structural device which may or may not be useful. Generally, such documents include the following types of information: statement of general purposes; bases and conditions of membership; times, places of, and procedures for calling meetings; how meetings are conducted (e.g., using Robert's Rules); the definition of a quorum; descriptions of executive roles, the qualifications required for office, and procedures for elections or appointments; standing committees and their function; procedures for financial accounting; and methods by which by-laws may be changed. The list suggests those features of organizational structure which require attention. If that attention is not to be ritualistic, however, it must take into account the stage of the group's development. Inexperienced participants find some procedures discomfiting because they are foreign, and thus need time to work at them before the procedures are sprung full-blown into by-laws.

Essentially, the question of degree of formality poses another of the many community work dilemmas. On the one hand, informality

[26] Organizers ought avail themselves of General Henry M. Robert, *Robert's Rules of Order* (New York: Pyramid Books, 1967).

[27] Collins and Guetzkow, *A Social Psychology of Group Processes*, p. 117.

is essential to permit expressive relationships to develop and for members to find satisfaction in the group. Conversely, however, if groups are to develop into institutional-relations organizations, rules have to be explicated, roles specified and defined, and other formal mechanisms evolved. Indeed, to be recognized by the State as a legal entity, formal structure (e.g., articles of incorporation) must be developed. As with the tension between expressive and instrumental leadership and activity, so too is there tension between the development of formal structure and the need for informality. The task of the organizer is to ensure the balance.

INSTITUTIONAL RELATIONS:
THE END PHASE OF THE PROCESS

We have, until now, focused our attention on community groups which function largely outside the established system of voluntary associations and government as they move through the process of becoming institutional-relations organizations (i.e., those formal bodies, such as trade unions, professional associations, social agencies, community corporations, social planning councils, and parent-teacher associations, whose function is to advance the interests of their constituency and provide a link between constituents and institutions). It has been observed that these "outside" groups, for example, Alinsky's People's Organizations, civil rights bodies, and community groups of the poor, do not develop long-term properties.[28] Although the observation is well founded, it need not be taken as an ascription of failure. The organization of groups outside the established institutional framework is a means of influencing those within, not an end in itself. When such groups do not achieve their goals or satisfy their members, they have, of course, failed, and participants will seek other means to accomplish their ends. But such groups may also win their point, and in the very winning, dissolve. Or they may serve as conduits into the institutional framework, and subsequently disband. In neither instance can it be said that they were unsuccessful.

[28] Frank Riessman, "Self-Help among the Poor: New Styles of Social Action," *Trans-Action*, Vol. 2, No. 6 (September/October 1965).

There are two organizational means by which the consumers of service may influence service programs and policies. One is the development of consumer-oriented groups, independent of the service institution but empowered to negotiate with its officials. Such a mechanism, institutionalized in much the same way as collective bargaining is in labor-management relations, would be highly desirable, and although not yet achievable in American society, is an objective for which to reach. The second means to modify service provisions is through the absorption of the challengers into the system. With successful organizational development, community groups (or individuals in them) are often incorporated into the established organizational life of the community, thus infusing new organizational interests and new leadership into community decision making.

If the community work process was as orderly as we may have made it seem, its outcome would be the transformation of a diffuse group of constituents into an institutional-relations organization. In an ideal model of the process, neighborhood groups would be organized, struggle to achieve their independence from their original sponsors, establish their organizational status, influence the sector in which they were interested, and would, sometimes, like community corporations, begin themselves to foster and sponsor community action groups. Ultimately, as new structures and roles were integrated into the institutional framework of society, the new organizations (e.g., the community corporation) would become part of a new *status quo,* and we might expect that leadership would be coopted, fervor dissipated, and change goals tempered. And thus the process might begin again.

In working with institutional-relations organizations in this end phase, the organizer's activity becomes increasingly managerial. The point has been aptly described by the authors of a volume on social movements and social change:

If the cause is to survive and grow, its adherents must eventually recognize and accept the necessity of management. The cause must be turned into function. This is recognized universally by groups as far apart in their objectives as conservationists, prohibitionists, abortionists, and revolutionaries.[29]

[29] Gerald Zaltman et al., *Creating Social Change* (New York: Holt, Rinehart, and Winston, 1972), p. 466.

The technical task of the worker is the implementation of program objectives: the organization and evaluation of programs, the supervision of staff, the maintenance of public relations, and the management of budgets, facilities, and records. He needs, in short, to know and use the theories and techniques of administration.

The worker's interactional concerns are tactical. Through interventions ranging from the educational to the disruptive, he attempts to help his organization influence the distribution of institutional resources and the allocation of institutional authority. He will educate, cajole, persuade, maneuver, bargain, and pressure target institutions together with his constituency. And in what may be an even more difficult task, he has to obtain the sanction of his "home base" organization (the sponsor) to use these tactics.

Indicating the technical and interactional tasks of the worker in the "final" phase of the community work process serves as an introduction to the remainder of this volume. In Part III, we use the sponsoring agency or organization which initiates, guides, and/or obtains support for community work as our case example of an institutional-relations organization. Because there is a rich literature on the theory and practice of administration, however, we shall not focus on managerial matters—but rather on how sponsor values and structure influence community work objectives and reflect the interests and aspirations of its constituency. A worker's skill, in this regard, may be measured by his adeptness at maximizing the opportunities and minimizing the constraints which stem from the auspices of the effort. Part IV then, is devoted to the tactics which are available to influence target institutions (or the sponsoring agency, as the case may be).

Our discussion of the community work process has up to now focused on the consumer constituency, on how clients (and workers) "get themselves together." We now turn our attention away from organizing people, so that they may express their will, to affecting the sponsoring organization and influencing target institutions.

Part III

INSTITUTIONAL RELATIONS:
THE SPONSORS OF COMMUNITY WORK

CHAPTER EIGHT

SPONSORSHIP AND CONSTITUENCY RELATIONS: MANAGING "DOMESTIC AFFAIRS"

INSTITUTIONAL-RELATIONS ORGANIZATIONS, we noted earlier, are formal organizations whose primary function is to mediate the relations between institutions and individuals. They include a wide variety of organizational types, such as trade unions, civil rights groups, professional associations, welfare councils, and boards of education. Frequently, these organizations are the targets of change of organizing efforts. Sometimes they are the sponsors of community work, and sometimes they are the initiators of the community activity, or the outcome of the community work process. Our interest in Part III is limited to institutional-relations organizations which sponsor community activity.

Sponsors may or may not be indigenous to the constituency that is organized. A sponsor may be an outside group—an agency that reaches into a community to organize residents in support of the agency's program, such as urban renewal agencies. Or it may be an organization which enters a community with the offer of staff help, technical assistance, and funds to encourage indigenous development, as in the case of some Model Cities programs. Sometimes, the sponsor is *in,* although not necessarily *of* the community, such as settlement houses which, though serving a particular locale, are managed by outsiders. Or sponsorship may derive from community people pursuing a segmental goal of a reformist or radical character, for example, the welfare rights movement.

Whatever its purpose or origin, sponsor interests significantly influence the organizing effort. And in being formally organized, the very structure of the sponsor limits the autonomy and control of the community worker. Yet if his commitment to the professional goals of community work is high, he must ensure the input of constituents in the decision-making process, and maximize their "degrees of freedom" in their relations with sponsors. Moreover, the worker's and the community group's ability to influence service-providing organizations is directly related to the sponsor's resources. It is the community worker's task to mobilize these resources to achieve constituency purposes, a task which is exceedingly complicated when the group's purposes are at variance with the sponsor's.

Although social work of all methods is practiced almost entirely in an organizational context, knowledge about the ways in which organizational values and structure affect the performance of practitioners is underdeveloped. For example, of the almost 100 articles in the *Social Service Review* (which is considered the most social-science-oriented of social work journals) for the years 1965–1967, only one had the social work organization as its central focus.[1]

The discussion of agency sponsorship which follows is intended to sensitize the worker to some of the organizational determinants of community work. In this chapter, we explore the ways in which a sponsor's value system and structure affect its relationship with its constituency.[2] Sponsor goals, we believe, shape the ways in which it perceives its client population, the type of social relations which develop, and the degree of commitment the sponsor has to constituency involvement in community affairs and internal decision making. But

[1] Andrew Eklund, *The Agency-Student Encounter,* A Report of the C.O. Curriculum Development Project, Columbia University School of Social Work, 1969, p. 2. (Mimeographed)

[2] We make no distinction between an organization's values and its goals. The first term refers to the official or informal sentiments which constitute its way of viewing the world; the second defines a desired future state of affairs which the organization hopes to realize. Together, they may be considered the organization's value system.

goals are not the only determinant of sponsor-constituency relations. The ways in which these relations are structured also affect the autonomy of community groups. An understanding of these factors is necessary for organizers to assess the perimeters of the organizing effort and to maximize the influence of the community group.

SPONSOR VALUES AND
CONSTITUENCY RELATIONS

Frequently, organizers are cynical about the goals espoused by organizations which sponsor community work with service recipients. Often, the agency's stated purposes are considerably more appealing than reality merits. Goals may be so global as to be meaningless, or so ambitious as to outrun the resources the organization commands. An illustration of the former is the Economic Opportunity Act's call for "maximum feasible participation" of residents served by Community Action Programs. "Maximum" is subject to conflicting definitions; "feasible" is vague; and as we noted in chapter 2 "participation" means many things. Thus the goal is so broad as to mean almost anything and therefore, as a behavioral prescription, it means little. A pungent illustration of a goal outrunning organizational resources is provided by Bayard Rustin in his characterization of the *Manifesto* of the National Black Economic Development Conference as "bombast." According to Rustin, the exaggeration of language in the *Manifesto* ("We say think in terms of the total control of the U.S.") is directly proportional to the isolation and impotence of those who drafted it.[3]

Stated values and goals may also be a device to hide the real, sometimes malignant, purposes of an organization, in which case the gulf between performance and pretence will be vast. Thus, when the New York City Department of Social Services organized welfare recipients, ostensibly to assure client input in agency policy making, some raised question about whether less benign objectives were at work. The question was not inappropriate in that the Department's

[3] Bayard Rustin, "The Failure of Black Separatism," *Harpers,* Vol. 240, No. 1436 (January 1970), p. 31.

organizing effort followed the growth of welfare rights groups in New York City.

In decision making, agency goals vie continuously with the maintenance requirements of the organization. The day-to-day activities of the sponsor often have little to do with its overriding purposes, and internal problems may deflect the organization from its original objectives. Because community work often generates controversy, the sponsors of community organization are especially prone to abandon their purposes in favor of self-protection. Although some "cause-oriented" sponsors require conflict to maintain themselves, by and large a sponsor's change objectives tend to be diluted by a quest for environmental peace.

In chapter 3 we identified three goals of community work sponsors along the dimension of the sponsor's orientation to social equilibrium and change: *integrative goals* are sought by sponsors concerned with social stability or the improved juxtaposition of service givers and service users, such as urban renewal agencies, community health and welfare councils, youth boards and bureaus, the parent associations in the public schools; *sociotherapeutic goals* are held by sponsors seeking to educate or to improve the self-image of participants, such as settlements, community development agencies, and some anti-poverty programs; and *environmental-change goals* are those by which sponsors seek a specific and substantive change in a problem area, for example, some Model Cities agencies, special interest or "cause" organizations, and social movements.

The value systems of organizations develop in patterned ways. For example, there is a pattern in the association between the goals of agencies and their means of obtaining them. Sponsors which have integrative and sociotherapeutic objectives manifest a preference for consensual means, while those with environmental-change goals view the generation of conflict as a more acceptable and necessary tactic.[4]

[4] There is little research which bears on this matter, but one study of neighborhood organizations under settlement house auspices in 120 neighborhoods calls forth this observation, "Agencies . . . which emphasize person and social development and the provision of services *almost always* employ the strategy of consensus." *Making Democracy Work, a Study of Neighborhood Organization* (New York: National Federation of Settlements and Neighborhood Centers, 1968), p. 36. (Emphasis added)

Similarly, sponsor goals influence (and are influenced by) relationships with constituencies.

Who Benefits? One basis for classifying organizations is the identification of the organization's prime beneficiary.[5] Although many groups may profit from an organization's activities, the benefits to one party (its prime beneficiary) furnish the basis for an organization's existence, whereas the benefits to others may constitute a cost.

When participation of the recipients of service is designed to enhance or stabilize agency and community services (i.e., integrative goals), then the beneficiaries of the activity are the agency, community, or the public-at-large. In the desire to satisfy both maintenance needs and program needs, sponsors with integrative goals will more often opt for the former than other sponsors will, since the agency is the prime beneficiary of the organizing effort. If a sponsor's objective is to contain conflict, as in the instance of the welfare department's organizing clients, the prime beneficiaries of the effort will be those for whom peace is desirable, which may not be the welfare recipients. A striking example is the delinquency prevention program whose function is to promote social control. The benefit to the potential delinquents is inevitably accorded lesser priority than the benefits to the community-at-large. Thus, an issue that was argued in street gang programs—should workers maintain confidentiality or report infractions of the law to the police—was by and large decided in the community's favor rather than the offender's.[6]

This does not mean that clients may not also benefit from the programs of sponsors with integrative goals. Nor would we assert that all decisions are made in favor of the agency or community. There are times when the interests of agency, community, and client are similar. Furthermore, staff in agencies with integrative goals—either because the goals are ambiguous, or challenged by the staff—often make client-oriented decisions, particularly when their actions are

[5] Peter M. Blau and W. Richard Scott, *Formal Organizations* (San Francisco: Chandler, 1962), pp. 42–58.

[6] We do not mean to imply that it is in the best interest of the youth to protect him from existing sanctions against his destructive behavior. But clearly, a blanket policy on reporting infractions does not allow the worker to decide when and if it is in fact in the youth's best interest. The policy is, however, *always* in the community's best interest.

not readily visible. Thus many street gang workers did not report infractions to the police although it was agency policy to do so. The
point is that organizations with integrative goals are more likely than
other sponsors to make decisions in favor of the agency or public-at-
large when there is a conflict of interests between the agency and its
clients.

Integrative agencies, more than other sponsors, look upon the ser-
vice-user instrumentally. That is, when a purpose of the agency is to
smooth-over or cool-out, or when the objective of community work is
to "sell" a program to residents (however salutary the program may
be), then the service user needs smoothing, cooling, or selling. When
agency considerations are paramount, the service recipient becomes a
means-to-an-end. He is, in other words, a political target. This, we
would submit, is one of the dangers in workers identifying strongly
with their agencies, whatever the nature of agency goals.

Sponsors with sociotherapeutic goals view the prime beneficiary as
the "client." Those who are helped, educated, or changed are clearly
intended to be the ones to profit most from the program.

Underpinning its view of the client is a belief in the intrinsic
worth, uniqueness, and strength of each individual, and the ability of
every person to maximize his growth potential. Thus the Biddles
offer these principles:

When community developers work on a friendly basis with people, in activities that serve the common good. . . .
When their actions affirm a belief in the good in people. . . .
Then people tend to develop themselves to become more ethically competent persons:
Then they may become involved in a process of self-guided growth that
   continues indefinitely.[7]

There is some discomfort among community workers with the
term "client," however valuable and unique a person he may be believed to be. Grosser suggests, for example, that the characterization
of a service user as "client" is invidious. It implies that social work's
conscientious respect for the integrity of the client has been neces-

[7] William W. Biddle and Loureide J. Biddle, *The Community Development
Process: The Rediscovery of Local Initiative* (New York: Holt, Rinehart, and
Winston, 1965), p. 62.

sary, at least in part, because from the field's residual perspective, clients are necessarily classified as helpless.[8] It is undoubtedly true that the engagement between a professional and a "client" suggests inequality, with one the giver and the other the recipient, whereas interaction between a professional and a "constituent" bespeaks greater parity.[9]

For sponsors with environmental change objectives, the prime beneficiaries are the "victims" of social injustice on whose behalf the action is undertaken. They are seen as "members" or constituents, that is, they are *in* the organization as much as they are served by it. But change-oriented sponsors have varying perceptions of who the victim is. Some perceive the victim to be the community group in interaction with the sponsor. Others have a notion of the victim which includes all people who fit a particular social category, whether they interact with the sponsor or not. This difference in perception often goes unidentified under the assumption that the participating group of victims and the category of victims are identical. In reality, however, this may not be the case, and the difference in outlook constitutes a source of tension between leaders and members within some organizations.

Staff or leaders who think in terms of a category of "victims" may be predisposed to consider the larger issues, whereas the group-in-interaction will almost always evaluate a potential action as it directly affects them. Sponsors who view a social category as its prime beneficiary, rather than the group with which it is in contact, are more likely to use participants instrumentally, as means to ends. In this respect they may be similar to integrative organizations.

Social Relations. The goals of sponsors and their view of their constituencies affect the kinds of relationships which develop between service users and agency personnel. There tends to be greater social distance between workers and constituents in integrative agencies, and least social distance in environmental change agencies. Sociotherapeutic sponsors fall in between.

Since the maintenance of institutional relationships is an upper-

[8] Charles F. Grosser, "Changing Theory and Changing Practice," *Social Casework,* Vol. 50, No. 1 (January 1969), pp. 18–19.

[9] That is, apart from fee for service.

most concern of integrative agencies, with service users likely to be
political targets, the relations between sponsors and constituents are
unlikely to be based on solidary ties. Exchange relations which are
devoid of social content often develop.

Organizations with sociotherapeutic goals are likely to draw upon
social work values in developing constituency-staff relations. Here, if
we generalize about concepts of appropriate professional role across
all social work methods, the ideal professional stance requires "identification and empathy on the one hand, but a sufficient degree of
separateness, self-awareness and discipline on the other, to permit
the professional worker to see the situation in a longer and broader
perspective than that of the client and group. . . ." [10] The "sufficient
degree of separateness" serves to protect client interest and simultaneously, in preventing workers from "overidentification," insulates
them from being unduly influenced by client desires.

A "sufficient degree of separateness" may be more appropriate for
clinical than for community practice, since the community work constituent is less dependent on the worker than the casework client, and
needs less protection. He is freer to withdraw from the relationship
than the client who needs specific, concrete, individualized help upon
which his own or his family's survival may depend. Since the organizer must have constituent support for community action, he is at
least equally dependent in the relationship, and therefore wields less
authority.

In any event, the identification, empathy, *and* separateness in the
role sanctioned for workers in sociotherapeutic settings supports social relations that are less affective than exist in membership organizations, and more affective than the exchange relations of integrative
sponsors.

Relations within a membership organization tend to be based on
solidary ties, that is, the act of joining indicates some agreement regarding the organization's goals. So too with environmental-change-
oriented sponsors. Their view of the constituent as a victim of social
injustice implies partisanship and "likemindedness" of purpose with
its participants.

[10] Harriet M. Bartlett, *Analyzing Social Work Practice by Fields* (New
York: National Association of Social Workers, 1961), p. 34.

This partisanship of the social worker in the environmental-change-oriented organization has been the subject of critical comment among some social workers, who argue that professionalism requires separateness and objectivity. However, singleness of purpose, if intense, makes it inevitable that there will be lesser social distance between participant and worker, and this may even be necessary for goal achievement. Sometimes, there is no real distinction between professional and participant with regard to the benefits to be derived from community action. The black professional, for example, has as great a personal stake in the achievement of a sponsor's goal of equal rights as other participants. This goes counter to the traditional perspective of the professional as someone who does not profit personally from the process. Although one might demand that the worker be self-conscious and disciplined, and that he eschew immediate gain, partisanship and strong solidary bonds are not avoidable, nor should they be.

Overzealousness does pose risks. All other things being equal, the more intense a commitment to change, the less concern there will be with the means of achieving the change, and the more likelihood that the rights of participants and others will be overlooked. Thus sponsors with environmental-change goals are more prone to manipulate constituencies for strategic gain than sociotherapeutic sponsors. This is particularly true of those who view a *category* of victim as their prime beneficiary. Claims that manipulation is in the constituency's long-range interest may mitigate a worker's own negative judgment about his behavior, but the claim does not justify the act. Mobilizing constituents to action by means of serious distortions, even though it is "for their own good," is treating them with patronizing disrespect even while purporting to rescue them from the disrespect and indignity meted out by "established" institutions.

The officials of an organization engaged in organizing tenants to demand housing improvements proposed to the worker that a "critical episode" was necessary to counter the tenants' apathetic response. They suggested that an eviction be contrived by advising tenants to take a series of actions, including rent withholding. The drama of the event, it was expected, would not only publicize the housing effort in the community but the incident would also propel further movement.

Anger induced by the eviction would serve as an incentive for action by a large number of residents. Furthermore, the proposal called for neighbors to block the bailiff which would commit them psychologically and generate consequences which would bind them to future actions. An aroused community would thus impel government intervention. The officials' analysis of the consequences of the proposed action may have been correct but it failed to consider two factors. The first was the risk to the tenants that they might spend a cold January in the streets. Of more dubious moral question is the second factor: the contrivance of an eviction without the tenants' full understanding and concurrence.

We do not mean to imply that constituents are necessarily manipulated in social-change-oriented agencies, seen as objects in integrative ones, or treated with detached neutrality by sponsors with sociotherapeutic goals. Obviously, there are other variables which affect these interactions: professional values; the personality of specific workers; the climate of particular work groups; special organizational circumstances; and the like. With that qualification, the worker should be prepared for the inevitable tendency for particular types of social relations to evolve from particular agency goals. It is only as community workers are aware of these agency influences that the option for dealing with them is available.

Constituency Self-determination. Values regarding the role of constituents in sponsor decision making vary with the orientation of the sponsoring organization. Integrative agencies, we adjudge, are least committed to involving consumers in either community or internal decision making. Environmental-change oriented sponsors are most invested in constituents having an impact on the larger community, but they are as reluctant as (or perhaps more reluctant than) sociotherapeutic sponsors to allow them internal authority.

Ultimately, sponsors are held responsible for the activities of groups organized under their auspices. When community organizations are challenged by the very people who are the recipients of their largess and therefore expected to be grateful, these organizations turn on the sponsor with charges of manipulating the "simple" client. To the extent that community groups are autonomous and free to "get out of hand," community participation is threatening to the sponsor of the program. Under these circumstances, participation becomes more or less expendable, depending on whether it is central to the sponsor's purpose or is instrumental to other ends.

Participation of the service user in community affairs is least central to agencies with integrative objectives. Autonomy is allowable only insofar as it facilitates mutual understanding in the community, since cooperation is its *raison d'etre*. For sponsors with sociotherapeutic goals, participation is also instrumental to other ends (i.e., as it helps the participant) rather than intrinsic to the agency's goals. For many sponsors with environmental-change objectives, however, the participation of the service recipient is an absolute necessity. Central to the achievement of these agencies' goals is a constituency of consumers acting as the source of pressure to promote desired organizational changes.

There is a distinction between sociotherapeutic and environmental-change conceptions of service which is often obscured in practice. In the former the group as a collectivity is important only so long as it serves as a mechanism for individual development. The collectivity is a tool, valueless in itself, and its achievements are considered secondary. When the goal is environmental change, the collectivity, rather than its members, assumes primary importance. It is not only the instrument through which goals are achieved but it may also constitute an end in itself (e.g., simply because it exists it may alter the distribution of power). The end result of collective action, rather than side benefits to participants, is primary. Although this may be a fine distinction, it affects sponsor attitudes toward community participation.

Sponsors of sociotherapeutic programs have various means by which to justify their control of community group decisions. The concept of "readiness" may be used, when necessary, to define the clients as "unready," and to prohibit action to protect them from themselves. The following report of an interview with a Youth Council worker illustrates the point:

[The worker] said that the major purpose [of the council] was to get the kids involved in community-wide social and political action, but these kids are not ready for this kind of thing. They first have to develop capacity to make effective decisions about their own affairs.[11]

[11] Irving A. Spergel, *Community Problem Solving* (Chicago: University of Chicago Press, 1969), p. 80.

Whether it is the youth or the agency that is unready is an important question which we will not presume to answer. The worker who is the arbiter of this capacity must be sure that the question is asked, however.

The concept of "representativeness" may also be used by the agency to limit client decision making; in this instance, it protects the community from its clients. The sponsor will allow action only if, as stated in these settlement house guidelines, "the group making the decision [to conduct a demonstration] is *truly representative* of the neighborhood." [12] Representativeness is a vague concept, impossible to define. "Truly" representative, then, is "truly" indefinite. In effect, it reserves for the agency the right to veto.

The picture is similar in regard to how different types of sponsors deal with internal decision making by service users. Sponsors with integrative goals have little incentive to accord decision-making responsibility beyond that which is required to legitimate agency program. Paradoxically, in light of their respective values regarding the participation of constituents in community action, sociotherapeutic sponsors, more so than those oriented to social change, emphasize broad involvement in internal decision making. There are two reasons for this, one professional, the other political.

When the goal of participation is the education or emotional growth of the participant, one is led to include the participant in decision-making. Professional thinking supports such involvement as a requirement of individual development. In part, this injunction stems from the democratic ethos of social work. In part too, it may be a residual consequence of the clinical base of social work. In clinical practice, intellectual understanding is viewed as insufficient for change to occur. The understanding must be internalized, made the client's "own." This is only a step removed from the idea that client decision making is necessary for client development.

In addition to professional sanction, there are political benefits in the notion of widespread involvement in decision making. When all are involved, the process is more time consuming and subject to considerable delay, thus reducing the force of urgency. But low-income people are rarely moved to adversary actions except by feelings

[12] *Making Democracy Work,* p. 60. (Emphasis added)

which are urgent, powerful, and immediate. In the words of Kozan-takis:

How can a man be made to struggle for freedom without an appeal to his deepest instincts: Hatred, hunger, thirst, and revenge are tremendous powers that must be mobilized. The virtues, bourgeois or not, are insufficient to shake off man's torpor.[13]

Thus for an organization which finds adversary actions threatening to its self-interest and which prefers consensual modes of practice, the involvement of *all* participants in decision making provides a professionally acceptable escape hatch, an "out" which is made more potent by its not being recognized as such.

The inclusive decision-making style of sociotherapeutic sponsors is not without its constraints, however. We have already identified two of them: the concepts of "readiness" and "representativeness," which act as undefined limits to client autonomy. In addition, as Ross suggests, the worker *guides* the group, "by encouraging verbalization, by patient listening, by skillful interrogation," [14] actions which frequently lend themselves to subtle direction setting by the worker.

Sponsors with environmental-change goals are at least as likely as sociotherapeutic ones to limit internal decision making by constituents for reasons uniquely their own. More than others, change-oriented sponsors tend to hold strong ideological commitments. These agencies are subject to the hostility of important interests in the community. One adjustment to that hostility is to intensify the conviction with which their beliefs are held. The difficulty of promoting community change also reinforces the intensity of the change-oriented sponsor's belief system, since mustering the necessary resources to pursue its ends requires intensity of commitment.

This intensity discourages widespread dispersion of decision-making responsibility. As we have already indicated, intensity of commitment to a position varies inversely with willingness to allow the position to be questioned, and may lead to overlooking the rights of others. Sponsors who are highly committed to environmen-

[13] Nicos Kozantakis, *The Rock Garden* (New York: Simon and Schuster, 1963), p. 19.
[14] Murray G. Ross, *Community Organization: Theory and Principles* (New York: Harper and Row, 1955), p. 212.

tal-change goals will thus limit the decision-making prerogatives of their constituency. Although its ideology and *need* for a constituency may lessen this tendency, community participants may be accorded only such internal influence as required to legitimate goals. To do this, the sponsor, overtly or covertly, may assign the worker or community leader the task of keeping the group "in line."

THE STRUCTURE OF SPONSOR-
CONSTITUENT RELATIONS

The structure of sponsor-constituent relations derives from sponsor goals. This is not the whole story, however, since the congruence of structure and goal is often imperfect. Structure has its own dynamic, and how relations between sponsor and constituents are patterned importantly influences the latter's latitude. Two aspects of the structure of sponsor-constituent relations are important in this regard: distance and staffing arrangements.

Distance. The structure of relations between sponsors and community groups vary in the degree of distance which they entail. Four points along a continuum may be identified: (1) When sponsor and community groups are the same entity, there is no distance. An example is the community corporation, composed of neighborhood residents. (2) Distance is minimal in the case of the community group which is an integral part of the sponsor's community work program and an extension of sponsor interests and values. (3) More distance exists in the case of the sponsor offering services and facilities to a purportedly independent, sometimes self-organized group. And (4) maximum distance exists in the contractual arrangement between sponsor and a community group, in which control of the program is delegated to the group. Here, the two entities are distinct and separate. The Community Action Agency which subcontracts a program component, such as a multi-service center, is an example.

Community group independence is greater at either end of the continuum. There are, furthermore, advantages to both of these arrangements which go beyond encouraging community self-direction. Both patterns provide opportunities for program management by community groups, thereby increasing their competence to administer their own affairs. They offer possibilities for ongoing program activity which enhance group stability and enrich the organizational and political life of the community. Clearly, the structures of choice for community groups are those in which sponsor and group are one, or short of that, those in which authority has been formally delegated, through contractual arrangements, to the community group.

The midpoints on the continuum provide only shades of difference. When the community group is an integral part of the sponsor's program, its survival rests on a heavy infusion of sponsor resources, sharply limiting the group's freedom of action. In the other instance, although the group is nominally in charge of its own affairs, and stated sponsor policy affirms its right of autonomous action, it is similarly dependent.

Yet, even though this informal "contract" regarding the community group's autonomy may be rhetorical, public pronouncements of constituency independence are useful. Such public expressions allow the sponsor an "out" if it wishes one. It can justify the controversial actions of constituents to its important reference groups on the grounds of the constituents' rights rather than the sponsor's agreement with the action. Furthermore, stated policy leads the community group to expect independence, and in that expectation, to offer stiffer resistance to attempts to curb it.

In practice the sponsor often organizes a group and, with time, the group assumes greater independence, develops a "life of its own," and is accorded nominal autonomous status. The task of the community worker is to encourage and, when possible, to accelerate this process. To the extent that conditions permit, he may ultimately move the relationship to one in which delegated authority is formalized.

The characteristics and commitment of the group's membership may also affect the structure of these relationships. Sponsors are likely to be chary of limiting community groups which have significant neighborhood support and committed and well-organized participants. Members who believe in their group's right to autonomy, and who are willing to risk and rail to achieve it, are more likely to earn independent status for a group, at least to the extent that the cost to the sponsor of granting self-direction is less than the cost of with-standing its militance. The backing of a well-organized constituency is also important for leaders of community groups who serve on the policy-making structures of sponsoring organizations or on other pol-icy-setting community associations.

Staff Arrangements. The structure of sponsor-constituent relations is defined by staff arrangements to a considerable degree. Who em-ploys the worker, and to whom he is accountable, has significant bearing on community group autonomy.

At one extreme, the worker is hired by the sponsor, supervised within its normal hierarchical channels, and responsible for his per-formance to the organization. Since sanctions in regard to worker be-havior rest with the sponsor, this arrangement inevitably limits com-munity group independence. To some extent, community-identified, skillful, and freewheeling workers may enlarge the group's prerog-atives, even as employees of sponsoring agencies. But they are no substitute for arrangements which put greater staff control in the hands of the community group itself.

At the other extreme are those patterns in which the group hires, fires, and holds the worker accountable. A community group can be said to be independent of sponsor control only insofar as it has effec-tive choice over who provides it with staff and technical assistance, on what terms, and in what ways. This usually occurs when sponsor and group are the same entity, or when program components are subcontracted to the community group. In some Model Cities pro-grams, for example, neighborhood-dominated groups have won funds from the program to engage their own technical planning staffs.[15]

In between these two extreme arrangements are those wherein community groups or their representatives may be involved in, if not in fact in charge of, the staff selection process. Some sponsors have developed joint committees composed of sponsorship personnel and community representatives to screen and choose professional candi-dates. Indeed, there is no reason—except custom and the desire of an agency to control the reins—why even traditional social agencies

[15] Melvin Mogulof, "Coalition to Adversary: Citizen Participation in Three Federal Programs," *Journal of the American Institute of Planners,* Vol. XXXV, No. 4 (July 1969), p. 230.

cannot significantly involve their clientele in staff selection or grant community participants veto power in the actual choice.

Community workers, employed by sponsors for whom the above is too "heady" stuff, have a minimal responsibility as professionals to give community groups a choice themselves, whenever feasible. One means is for the worker to raise with the group its right to accept or reject him before the assignment is made final. He might encourage an "interview" that is, a discussion regarding his abilities and beliefs, following which the matter of his assignment is submitted for group decision. The choice must be real to be meaningful, so that the worker must, in fact, be willing to risk rejection.

In sum, the degree of community group independence from sponsorship control is determined by the goals of the sponsor, some of the patterned value tendencies which are associated with those goals, and the structure of sponsor-constituency relations. It is well, however, to conclude this chapter with a note of caution. No organization is an "ideal type," purely integrative, sociotherapeutic, or social-change-oriented. Goals, value predispositions, and structured relationships exist along a continuum, rather than at fixed points. Nor do values or constituency-relations spring full blown. They are developed in response to and are influenced by the internal and external relations of the sponsor. It is to the latter that we turn in the next chapter.

CHAPTER NINE

SPONSORSHIP AND
COMMUNITY AUTONOMY:
MANAGING "FOREIGN AFFAIRS"

AN ORGANIZATION'S EXTERNAL RELATIONS ("foreign affairs") and internal operations ("domestic policy") are interdependent. Goal setting, usually considered an internal matter, defines a sponsor's relationship to its environment; and even agency structure is, in part, a response to external conditions. Community opposition, for example, tends to encourage the formalization of organizational activities. Thus Rose found that voluntary associations in hostile environments were more likely to develop formal structures than those in environments that were benign.[1]

Our interest in the "foreign affairs" of the sponsor is circumscribed by the question: How do external relations affect a sponsor's ability and willingness to grant autonomy to constituent groups? Important in this regard is the sponsor's own degree of independence. Many sponsors would be more likely to support the right of constituent groups to autonomous action if such autonomy did not pose a threat to their own survival and developmental needs.

Sponsors which are well endowed with money or other societal resources are more powerful, and thus have a greater number of op-

[1] Arnold M. Rose, "Voluntary Associations under Conditions of Competition and Conflict," *Social Forces,* Vol. XXIV (December 1955), pp. 160–61.

tions. Those with minimal needs require less from the wider community, and are therefore more independent too. In both cases, the
organization need not trade its freedom of action in return for external resources.[2] But the similarity ends there. Sponsors that are well
endowed and those that need little may be comparable as regards
autonomy, but their ability to influence policies and programs is
quite different. In the main, of course, community work sponsors are
neither completely independent nor totally impotent. They are
only more or less free of environmental restraints. An understanding
of what makes for these differences is important in assessing how
much constituency self-direction will be permitted, or how much resistance can be expected when community groups struggle to wrest
their independence from the sponsor.

In this chapter we explore some of the factors affecting sponsor
autonomy and potency: the organization's funding patterns and
sources; the influence on the voluntary agency of its organization set;
the characteristics of the sponsor's constituency; and local community
conditions.

FUNDING PATTERNS

Conventional wisdom has it that "he who pays the piper calls the
tune." But it is not only he who pays who counts in tune calling, but
where and how the payments are collected. That is, the structure of
fund raising influences the freedom with which sponsors may dispense funds.

The degree to which sources of funds are disbursed or centralized
affects the kinds of community activity the sponsor can support. For
example, universities became more flexible in their pursuit of educa-

---

[2] A similar dynamic operates with individuals as well. Thus it has been observed that militance is more possible for members of the lower and upper
classes than for the middle class. Lower class persons risk less because they
have less; upper class persons can afford to risk because, in the richness of
their resources, they can stand a loss. N.J. Demerath III and Victor Thiessen,
"On Spitting against the Wind: Organizational Precariousness and American
Irreligion," *American Journal of Sociology,* Vol. LXXI, No. 6 (May 1966), p.
682.

tional objectives as they became less dependent on the support of a single individual or class. Similarly, as the funding of community work is disbursed, with contributions from the public and private sectors, from federal, state, and municipal auspices, greater flexibility ensues. When its funding sources are diversified, a sponsor is freer to avoid the strictures of a single giver. Givers too are more restrained in their demands on sponsors when they know their contribution is not fiscally central to the organization's operation.

An amusing example is provided by the experience of one poverty agency which had multiple-fund sources. Groups organized under the aegis of the agency were engaged in a rent-withholding campaign, which prompted a telephone call to the agency executive from an official of a supporting foundation. "You fellows must be doing a great job," the foundation official said, "I have a letter of complaint from the real estate association." He went on to read the letter, murmured something about "keeping up the good work," and then added in passing, "Of course, you're not using foundation funds for that campaign, are you?" Because the agency had a number of funding sources, the executive was free to reply that, in truth, they were not.

Distance between funder and sponsor allows greater sponsor autonomy. The greater the distance both geographically and politically, the less the spender is likely to be observed, and the less attention the funder is likely to pay. Thus, according to one observer, "the agency which receives substantial funds from a national office . . . is more likely to allow its staff freedom for organizing on controversial matters than one which is entirely dependent on . . . local sources." [3]

Congressional action to tame the poverty program reflects an awareness of the relationship between control and distance. The Green amendment, a major congressional "corrective" to the Economic Opportunity Act in 1968, gave local municipal authorities the option of controlling the management of Community Action Agencies. Previously, some of these agencies had been able, against all the odds of political life, to involve the poor as planners, policy makers,

[3] *Making Democracy Work: A Study of Neighborhood Organization* (New York: National Federation of Settlements and Neighborhood Centers, 1968), p. 37.

and staff, an accomplishment made possible in no small part by skirting over, under, or past municipal officials with tacit OEO support. One might hazard the hypothesis that federal support for activities generating local tension is available in direct proportion to the distance of federal officials from the battleground. The federal official's own ideology or commitment to principle has room for greater play because his participation takes place in a more distant arena and he is less directly involved in the program. Local officials, on the other hand, must be more attentive to the reactions of local interests, not to mention their ubiquitous interest in protecting their "turf."

As the Green amendment demonstrates, the advantage of distance may be short-lived. Over time, controversial actions become increasingly visible, even at long distances, since local interest groups which have influence with national officials quickly involve them in the fray.

More important perhaps, differing geographic locations represent differing political alignments and power. In this context, local community control of programs could be something of a mixed blessing. For example, community self-determination is potentially advantageous to black interests in largely black communities. In communities where blacks are a minority, however, local—as opposed to national—control of the expenditure of funds is more likely to lead to the distribution of resources in ways which are disadvantaging to the minority group. Local communities represent local majorities; state and particularly national administrations in the United States are likely to be responsive to minorities whose "swing" vote in state and federal elections is important.

Sponsor autonomy is affected by the degree to which the sponsor's program impinges on the funder. Programs which have minimal consequence to the supporter will generate less interference than those which are either meaningful or threatening. The scope of the program and its resultant expense is relevant in this regard. The larger the contribution, the more attentive the contributor. The more comprehensive the program, the greater the number of community interests it will affect. Thus mayors who were satisfied to allow the two-to-three million dollar per year projects of the President's Committee on Juvenile Delinquency to escape their purview were activated by the promise of the vastly expanded funds of the war on poverty, although their arguments were often couched in ideological terms.

Funds granted to agencies on a time-limited or ad hoc basis can ordinarily be expended in ways which are more innovating or threatening to powerful other institutions than on-going or regular grants. Ad hoc funding is used extensively as a technique to permit experimentation or to neutralize opposition. A time-limited grant suggests that the program will be temporary unless its value is proved. The criteria for "proof" of effectiveness are often left indeterminant, however, subject to later political circumstances. (In some cases, the program's value is "proved" simply by being acceptable to those in a position to veto it.)

Impermanence may also lull opposition, for in being temporary, a program is less threatening. However, as both the advocates and the opposition are aware, even temporary programs die hard.

The classic example of this strategy is the demonstration project, a technique which came to full flower in the 1960's in the juvenile delinquency projects, the war on poverty, community mental health, Model Cities,[4] manpower retraining, and a host of other programs. The success of the "demonstration" as a political ploy is evidenced in the contagion of the delinquency and community action projects across the country before the first demonstration was two years old. This barely allowed time to organize the research which was to be used to evaluate the programs, much less to conduct the evaluation itself.

The granting of temporary funds as a first step in the process to garner acceptance for larger and more permanent expenditures is nowhere more clearly manifest than in the Nixon administration's family assistance proposal in the early 1970's. As Congressional opposition mounted, the administration hoped to forestall the program's defeat by proposing a demonstration of the plan, to be followed automatically, and without further Congressional action, by its complete adoption.

[4] The Model Cities Program was originally called "Demonstration Cities." However, when the legislation was being prepared in the mid-1960's, the word "demonstration" had achieved a different (and militant) popular meaning, thus the change in language.

A funding structure in which the constituents either contribute or otherwise control the funds most clearly assures the sponsor's responsiveness to constituents and respect for their autonomy. Obviously, when support comes from the beneficiaries of the program, sponsors must be responsive to them. There are some who suggest that organizing the poor in their own interests is impossible unless the poor foot the bill. Thus Warren Haggstrom, in advising "how the poor might transform the world," observes that an organization of the poor inevitably becomes the object of attack by opponents who commonly challenge the program at its source of funds. The threat can be avoided, according to Haggstrom, "by securing funds *solely* from the poor, who will pay the costs associated with their movement because their movement will be regarded by the poor as effective and important enough to be worth the expense." [5]

The assumption that the poor can pay if they are sufficiently motivated is neither very different from, nor more rooted in reality than, the assumption of welfare critics that welfare clients can work, and all that is required is incentive. Even if the poor could and would pay once they regarded the organization as sufficiently important, the question of how the organizers support themselves and who would pay their salaries until a movement's worth became apparent, is left unanswered.

Financial support by constituents is highly desirable, since external sources of funding inevitably compromise the integrity of an organizing effort. A community group's program must be shaped to anticipate the objections of financial supporters, and the vested interests of fund-givers inevitably constitutes a serious inhibition to the autonomy of the community group. But since, in an imperfect world, service recipients do not ordinarily have the financial resources to contribute significantly to the effort, such an arrangement, for all practical purposes, is impossible.

Arrangements other than direct support have been proposed to eliminate the anomaly of community work intended to be responsive to its constituency on the one hand, but controlled by fund dispensers

[5] Warren C. Haggstrom, "Can the Poor Transform the World?" in Ralph M. Kramer and Harry Specht, eds., *Readings in Community Organization Practice* (Englewood Cliffs, N.J.: Prentice-Hall, 1969), p. 313. (emphasis added)

on the other. In such alternate patterns, the constituents control rather than contribute the funds. An example is a fee-for-service plan. Instead of public support for an organization, as for example a legal aid society, the person who needs a lawyer is given the funds or a chit, so that he can purchase the assistance. In that way, the service-giving organization must seek, and therefore be responsive to, its "customers." However, fee-for-service plans do not ensure responsiveness to clients. Universities, although they operate on a fee-for-service basis, have not been acclaimed by their student-customers for their responsiveness to students, much less for the high degree of student autonomy they allow.[6] It is unlikely, in any case, that fee-for-service arrangements would be practicable in community work, since organizing does not constitute a delineated service.

An arrangement more relevant to community organizing is one that gives constituent groups the right to pass on proposals for community programming. In some Model Cities programs, for example, community groups have won *de jure* veto power. Here, procedures require that the city council or mayor submit programs for funding only with the prior approval of an advisory committee composed of neighborhood residents.[7] Similarly, legislation which mandates community participation offers a structure which, in some measure at least, promotes constituent control of expenditures.

Even more significant is the pattern set by some Model Cities Programs in which resident organizations receive budgeted funds from the City Demonstration Agencies to engage their own organizing and planning staff. In these arrangements may be found a recognition by government that it has a responsibility to provide the resources required for community participation to citizens who do not have them.[8]

[6] It should be pointed out that student fees constitute a limited percentage of university budgets, and this fact may account, in part, for administrative reactions to student-customers.

[7] Melvin Mogulof, "Coalition to Adversary: Citizen Participation in Three Federal Programs," *Journal of the American Institute of Planners,* Vol. XXXV, No. 4 (July 1969), p. 230.

[8] James L. Sundquist, *Making Federalism Work* (Washington, D.C.: Brookings Institution, 1969), chapter 7.

PUBLIC OR PRIVATE FUNDING?

The distinction between public and voluntary agencies has long been considered of major significance. As government support for social programs has become pervasive, however, the role of the voluntary agency has undergone critical examination. Whereas it was once largely accepted that the primary function of the voluntary agency was to innovate in regard to new needs and techniques, it has become increasingly clear that voluntary agencies have no monopoly on innovation. If anything, the reverse is true: trail blazing in the 1960's was performed largely under public auspices.[9] Indeed, the press for citizen participation in institutional decision making came from government and was met with resistance from many in the private sector. In reacting to the poverty program, Schorr has observed that "voluntary agencies that had been teaching participatory democracy for many years found themselves arrayed against its most vigorous manifestation." [10]

Voluntary financing necessarily sets sharp limits to the scope of social programs. It does not assure their pioneering character, as noted, and has even sometimes been allied against participation of the poor in community decision making. Nevertheless, proponents of community action are often counseled to eschew public support for community work with the poor. The case against the granting of public funds for the purpose of organizing the poor is a strong one. It has two bases: one moral, the other strategic.

The moral case has been put as follows:

The emotional thrust behind nearly all such [community action] programs is bound to carry them over into the field of political action. Voter

[9] Alvin L. Schorr, "The Tasks for Voluntarism in the Next Decade," paper presented at the Centenary Conference on Voluntary Organization in the 1970's, sponsored by the Family Welfare Association, June 1969, at the University of Sussex, Brighton, England. (Mimeographed) Schorr cites five pioneering ventures of the 1960's (the juvenile delinquency programs, community action, amendments to social security, community care of the mentally ill, and Model Cities), and notes that these were largely inspired and set in motion by government, p. 3.

[10] *Ibid.*, p. 10.

registration, civil rights, tenant councils, and the like are programs possessing a strong political color. What the government through its subsidization of such programs is in fact doing is providing them with an organizational framework and a degree of legitimacy. This is not only contrary to American political practice and tradition, but serves as a potentially dangerous precedent. "The poor today and some other group tomorrow" is a slogan that flows easily from the premise of government sponsored social-action programs. Such programs, finally, could be exploited by unscrupulous or overzealous persons for their own partisan or personal ends. [11]

These risks inhere in government support of community change efforts, since the line between social action and partisan political activity is thin. The proponents of public support argue that although publicly funded community action should avoid partisan political activity, the risk of political abuse is worth taking on the premise that the poor must develop a stake in their society, contribute their special perspective and experience to devising solutions to community problems, and acquire the political influence necessary to bring about a more equitable distribution of resources, ends which can only be accomplished by programs of great magnitude. At some point in the sociopolitical history of the nation, these proponents would say, the risk might become too costly for the desired end. At present, however, there is a sufficient check within the political processes, and service-recipients are so severely underrepresented in decision-making councils as to warrant courting the danger of abuse.

A second ethical objection to the use of public funds is less telling. Taxes, it is argued, should not be used to the advantage of one group of citizens at the expense of another. So, for example, it would be deemed inappropriate to use public funds to organize citizens against tax-paying landlords. However, tax funds are frequently used for the advantage of one group to the detriment of another; farm subsidies, for example, hardly benefit the taxpaying consumer. Nor is there a dearth of examples of government succor to special groups on the basis of age, occupation, industry, and military status.

[11] Murray Silberman, "Securing Change through Government-Supported Social Action Programs," Columbia University School of Social Work, March 6, 1965, p. 9. (Mimeographed)

The pragmatic argument against public support for community work is more troublesome. It was summarized by one poverty program official who suggested that "If Jesus had been on the Roman payroll, the history of Christian civilization would have been different." [12] Since the interests of the funder are primary, so the argument goes, publicly financed community work must serve the interests of government rather than the interests of politically powerless citizens. These interests are likely to conflict, since the major service institutions are public ones, and are therefore standing targets for community action. As put by a critic of the anti-poverty wars, "Social radicalism is not a civil service calling." [13]

Nevertheless, governmental support for the participation of the poor and other service recipients is now embodied in most federal legislation dealing with the human services. And although public support may be expected to impose significant constraints on community groups, public control is not absolute. Officials who dispense funds do not have complete information (particularly of behaviors as complex and subtle as community work). They are neither always rational nor consistent. They may hold values which encourage them to make decisions in other than utilitarian terms. Most important, they are subject to the pressures of conflicting jurisdictions and reference groups.

One factor that limits the autonomy of publicly financed sponsors is that their location in the political arena inevitably provokes political pressures. Elected officials are ordinarily impelled to react to public criticism of community work programs which are government supported. Thus the sponsor is accountable to the politician, and public pressure on the politician is transformed into constraints on the sponsor.

In addition, controversy in publicly financed programs is proscribed, because it is considered politically unpopular. Thus Burke declares that "conflict-oriented strategies . . . are inappropriate in governmentally sponsored programs which demand coordination and coop-

[12] George A. Brager and Francis P. Purcell, "Conclusion," *Community Action against Poverty* (New Haven: College and University Press, 1967), p. 334.

[13] Daniel P. Moynihan, *Maximum Feasible Misunderstanding* (New York: Free Press, 1969), p. 187.

eration." [14] But community work which seeks to influence the policies of public institutions must necessarily run the risk of engendering conflict. To limit such programs *solely* to coordination and cooperation is to guarantee their impotence.

Whether these constraints are greater in publicly financed than in privately financed programs is another matter, however, and is by no means clear. There is some research that suggests that they are not. Lazersfeld and Thielens, in a study of public and private academic institutions, assessed the perceptions of faculties regarding increases in political pressures during the McCarthy era. Interestingly, the findings reveal no clear-cut difference between the faculties at public and private institutions. [15]

Sources of pressure differed, however. At the public colleges, politicians were most frequently identified as the source of new pressures, whereas teachers at the private institutions reported increased pressure from a greater variety of sources. In the latter instance, alumni who had been largely quiescent came to the fore in urging a new pattern of conformity on their schools. [16]

Administrative responses to pressure differed as well. In tax-supported schools, the greater the political pressure, the less the administrative protection perceived by the faculty. In privately endowed schools, on the other hand, the case was exactly the reverse: the greater the political pressure, the more ready the Administration was to protect its faculty. [17]

These findings suggest that community work sponsors supported by voluntary funds may be no more immune from external pressure than private academic institutions. Differences between public and private social agencies on this score are minimal, we suspect, and have generally been overstated. But sources of pressure are likely to be different. Public agencies must necessarily be more responsive to elected officials, whereas in the private institution it is the business man-philanthropist who carries the weight. The issues which impel

[14] Edmund M. Burke, "Citizen Participation Strategies," *Journal of the American Institute of Planners,* Vol. XXXIV, No. 5 (September 1968), p. 293.

[15] Paul F. Lazersfeld and Wagner Thielens, Jr., *The Academic Mind* (New York: Free Press, 1958), p. 40.

[16] *Ibid.,* p. 41.   [17] *Ibid.,* p. 183.

either the politician or the philanthropist to exert pressure depend, similarly, on the current community agenda as well as the interests of their respective constituencies.

Evidence against the view that government cannot initiate controversial programs is provided by a study conducted by Warren and Hyman. In their review of 35 published episodes of purposive community change, they found that actions originating under private auspices tended to be associated with consensus situations, while those under government auspices were overwhelmingly associated with dissensus. They conclude:

> . . . the finding casts grave doubt on the assumption that government offices and agencies tend to be conservative, dodging the controversial actions, while non-governmental agencies are the fearless protagonists of conflicting points of view. Taken aggregately, governmental auspices are handling a much greater proportion of controverted issues than are non-governmental auspices.[18]

Furthermore, they suggest that governmental involvement in controversy is not spurred solely by elected officials "engaging in a loose, free-swinging type of contest activity." And conversely, consensual activities are not the exclusive province of cautious government bureaucracies. Rather, the initiation of the conflictual cases in the public sector was about evenly divided between political leaders and bureaucratic officials.[19]

If the constraints of political pressure and conflict avoidance are shared by both government and voluntary agencies, the choice between public and private financing is not central in regard to sponsor independence. Some theorists contend that a modern function for voluntary agencies ought to be to "watch dog" public services and public policies, to provide "a countervailing force against the power of central government." [20] We would add that this function is also a

---

[18] Roland L. Warren and Herbert H. Hyman, "Purposive Community Change in Consensus and Dissensus Situations," in Terry N. Clark, ed., *Community Structure and Decision-Making: Comparative Analyses* (San Francisco: Chandler, 1968), p. 417. It should be noted that Warren and Hyman point out that although the 35 cases represent a wide variety of settings and circumstances, they cannot be assumed to constitute a statistically representative sample.

[19] *Ibid.,* pp. 417–18.   [20] Schorr, "Tasks for Voluntarism," p. 16.

responsibility of government. Myrdal has contended that the active participation of all groups of citizens in the operation of the welfare state will minimize bureaucratic malfunctioning and prevent the erosion of individual freedom.[21] Since the constraints appear similarly large with both voluntary and government auspices, there is little basis for advocating one or the other arrangement. If anything, the balance of choice leans toward the public sector because it has the resources to undertake the task.

The distinguishing characteristics of public and private agencies are more ambiguous than our discussion has implied thus far. Traditionally, the distinction between public and voluntary agencies has been made on the basis of their management as well as their financing (i.e., voluntary agencies are supported by nongovernmental funds and managed by private citizens.) However, few voluntary agencies currently meet this criteria and, as Schorr comments, the distinction is hardly more than a state of mind. Thus few social welfare agencies could survive without government funds, and many agencies which are considered private (e.g., Community Action Agencies) have their full complement of public managers.[22]

There are both advantages and disadvantages to this overlap for community work although, on balance, the advantages probably outweigh the liabilities, at least at the present time. The ambiguity of the arrangement contributes to sponsor autonomy. The private management of public funds represents an attempt to have the best of both possible worlds in community work. Access to public funds allows greater programmatic scope. The participation of public officials in private organizations may provide their support while it limits their responsibility for, and authority over, the program. The ideal situation for community action groups is to simultaneously obtain public resources while avoiding the constraints of public accountability and the rigidities of public organization. (The potential

[21] Gunner Myrdal, *Beyond the Welfare State* (New Haven: Yale University Press, 1960), chapters 4 and 6; as noted by Charles Grosser, "Staff Role in Neighborhood Organization," in John B. Turner, ed., *Neighborhood Organization for Community Action* (New York: National Association of Social Workers, 1968), p. 137.

[22] Schorr, "Tasks for Voluntarism," p. 2.

for the Shavian nightmare is inherent in these arrangements: the vagaries of politics can result in quick cutting of purse strings and public investigations resulting in the delay and demoralization of programs.) [23]

Robert Levine concludes from his research that the most effective Community Action Agencies were in cities in which the public establishment participated but allowed the directors flexibility and influence in operating the program. "The abdication of some real power by local officialdom," Levine observes, "can . . . add to program effectiveness for the purposes desired by both officialdom and the poor themselves." [24]

Most important in this regard is the political climate of the community and the stance of its political figures. In the study of 11 Model Cities programs, referred to in chapter 3, it was found that the role of the city's chief executive was an important determinant in the planning process. Where there was a high degree of political integration in the Model Cities area *and* a chief executive who was actively committed to the Model Cities Program, a planning system in which there was "parity" between the program staff and residents of the neighborhood was more likely to evolve.[25] Obviously, in communities where the service recipients are a political force, or in which officials value their participation, sponsor accountability to the public encourages community group participation. When these community conditions are not present, ambiguous accountability will be more likely to aid community group autonomy.

[23] This point may explain the reaction of 155 executive directors of privately managed Community Action Agencies in responding to a survey which asked whether they thought their CAA would be more effective if it were a public agency. Ninety-five per cent answered "no." The directors of publicly run CAA's were less positive about their own current arrangements, since 21 per cent of them advocated a change to private auspices. *Intergovernmental Relations in the Poverty Program,* Advisory Commission on Intergovernmental Relations, April 1966, p. 30.

[24] Robert A. Levine, "Evaluating the War on Poverty," in James L. Sundquist, ed., *On Fighting Poverty* (New York: Basic Books, 1969), p. 210.

[25] Department of Housing and Urban Development, *The Model Cities Program* (Washington, D.C.: U.S. Government Printing Office, 1970).

THE VOLUNTARY AGENCY
AND ITS ORGANIZATION SET

Voluntary organizations are not, of course, as singular as the discussion above implies. Our referent has been the established philanthropic agency, but no discussion of sponsor autonomy is complete without taking note of "cause" organizations which come into being to serve a specific reformist or radical objective.

The strictures on "cause" organizations are different from those placed upon voluntary agencies. They need be responsive, not to the businessman-philanthropist, but to their members or to the supporters of the "cause" who contribute the necessary resources. As such, they are not only freer to pursue constituent interest; they are *required* to do so.

Although such organizations provide greater constituent autonomy than other voluntary associations, there is a price they pay for their relative freedom. "Cause" organizations usually suffer financial problems, so that maintaining themselves becomes a major organizational task, directing organizational attention inward, away from substantive, outwardly focused ends.

The need to raise funds is not entirely without benefit to an organization. Fund raising constitutes a programmatic activity which involves members and strengthens their own sense of importance and commitment to the group. It provides task-oriented groups with an excuse to engage in expressive activities such as fund-raising social events, thereby increasing sociability, as well as serving to publicize the organization. Nevertheless, when a group is absorbed in fund raising for survival, it is deflected from its community action objectives.

Foundation financing ordinarily allows greater sponsor latitude than do other sources of voluntary support. This is because, by and large, foundations subsist on endowments. Although a foundation's interest in impressing some public with its good work inevitably constitutes a spur to certain types of activities and is a restraint on others, the fact that it need not engage in on-going fund raising offers some insulation from the vagaries of fashion or responsiveness to contributors. With greater latitude the foundation can, in turn, allow the sponsor greater latitude.

Furthermore, foundation grants are ordinarily made as lump sums. Since they are not restricted to line by line budgetary items, greater administrative flexibility in their expenditure is permitted. Little on-going surveillance over spending is exercised by the foundation. The sponsor need be accountable only through sporadic reporting or when it seeks renewal. Many grants are time-limited and nonrenewable and provide even further room for sponsor maneuver.

Since one major justification for the existence of foundations is program innovation, awards of foundation grants tend to stress the new and the innovative, so that they sometimes fund programs on the basis of glamour rather than quality. Community work with the consumers of services is often not glamourous, and sponsors are impelled to invent appealing "gimmicks" in their search for foundation funds. A whole specialty, "grantsmanship," has evolved as a result of this dynamic, a profession of consultants who shape proposals to meet the penchant for gimmicks or who refurbish old ideas with new trappings.

Just as individuals are involved in a whole set of role relations, one can speak of "organization-sets," that is, the constellation of other organizations to which a particular organization is related and to which it must be responsive.[26] The interests and ideologies of their organization set condition both the degree of autonomy community work sponsors have and the substantive areas in which they can be more or less free. The Community Action Agency, often an amalgam of other community organizations, is an obvious example. In sponsoring community organizing with service recipients, the CAA is sharply constrained when the organizing affects the primary interests of the organizations which are its constituent members. So too with other representative organizations, such as Health and Welfare Councils. Because in these instances the organization set is visible and highly attentive, its constraints are likely to be greater than for nonfederated organizations. Thus representative organizations (except

[26] Peter M. Blau and W. Richard Scott, *Formal Organizations* (San Francisco: Chandler, 1962), p. 195.

those forged on an ad hoc basis to combine against a common enemy or to pursue a segmental common interest) tend to be more restrictive sponsors, at least as far as community work impinges on any part of its organizational network.

But all sponsors have an organization set, however much of its visibility may vary. And in every instance the nature of the set limits the freedom with which particular issues may be pursued. We wish to conclude our discussion of voluntary funding by noting that church-related sponsors offer greater autonomy for community work than traditional social work agencies.

Grosser, among others, calls attention to the special advantage of the church as a source of support for citizen organizing.[27] As the bearer of societal values, the church has a resource which accords it influence, certainly more influence than social welfare agencies. As such, it is freer to permit community groups greater rein. Neighborhood groups, in turn, offer a tool that helps the church express its historic concern for social justice (and also extend its membership). More importantly, the organization set of the church is less threatened by the issues likely to be raised by the social welfare consumer than is true of a social agency. For example, a welfare department is less likely to be within a church's organization set than it is to be within the organization set of a social agency. This helps to explain why, in Ohio, the church was able to sustain the hostility of the welfare system and to support community activities that made the inadequacy of the state's welfare system a matter of public record.[28]

Interlocking board directorates discourage service institutions from aligning themselves with adversary actions by community groups directed against other service institutions. Social obligations, mutual favors, and minor accommodations among the personnel of a sponsor's organizational set further reduce freedom of action which impinges on those in the set. In other words, community groups are more autonomous as their interests move farther away from the interests of the sponsor's organizational role partners.

[27] Grosser, "Staff Role in Neighborhood Organization," p. 138.
[28] Ibid., pp. 138–39.

THE SPONSOR'S CONSTITUENCY

Another factor which affects a sponsor's autonomy is the character and commitment of its constituency.[29] A politically potent constituency allows greater organizational independence. Obviously, constituents with wealth, formal position of authority, or access to other influentials, who also are supportive of the interests of service users, increase the potency quotient of a community work program.

Size and location are other characteristics of constituencies which affect the sponsor. The larger the number of supporters or persons served by the organization, and the more they are dispersed throughout relevant populations, the stronger the sponsor. Rourke makes this point in regard to the administrative agencies of government. He notes that the Corps of Engineers has greater influence on water resource policy than the Bureau of Reclamation because it has a larger and more strategically located constituency.[30] When, in the early 1960's, the President's Committee on Juvenile Delinquency made a considerably larger number of planning grants than it had program money to expend, it did so with the knowledge that it would thereby expand its constituency, and thus encourage congressmen from planning grant cities to vote for increased delinquency allocations.

The constituency's commitment is a factor in determining how influential and independent a sponsor can be. Powerful organizations are composed of powerful participants for whom the organization has a high salience. That is, the influence of participants is transferable only if they are willing to exert it on behalf of the organization. Unfortunately for community work, influentials are not likely to feel unreserved adherence to social change goals. If they are committed to

[29] Warren uses the term "input" and "output" constituencies, by which he means those who provide the resources necessary to maintain the organization ("input constituency") and those who benefit from the organization's program ("output constituency"). The former are, of course, considerably more influential in internal matters. Roland L. Warren, "The Interaction of Community Decision Organizations: Some Basic Concepts and Needed Research," *Social Service Review*. Vol 41, No. 3 (September 1967), pp. 261–70.

[30] Francis E. Rourke, *Bureaucracy, Politics, and Public Policy* (Boston: Little, Brown, 1969), p. 64.

the sponsor, it is more often to the organizational mechanism than to the values of the agency.[31] Or when they are committed to its values —which is possible, since ideology may transcend immediate self-interest—the commitment must inevitably be felt less personally than it is felt by service recipients.

Nor are the numbers of people served by an agency sufficient to insure its influence. Unless those numbers self-consciously identify themselves as a group (consumers ordinarily do not, for example, unless runaway inflation and the work of "Nader's Raiders" change things) or they have a strong identification with the agencies which serve their interests, size of constituency is of no consequence. What is required, then, is a constituency which is both large *and* cohesive, dedicated to the organization's interest, and convinced of the crucial nature of its program. In community organizing, the development of a well-organized and cohesive constituency is ordinarily costly in terms of the time and energy that it requires to be devoted to internal matters. As with the need to raise funds to guarantee survival, emphasis on constituent building risks an inward concentration which is deflecting of an organization's community action interests. The sponsor's need is for a dual focus since, if it neglects its ultimate purposes, it may lose its sense of mission and its constituency as well.

COMMUNITY CONDITIONS

It is beyond the scope of this chapter to indicate the numerous ways in which community organization is influenced by community characteristics and processes. We wish only to make some general comments on the relationship of local community conditions and the broader social climate to sponsor autonomy and influence, and the opportunities for effective organizing.

Communities may be conceptualized as falling somewhere along a

[31] For example, it was found that the Board of Directors of Mobilization for Youth, composed largely of community influentials, evidenced less commitment to the agency's community action values than any of the organization's other constituent groups. George Brager, "Commitment and Conflict in a Normative Organization," *American Sociological Review,* Vol. 34, No. 4 (August 1969), pp. 482–91.

continuum between the two extremes of centralized decision making and decentralized decision making or, in other words, between a monolithic power structure and a pluralist form of organization. At one end of the scale is the local community as described by Hunter, consisting of a small covert business elite who make the major decisions in a wide variety of issue areas, who generally do not hold political office, and who are unrecognized by the community-at-large as key decision makers.[32] Another conception of community influence views decision making as widely dispersed, with variations among influentials depending on the particular issue to be decided, and with those who hold formal office in fact answerable to an electorate that is responsible for wielding power.[33]

Few communities exist that qualify as either of these ideal types, and a wide range of patterns is reported by empirical studies of communities. Many hypotheses have been advanced to account for differences in community influence structures, and we shall mention only a few. For want of more specific guidelines, community workers may find them suggestive for tentative diagnosis.

According to Rossi, "the greater the diversification of the economic control [of the community] the less likely the concentration of power and the more likely a 'healthy competition' for leadership among different social positions." [34] One-company towns, he hypothesizes, are controlled by the single industry, so that diverse bases of power will be nonexistent.[35] When industries are owned and managed largely from outside a community, Clark suggests, the executives "are usually less involved in local decision-making processes than those of locally owned and managed enterprises." [36] When officials from absentee-owned companies do become involved in community affairs, they tend to choose charitable, educational, and cultural

---

[32] Floyd Hunter, *Community Power Structure* (Chapel Hill: University of North Carolina Press, 1953).

[33] Nelson W. Polsby *Community Power and Political Theory* (New Haven: Yale University Press, 1963).

[34] Peter H. Rossi, "Theory, Research and Practice in Community Organization," in Charles R. Adrian, ed., *Social Science and Community Action* (East Lansing: Michigan State University, 1960), p. 21.

[35] *Ibid.*, p. 21.

[36] Clark, *Community Structure and Decision-Making*, p. 102.

activities—those with minimal possibilities for conflict. In small, economically specialized communities, the owners of the largest locally owned enterprises tend to dominate community decision making.[37]

Summarizing the major results of studies of 166 American communities, Gilbert concludes that economically diversified cities tend to be led by politicians and government officials (i.e., an overt power structure), whereas cities dominated by a few industries are less likely than others to have politicians as the most important figures in community decision making.[38] Cities where pyramidal structures do exist usually have elected officials at their apex, although this tendency is most apparent in cities of a large population.[39]

The size and stability of a community's population are other factors which are related to its influence system. The larger and more heterogeneous the population, the more likely a pluralist structure. Clark formulates the issue of size as follows:

The larger the number of inhabitants in a community, the more demands for government activities, the larger the government bureaucracies, the larger the political parties, the more numerous the full-time political roles, and . . . the more direct the implementation of the values and interests of political leaders on community outputs.[40]

A relatively stable population, since it has had time to build commitments and "learn the ropes" is more likely to affect community policy, and therefore to be found in pluralist-tending communities. This hypothesis is supported by a study of four communities, where it was observed that a large population influx was associated with the existence of a covert community elite.[41] The same study also reports an association between a high incidence of poverty and a covert power elite—possibly because the poor are both less attentive to community issues and are accorded less attention as well.

A sponsor's independence and influence, and its ability to support

[37] *Ibid.*, p. 103.

[38] Claire W. Gilbert, "Community Power and Decision-Making: A Quantative Examination of Previous Research," in Clark, *ibid.*, p. 153.

[39] *Ibid.*, p. 151.   [40] *Ibid.*, p. 124.

[41] Charles M. Bonjean and David M. Olson, "Community Leadership: Directions of Research," *Administrative Science Quarterly*, IX, No. 3 (December 1964), pp. 298–99.

autonomous action by community groups, are obviously determined by who controls the community's decision making and how the decisions get made. A covert elite with centralized power, controlling decisions over a wide ambit of problem areas, is less accessible to being influenced than identifiable decision makers who are publicly accountable and whose authority is limited and dispersed. Undoubtedly, every community worker knows this. What is sometimes overlooked, however, is that the dynamic works in reverse as well. A centralized elite is not only less subject to influence but can use its influence to abort a sponsor's (or community group's) effort before it is begun. The powerful are, at once, less open to change, and less likely to be challenged.

The single most important sector in this regard is the community's political system. Social-change-oriented organizations which rely on constituent action are potentially more able to influence politicians than to influence other community actors. Organized groups may have something to trade that politicians, more than other decision makers, need: votes, a humanitarian image, and community peace. However, in communities where politicians are front men for a covert elite, where they are the implementors rather than the decision makers, sponsor and community group leverage is drastically reduced, and may be nonexistent.

Communities in which there is political competition are more conducive to the emergence of new leadership, and serve sponsor independence and influence as well. With competition, there is less likelihood that decision making will be covert—since there is greater probability that it will serve the interests of one or another contender to expose decisions to public view, thereby making them more controllable. More important, however, is the fact that there are two resources which politicians need more than any others: money and votes. In populist movements, the time and energy of volunteers substitutes for required funds. Money, of course, is readily transformed into votes and is important to the politician in almost every instance. Where competition is minimal, the desires of larger numbers may be overlooked in favor of the wishes of bigger givers.

A fragmented political system has some of the defects of its virtues. Although decision making in an elitist or executive-centered system tends to be covert and is often unresponsive to the needs of disadvantaged citizens, it can at least make decisions and get programs moving (assuming the acquiesence of the ruling group). To achieve consensus or build a winning coalition in competitive political systems is a difficult task. As a consequence, organized groups may more easily veto programs of which they disapprove than gain the acceptance of those which meet their unmet needs.

Nonpartisanship in local community politics, such as "good government" and city manager arrangements, has been equated with effective city administration by many reformist, middle-class intellectuals. But as Clark suggests, "Non-partisanship tends to favor the better organized (and wealthier) segments of the community population over the amorphous (and less-well-to-do) segments." [42] Nonpartisanship, he reasons, requires that candidates depend on business organizations and wealthy private individuals for campaign contributions more so than when financial support is derived from a political party. Even more important is the fact that in a nonpartisan political system issues tend to be flattened and made imprecise, and so favor the more privileged social strata who need less inducement to bring them to the polls. Thus, in a study of 26 California communities of over 50,000 inhabitants which had nonpartisan administrations, it was found that 80 per cent of the mayors and 68 per cent of the councilmen were registered Republicans, although the great majority of the registered voters in these same communities were Democrats.[43]

There is a qualifying factor, relating to the historical development of nonpartisan arrangements. At its inception, the city manager system constituted an important reform. "Technism" was used to break the back of corrupt and unresponsive political machines (i.e., "leadership"). In time, however, it too becomes the creature of vested interests and the reform movement (i.e., "participation") comes along, as a new broom to sweep clean. Ultimately, the reformers themselves become the rascals who have to go, perhaps to be replaced by an "expert," . . . that is, a city manager or general admin-

[42] Clark, *Community Structure and Decision-Making,* pp. 108–9.
[43] Eugene Lee, *The Politics of Nonpartisanship* (Berkeley: University of California Press, 1960), pp. 56–57, as noted in Clark, p. 109.

istrator. As our hypothetical history illustrates, political structures cannot be evaluated apart from their social context.

The rate of social change within a community is another factor which affects sponsor encouragement of community work. In communities undergoing rapid change, the incentives for community organizing are increased, and the opportunities for sponsor independence and influence are greater.

Change, whatever its source, takes place in response to strains within a system, and breeds strain in return. Conditions of uncertainty occasion innovation and creativity. Change, of course, is neither good nor bad in itself; one's evaluation of it depends on the specifics of the change. But when there are dramatic alterations within a community, the community system tends to "unfreeze," allowing for planned changes which seemed impossible only a short time before. Generally, the search for mutual adjustments to reestablish equilibrium favors the have-nots of the community.

Change on a local level is related to the stirrings within the broader society. How far a sponsor may go in encouraging autonomous organizing, what restraints it will impose, which issues can be addressed, and what strategies pursued, all of these questions are influenced by the social conditions extant at a particular point in time. Social climate shapes, but also transcends, a sponsor's value system, structure, or immediate community environs as a force for organizing. The contagion of organizing in community after community across the country in response to the press for civil rights is a case in point.

Since the social climate is intangible and pervasive, it is barely noticed. Thus the difficulty or ease of organizing or optimizing programs in a constituency's interest tends to be ascribed to the "justice" of the cause, "effective" strategy, or "responsive" community conditions. All, of course, contribute to the success or failure of a community effort and are important. But it is the wider environment which provides more or less receptivity to the effort, which conditions judgments about the validity of organizing itself, and which sets the expectations for its accomplishment.

We have, in this chapter, considered some of the factors which affect sponsor autonomy and influence, particularly its funding patterns, the source of funds, the sponsor's organization set, the characteristics and commitments of the organization's constituency, and the influence of community and broader social conditions.

Sponsors "sense" their environment with internal mechanisms. They sense, or assess, environmental changes indirectly, as these changes are presented to the organization through the demands of its members.[44] Organizational participants get their cues and take their opportunities from the wider community as they struggle internally to gain ascendancy in the organization. We devote the final two chapters of this section to a discussion of this struggle.

[44] James Q. Wilson, "Innovation in Organization: Notes toward a Theory," in James D. Thompson, ed., *Approaches to Organizational Design* (Pittsburgh: University of Pittsburgh Press, 1966), p. 198.

CHAPTER TEN

THE STRAIN FOR ASCENDANCY: BOARD AND EXECUTIVE

THE ACHIEVEMENT OF ORGANIZATIONAL PURPOSES depends on two somewhat contradictory characteristics. The first is the need for organizations to exercise control over their members; the second is the need to encourage creativity, so that the organization may change in response to a changing environment.

Far greater attention has been given in the literature to the organization's means of maintaining control of participants. Organizations must be able to reward participants for (organizationally) proper behavior and to punish and resocialize them for (organizationally) improper acts. Participants must be supervised, the supervisers themselves supervised, and so on to the top of the organization. The hierarchy of control, according to Etzioni, is the central element of organizational structure,[1] and empirical studies abound exploring the ways in which conformance and compliance are induced among lower-ranking members.

The second and somewhat different perspective only occasionally appears in the literature. This alternate theme emphasizes the need for organizational responsiveness to a quickly changing environment, with greater value placed upon means of encouraging creativity among participants. Thus, one theorist observes, "The rituals and

[1] Amitai Etzioni, "Organizational Control Structure" in James G. March, ed., *Handbook of Organizations* (Chicago: Rand McNally, 1965), p. 650.

teachings of administration have been fixated on *control* . . . an ideal of a static world. . . . An innovative atmosphere requires a non-hierarchical climate, especially a non-hierarchical communication structure, and 'loose' organization in general." [2]

In reality, an organization requires both control and creativity to achieve its purposes. Although the point is applicable to all organizations, there is none for which it is more true than the community work sponsor because its technology is uncertain and its environment changeable. The inherent strain between the need to control participants and the need to promote their creativity is explicated by Blau and Scott. They cite a number of studies which demonstrate that the free flow of communication (e.g., criticisms, suggestions, manifestations of respect, and expressions of approval) increases the problem-solving capacities of organizations and that hierarchical organization impedes free communication. Blau and Scott also found that hierarchical differentiation facilitates coordination, and that when the organization needs to coordinate opinions to achieve consensus, the free flow of ideas may be counter-productive.[3] Thus effective administration requires structures sufficiently flexible to balance these two contradictory values, allowing the maximization of one or the other, depending on whether the need is for coordination or innovation in a particular instance.

FROM THE PERSPECTIVE
OF THE WORKER

In chapters 10 and 11 we deal with the components of a sponsor's hierarchical system: its board of directors, executive, and staff. First, our focus is on the board and executive and their resources for control over the agency. In the next chapter, we consider the staff as it too vies for ascendancy over organizational direction.

Our interest is not in effective administration, however, or in the

[2] Victor A. Thompson, "Administrative Objectives for Development Administration," *Administrative Science Quarterly*, Vol. 9 (June 1964), pp. 93–94.

[3] Peter M. Blau and W. Richard Scott, *Formal Organizations* (San Francisco: Chandler, 1962), pp. 121–28.

ways in which workers are induced to conform or create. Quite the reverse. Our discussion of the resources located at different levels of the organizational hierarchy is intended to sensitize organizers to their opportunities to affect sponsor program and policy. By and large, our interest is in the sources of influence available to lower ranking members to affect the actions of higher ranking ones, that is, the executive's source of influence with his board, and the staff's with the executive. Our intent is to provide a basis for assessing when and how exertion of influence is possible.

Our attention to the influence of the community organizer does not stem from a romanticization of the "Noble Worker." There is a kind of neo-populist myth that correlates integrity with position on the organizational totem pole. The lower in the hierarchy, the notion goes, the more socially concerned the person will be. Implicit in this idea is the belief that the desire for social change to benefit the poor is disproportionately held by those of lower status, that indigenous workers (nonprofessionals) are "better" or "more activist" than professional workers, line professionals are "better" or "more activist" than their supervisors, and so on. Although this class-distinction-in-reverse may fill workers' needs for in-group celebration, it is an oversimplification of reality.

Like many myths, this one also contains elements of truth. Low-ranking members may be freer to act on principle because the costs to them are less; that is, perhaps being younger and without families they may be risking less in job and money than higher-ranking participants. Persons with lesser material resources (e.g., the poor who are hired as indigenous workers) have more to gain from change, and thus may generate a greater sense of social injustice. Furthermore, since their interests are more closely allied to the interests of the poor, lower-ranking personnel can be expected to represent the yearnings of impoverished clients more than those in the upper reaches of agency hierarchy.

Interestingly, however, in a study of the students entering The Columbia University School of Social Work in a single year, it was found that family income alone did not explain students' motivations for effecting social change. Students whose families earned $8000 or less, $12,000 or less, and $20,000 or less showed no significant difference in motivation to pursue social change. What did emerge as a determining factor was an imbalance between family income and educational attainment. Students whose fathers were "underpaid" in contrast to their educational peers were more committed to social change than others. When the educational level of the parent was controlled (high school or less, college, and beyond college), the offspring of the more poorly paid fathers in each of the educational groups were generally more change-oriented. Thus the disparity of socioeconomic status within educational ranks rather than income alone appears to explain the desire to challenge the social order, at least among these particular neophyte social workers.[4]

But the major inadequacy of the idea that the lower the rank, the more the social concern is that it is structurally blind. It ignores the influence of organizational structure on the occupants of organizational positions. All other things being equal, we would expect that those with greater responsibility for an organization would be more committed to its purposes, *even when its aims are militantly change-oriented.*

Sponsors with differing objectives require the performance of different worker roles and, therefore, they recruit workers with differing motivations, attitudes, styles. Sponsors which demand bureaucratic fealty tend to attract organization men; administrators who value professional expertise select professional experts; and the desire for activism brings forth activists. Although the correlation is hardly exact and many other factors intervene, sponsors with integra-

[4] George Brager and John Michael, *The Student Community Organizer and His Training in the Field* (New York: C.O. Curriculum Development Project of the Columbia University School of Social Work, 1969), Part II, chapter 3, pp. 35–37. (Mimeographed) The literature on "rank equilibration" states that individuals with disparate ranks on two salient characteristics will attempt to equalize these ranks by raising the lower one. Apparently, the dynamic holds for community organization students. See Emile Benoit-Smullyan, "Status, Status Types, and Status Interrelationships," *American Sociological Review,* Vol. IX (April 1944), pp. 151–61; G. H. Fenchel, J. H. Monderer, and E. L. Hartley, "Subjective Status and Equilibration Hypothesis," *Journal of Abnormal and Social Psychology,* Vol. XLVI (October 1951), pp. 476–79; Gerhard F. Lenski, "Status Crystallization: A Non-Vertical Dimension of Social Status," *American Sociological Review,* Vol. XIX (August 1954), pp. 405–13); and Elton F. Jackson, "Status Consistency and Symptoms of Stress," *American Sociological Review* (August 1962), pp. 469–80.

tive, sociotherapeutic, or environmental change objectives are likely to employ workers with similar goals. But—and this is the crucial point—whatever his orientation, the higher the worker is located in the hierarchy, the greater will be his commitment to the *sponsor's* value system, whether integrative, sociotherapeutic, or environmental change.

The argument is supported by research on the commitments of staff conducted at Mobilization for Youth (MFY), the community project which served as the forerunner of the anti-poverty program and the Community Action Agency concept.[5] High scorers on an index of commitment tended to agree with the following MFY values: institutional arrangements bear a major responsibility for the estrangement of the poor from community services; low-income people need power in order to force institutions to respond to their demands; social protest is an effective social action strategy; and sponsoring agencies ought not to impose constraints on low-income social action because of the risks such action entails for the sponsor.

If lower-ranking participants are more closely identified with the poor and more eager to change social conditions, one would expect line staff to be more committed to the MFY value system than upper-ranking members of the agency. The outcome was exactly the reverse. It was found that 48.1 per cent of the executive staff fell within the highest commitment group compared to 39.4 per cent of the supervisory staff. The percentage of practitioners in the high-commitment group was only 26.1 per cent, and nonprofessionals were the least committed to MFY's "activist" value system.

Whether or not one wishes to maximize the influence of line staff, therefore, would depend on one's agreement with the purposes of the organization rather than on the concept of worker virtue.

[5] MFY was the subject of a very nearly fatal attack which occurred because of its crusading zeal. The attack was signaled by a front page article in the powerful *Daily News* which accused it of using "its facilities—and juveniles —to foment rent strikes and racial disorders." To measure the extent of commitment of MFY's constituent groups to the agency's value system, an index was constructed, consisting of 20 items which were for the most part direct quotes from the organization's official documents. For specification of the research methodology, see George Brager, "Commitment and Conflict in a Normative Organization," *American Sociological Review,* Vol. 34, No. 4 (August 1969), pp. 482–91.

There is no moral rightness in the accrual of influence by any set of the organization's members apart from the purposes to which the influence is put.[6]

Nevertheless, there are two reasons to search out factors which increase a worker's edge in the sponsor control system. One has to do with the sponsor's responsiveness to its consumers. The other concerns the disparity in influence between upper- and lower-ranking participants.

Our assumption throughout this volume has been that a community work sponsor ought be maximally responsive to the interests of its consumer group. If one accepts the assumption, the desirability of increasing line-staff influence follows. Practitioners are likely to be more in touch with consumer interests than higher-ranking staff, the MFY findings notwithstanding. The MFY data deals with the poor as a social category, but it does not measure knowledge about, or responsiveness to, particular service recipients who are in contact with the agency.

The closer agency decision making is to the source of information, the more likely will the decisions accurately take account of the information. The greater the number of ranks through which information passes, the more distortion there is at the point of decision making. For example, research in a large welfare department disclosed that executives had more accurate perceptions of how the community-at-large viewed the agency, but line staff were more informed about client views.[7] In effect, the availability of information depends on location in an agency's structure, so that one means of increasing responsiveness to consumer interests is to locate decison making closer to line staff.

Furthermore, line staff gets the full impact of client feelings. It is considerably more difficult to deny the claims of unhappy or angry persons in face-to-face interaction than when it is mediated through

[6] The same may be said in regard to the avoidance of influence. There is no virtue in eschewing power, if that power would be used in the service of "good" ends. Indeed, one could argue that its avoidance in such an instance constitutes an act of irresponsibility.

[7] Morris Janowitz and William Delany, "The Bureaucrat and the Public," *Administrative Science Quarterly*, Vol. II (September 1957).

less involved sensibilities. This is one reason why administrators desire "gatekeepers," for it is easier to say "no" to the worker who pleads a client's case than to face the client with a refusal. For this reason, wise client-oriented workers try not to shield their administrators from direct client impact, if the contact can be managed without undermining the administrator's confidence in the worker.

The second reason for interest in increasing the influence of lower-ranking participants is because their actual power is limited. Were agencies to be run by worker commissariats, such attention might be misplaced. The attention seems to be appropriate, given current arrangements and the paucity of theoretical interest in the subject.

At best, one cannot be sanguine about the ability of lower-ranking members to move or shape a sponsoring organization. Whatever cards they hold, or how skillfully they play the game, they are least likely to hold the winning hand. Thus, while they may influence programs or contribute to policy setting, they are not likely to decide on or control either. It is in the context of relative professional powerlessness, then, that we are interested in the means to maximize staff influence.

The above argument implies that the diffusion of power within community work agencies is a desirable condition. But diffusion of power makes affirmative action difficult, and often impossible. If any of a number of groups can veto a proposition, it is likely to slow or prevent change. Since some of the decisions of a "ruling elite" may be "good" ones, to the advantage of all, they are better than no decisions at all, as often occurs when power is diffused.[8] In balancing the respective risks, however, we favor the diffusion of influence, at least in regard to how sponsoring organizations are currently structured and operated.

[8] The flouridation controversy is a case in point. In communities with centralized decision making, flouridation tended to be successfully introduced. Although a "good" decision, with particular benefit to low-income people who did not have alternate means of dental hygiene, it failed in communities with widespread citizen participation, or a diffusion of power. See Robert L. Crain, Elihu Katz, and Donald B. Rosenthal, *The Politics of Community Conflict: The Fluoridation Decision* (New York: Bobbs-Merrill, 1969).

ORGANIZATIONAL INFLUENCE
AND AGENCY HIERARCHY

The disaffection and resistance which so often results from attempts to change an agency is hazardous to the employee who makes the attempt. Our earlier analysis of the goals of community work sponsors suggests one reason why this is so. Agencies which pursue integrative, sociotherapeutic, or environmental-change goals tend to attract a particular staff and constituency, to establish styles of relating and ways of doing business together, and to employ certain types of means with some consistency. To change a sponsor's goals inevitably disrupts these patterned tendencies and the investments which participants have in them.

Not the least significant factor in the dislocation caused by change is its intended effect on the organization's distribution of control. For change to be successful, it is necessary to influence the powerful, while simultaneously trying to reduce their power—a difficult order. Central to an influence attempt, therefore, is an understanding of the relevant control structure and the skill required to manipulate it.

By control structure, we refer to the hierarchically defined individuals or groups who exercise authority over the affairs of the organization: its board of trustees, executive, and staff. The categorization is in part arbitrary and omits both the sponsor's funding sources (except when funders and trustees overlap) and other important reference groups. As Goffman has noted, organizations are surrounded by "a semipermeable membrane," with the degree of permeability varying with a particular organization.[9] Boundaries between an organization and its environment are unclear, and properties which can be defined precisely as internal or external are difficult to fix. Our decision to include reference to funding sources and constituents

[9] Erving Goffman, "Characteristics of Total Institutions," *Symposium on Preventive and Social Psychiatry* (Washington, D.C.: U.S. Government Printing Office, 1957), pp. 82–83.

in earlier chapters was made for stylistic reasons as much as for substantive considerations.[10]

Boards of directors, trustees, commissions, and government panels are generally viewed as policy setters, responsible for determining the major rules or broad-gauged decisions of the organization. They generally perform three major functions: to define organizational values and goals; to direct the organization's relations with its environment; and to approve plans for the utilization of organizational resources.

Staff members conduct the day-to-day operations, implementing agency program within the framework of the board's mandate. Line staff fulfill agency purposes in their contacts with clients, while supervisors oversee their work.

The executive spans the two groups. Whereas the board is said to "establish policies and make plans . . . executives take part in the formulation of policy, as they provide facts, clarify issues, make proposals [and] suggest action." [11] In regard to the board, then, the executive "clarifies" and "suggests," that is, offers guidance to the board and takes direction from it. Much of the literature on social agency administration obscures the hierarchical arrangement between board and executive by the notion of a "partnership." But the executive is actually staff, its super-supervisor, accountable to the board for implementation of all agency functions.

The above is an encapsulation of the usual definitions of board, executive, and staff responsibility. Nowhere, we hasten to add, do they exist in practice as described. However much one might endorse a particular division of responsibility or however powerful the endorser, in practice, responsibility is shaped as much by situational factors as by ideal conceptions.

There is variability among organizations, and influence may travel

[10] There are actually more than these three hierarchical levels in all but the smallest agencies. Considerable interpenetration exists among the three, e.g., executives may also be members of boards, and sometimes community representatives are both workers and trustees. Nevertheless, the three levels can generally be distinguished, and tend to represent identifiable functions.

[11] Ray Johns, *Executive Responsibility* (New York: Association Press, 1954), pp. 65, 32.

up the hierarchy as well as down. Thus some executives may control their board, and others may be prisoners of their staff. It is this variability which provides the incentive for lower-ranking members to try to increase their influence, and it is the reason why community workers sometimes succeed in managing it. Identifying these differences among organizations and, more importantly, the conditions which make for these differences, contributes to understanding the dynamics of organizational change.

Norton Long has written of the "galling nature" of a reverse control of themselves practiced by professional social workers. According to Long, among the various types of community games is the "civic game," which requires the legitimizing sponsorship of prestigious figures. The social worker's task may be self-assigned, and his perception of the problem and its solution may be his own, but he cannot gain acceptance in the "civic game" without mobilizing influentials. He thus engages in a thrust from below to organize top leadership, and thereby creates his own controller.[12]

It is not the perversity of social workers which leads to this reverse control, but the requirements of the "civic game." Although requirements differ from game to game, it is the very existence of requirements which explains the nature of organizational control. Essentially, who controls an organization depends on who controls the resources the organization needs.

BOARDS OF DIRECTORS

The resources available to boards, executives, and staff can be identified only approximately. Trustees ordinarily have access to, or control of, financial resources. However, sometimes executives contribute to or even control fund raising, and their influence in relation to their board is then more substantial. These arrangements vary from agency to agency and within specific agencies over time, but the principle remains the same, viz., access to financing is a major source

[12] Norton E. Long, "The Local Community As an Ecology of Games," in Mayer N. Zald, ed., *Social Welfare Institutions* (New York: Wiley, 1965), pp. 260–62.

of organizational influence. It is one of the principles which accounts for differentials in board, executive, and staff influence.

Zald states that "Boards of directors were created and recognized in law in order to insure continuity in the management of organizations, and to fix a locus of responsibility for the control of 'independent' organizations."[13] Its formal position as the legally responsible entity of the corporation constitutes another source of actual or potential power. In addition to resources which inhere in its legal right and its control over financial resources is the board's role as community legitimator. Boards which are mindful of their legal positions, which represent the diverse interests attentive to the agency's program, and which are its source of financial input are powerful indeed.

Access to Funds. Boards of community work sponsors which contribute or raise the agency's funds have a powerful lever for control. The authority to levy taxes (in the case of government) or to raise and receive funds (in the case of nongovernmental agencies) is central to the exercise of power in society. Conversely, the ability of constituents to withhold funds constitutes a threat to established government, as in the case of taxpayer revolts, and to nongovernmental agencies, as in the case of organizations which antagonize potential financial contributors by their change-oriented positions.

By and large, it is the voluntary social agency which is best suited to the model of the fund-raising board. As the philanthropic base has widened and community federations have conducted widescale campaigns, the concentration of power by individual members of these boards has probably been diluted. Essentially, though, the big donors to community funds are members of individual boards, and their importance to the community fund undoubtedly correlates with their importance to the agency. The class location of these givers and their considerable influence in the social agency network explain why these agencies favor integrative and sociotherapeutic objectives.

When fund raising is dispersed among many small givers and does not depend on the work or personal appeal of a few, the influence of

[13] Mayer N. Zald, "The Power and Functions of Boards of Directors: A Theoretical Synthesis," *American Journal of Sociology,* Vol. 75, No. 1 (July 1969), p. 99.

the board diminishes. The agency which collects its full budget from a mail solicitation and the sale of Christmas cards need not worry about its board as a source of funds, though it may be concerned about how its larger group of supporters views its behavior. Militant cause organizations are, of course, notoriously poor. Their goals are ordinarily not glamourous to established big givers. Both their ideology (i.e., to look to "the people") and their quest for independence turns them to the small giver or to big givers who prefer to remain out of the public spotlight. Money is obviously not a source of influence for the boards of these sponsors.

Increasingly, all or part of the budgets of community work programs have been funded with public monies. In such cases, power flows to those in the agency with the program ideas or political connections which bring about the allocation. Executive and staff are as likely as trustees to be in a position to do so.

When public agencies sponsor community work, such as the urban renewal agencies or the Model Cities Program, the conception of a board which fixes "a locus of responsibility for the control of independent organizations" is obscured. Both the board of directors and the executive director are likely to be accountable to higher administrators, such as a commissioner of housing, or to elected officials and their designees. The advisory committees or boards of these agencies, many of whom have more political authority than formal or statutory responsibility, act as agents for the chief executive. Although they are not income producers, advisory groups which have won the right to pass on applications for funds, or whose endorsement is required, have a potentially potent resource for influence in the funding process.

By and large, however, groups such as these are heard to the extent that they are perceived as "the voice of the community" and heeded when that voice is important to relevant officials. Their major source of influence—exemplified even in their having won the right to veto funding applications—is as community legitimators.

Community Legitimation. Community legitimation is the second major resource available to boards as a source of influence. Since it is a less concrete resource than money and more subject to conflicting definitions, it is more easily challenged, and probably more easily acquired than money. Our discussion above suggests that there may be an inverse relationship between money and community legitimation. Boards which produce their own income require only the legitimation of donors. For the latter, the quality of their mercy may be sufficient inducement to incur support. On the other hand, organizations which receive public funds are more likely to require broader community support and representativeness. Social change-oriented organizations also need to appear representative of "the people" in whose behalf the change is sought.

The ability to mobilize individuals, groups, and organizations that can affect the flow of organizational resources is more of a source of power than merely symbolic or nonpartisan representativeness. As Zald observes, "the more closely board members are linked to external groups, the more they 'represent' community legitimation and, therefore, the more powerful they are vis-à-vis the administrative leadership." [14] The proposition suggests that representatives of the service user are most influential when they have links to organized community groups.

There is a significant exception to Zald's proposition. When the interests of the external groups that are represented by a board are varied and conflicting, an administrator has the opportunity to play off one against the other or, in mediating the differences, give some edge to his own solutions. The representative board structure, with its resultant potential for disunity, constitutes a lever for executive influence.

Legal Authority. Boards with otherwise scant resources have a formidable source of influence in their legal authority, a resource which is ordinarily given insufficient consideration.

Differences in legal arrangements (i.e., an organization's charter, its "constitution" or legislative mandate) result in differentials of influence between boards and staff. The powers of boards of education, for example, are delimited by law, with considerable authority reserved for school superintendents. The same is true of executive officers of Model Cities programs in relation to Model Cities boards.

By and large, legal authority extends—minimally—to hiring (and firing) the chief executive. An incumbent executive, secure in his po-

[14] *Ibid.,* p. 103.

sition, might be unconcerned about the board's prerogative to hire and fire, although such unconcern may be less universal than many executives admit. However, the board's responsibility for hiring is a source of influence for another reason. Inevitably, the board's ability to hire the executive and fix his salary defines the norms which govern their relationship, because certain employer-employee behaviors are prescribed. The executive is expected to be deferential to the board chairman, although if he is an important professional in his own right, he must offer the deference subtly.

The rituals that frame interaction may be more important than other realities which govern communications among people. The risk of any ceremony is that persons will come to believe that it has intrinsic meaning, rather than being merely symbolic. Thus the norms which define the board-executive relationship as employer-employee potentially influence perceptions in the direction of supporting the board's superordinance. Professionals who prefer to think in terms of "partnership" and thus deny the actuality cannot deal effectively with the matter.

Power, to some extent, is in the eye of the beholder, that is, authority exists to the degree that one party accords it and the other expects it. Both are necessary for an act of authority to occur. Any patterning whereby one commands and the other obeys, or one decides and the other implements, constitutes an authority system *regardless of the respective resources of either party*. What is required is that each define the situation as legitimate.

Extremist challenges to governmental authority are based upon the withdrawal of this legitimacy. Nothing so outrages the "establishment" as the radicals' assumption that their "outlandish" demands and "impertinent" defiance of authority are wholly legitimate. The challenge often reveals, however, that the fortresses of power are not as impregnable as might be supposed, since one reason why the community awards legitimacy to government is because it can govern. When that belief is shaken the legitimacy of government may be undermined.[15]

[15] MacIver speaks of the "myth" of government, by which he means that the most important feature of government is the belief in the sovereignty (legitimacy) of those who rule. Sovereignty is just that, a belief and nothing else. Once a society loses this belief, it is no longer possible for men to rule other

A board's legal authority constitutes both a tangible and an intangible resource. It is tangible in that the board has personnel and monetary authority. Indeed, as its legal base, a charter often grants boards the right to decide *everything* pertinent to the organization's affairs.

Suppose, however, that other concrete resources are lacking. What if the executive obtains the funds through his governmental connections and/or the executive's constituency provides legitimation for the sponsor's program rather than the board? In that case, the usefulness of legal authority as a tangible resource diminishes. A board would hardly overrule an executive who has such "clout." A resource which cannot be spent is no longer a source of influence.

However, all may not be lost for board ascendancy. Legal authority, in its intangible manifestation, can operate as the definition of what is appropriate in particular circumstances. So, for example, if the executive accords legitimacy to the board's legal status, he may, in effect, be responsive to a nonexistent source of power because of his belief in the board's superior status. Legal authority creates the social circumstances in which such norm systems flourish.

The point is important for two reasons. Professionals who are employed by social agencies tend to award greater authority to boards which are nonrepresentative of service users than objective reality might require. Legal authority and professional values combine to unduly limit executive action, even in circumstances in which the executive's position is morally just and his resources are sufficient to obtain his end.

Drawing attention to this system of norms is important on another ground. Intangible resources are more manipulatable than tangible ones. Beliefs and values can be fashioned by participants, as concrete resources cannot. The strong executive with an inexperienced board (e.g., composed of the poor) can, if he wishes, set the perimeters of board authority by what he says and does, quite apart from the strictures of the agency's charter. His task would be considerably more

---

men *legitimately* (though the government may continue through force of arms or repression). The myth is, of course, powerful, and compels men to obey, but it is fragile as well, and may dissolve. Robert M. MacIver, *The Web of Government* (New York: Free Press, 1965).

difficult if the board's contribution were more concrete than mere legal authority.

Power may be viewed as the potential for influence, as well as its exercise. A party is no less powerful because it chooses not to use its resources, provided that it could. The use or nonuse of a resource by a board of directors is related to an organization's stability. A newly formed agency, in which the program is still unshaped and ways of working together not yet established, undergoes a shakedown period. Goals vie for acceptance, and participants "sniff" one another out. During times like these, the participants have greater incentive to put their resources to use, both to obtain their goals and to establish their influence. With numerous policies to be decided, a board is likely to be active and there will be less slack due to disinterest or inattention. During periods of stability, when decisions are more routine, the board will be less involved and the slack greater.

Controversy disrupts routine. The controversy-potential of community work is always high, particularly among sponsors with environmental-change objectives. When the sponsor is criticized or attacked, powerful others (e.g., government officials, foundations) will turn to the sponsor's legally constituted authority for answers and decisions. Whether or not the board has been co-opted by its executive or staff, the challenge will encourage its assertion of authority. If it has been inactive, it need not blame itself for the actions which called forth the criticism, only for its inactivity. And the way to deal with that is to pull in the slack. The fact that powerful others view the board as legally responsible for the actions which brought censure, encourages its assumption of full authority. In times of crisis, frequent for community work sponsors, latent power rooted in legal authority becomes actual power.

Individual Attributes of Trustees. Until now, we have discussed the resources of the board *as a group,* rather than those possessed by its individual members. Legal authority is, of course, a property of the collectivity, whereas individuals vary in the extent to which they contribute material resources and community legitimation. Obviously, those trustees who are richer in these resources will have more impact on board decision making. Other resources, such as socioeconomic status, prestige, knowledge, and energy also have a bearing on how much weight each board member swings within board counsels.

When Hollingshead studied Elmtown in 1949, he indicated that to be elected to the school board, a person had to be from one of the two upper classes, male, Protestant, Republican, a property owner, and preferably a Rotarian.[16] The situation has changed since then, although continuing studies have attested to the disproportion of those with higher socioeconomic status on boards of directors.

High socioeconomic status is a source of influence for the individual trustee. Prestige which is rooted in other than wealth or social position is also a source of influence. A public official, such as a welfare commissioner, may be influential on a board not only because of his political connections or potential contributions but also because his is a prestigious position. Prestige may also derive from intellectual attainment, from control over widely held values (e.g., a minister), and even from frequent appearances on the mass media.

Thus, all board members are equal; but the Orwellian truth is that some board members are more equal than others. For instance, if the five "top" members of a board of 40 agree on a particular course of action, the outcome may be predicted without knowing the positions of the other 35.[17] This augurs ill for the impact of the poor on heterogeneous boards. If influence flows from prestige, or from the contribution of material resources and community legitimation, the poor are disadvantaged in the contest for ascendancy. Only as they represent organized community interests, or if they serve in sufficient numbers to constitute a block on the board, are their leaders likely to be among those five top influentials.

Two resources which, in part, qualify the above are knowledge and energy. Knowledge about the community, community work strategies, the agency, and its program is a salable commodity that may be

[16] August B. Hollingshead, *Elmtown Youth* (New York: Wiley, 1949).

[17] However, power theory does not allow predictions of the outcome of issues with a high degree of specificity. The exact ratio of how many of the powerful can control decision making against the will of how many of the nonpowerful is unknown. Theory and methodology are insufficiently refined to allow more than make educated guesses.

traded for influence. Energy refers to the amount of activity and aggression available for investment in an influence attempt. (Aggression may be viewed, in part at least, as an assertive effort to redefine a situation, that is, the usual norms flowing from prestige, position, or contribution are ignored in favor of other standards on which to base the "right" to influence.) Energy is manifest through active participation. Together, knowledge and energy can be used to redress the balance of power in favor of the less prestigious participants.

One other factor should be noted: the more important a board member's contribution, and the greater his prestige, the more likely he will be to limit his concern to critical as opposed to routine decisions. This allows the knowledgeable and energetic participant room to maneuver. Thus he may take advantage of the greater slack in the system and, as we shall note in our discussion of the executive, he will also have greater leeway in defining the problems which require a decision. Both enhance influence.

EXECUTIVE DIRECTOR

Not all boards are similarly endowed, and the sources of influence at the command of the executive may allow him significant opportunities to direct policy regardless of the agency's formal hierarchical arrangement. Informal influence or control, patterened over time, can constitute a more real representation of power than appears on the organizational charts.[18]

Potentially, executive resources are considerable. We wish now to examine some of the major ones: the executive's greater knowledge, his location in the agency's communication network and formal structure, and the group nature of board decision making.

Knowledge. Social scientists and planners may be excused if they

[18] The point, though perhaps obvious, is often overlooked. Graduate students in schools of social work, for example, have little sense of their informal influence. The student "grapevine" is probably a more significant factor in assessing the use of field placements than any other, but unless they have formal authority to act on placements, students *feel* powerless to affect placement decisions. The problem with informal influence is that it is uncertain and indefinite.

overemphasize the importance of their unique contribution to problem solving,[19] but knowledge hardly constitutes power, and rationality as a source of influence ought not to be exaggerated. We suspect that a command of the facts is not so directly correlated with decision making as one might wish or expect but it is, nonetheless, a major resource for the executive, since organizational decision making can hardly take place without knowledge on which to base decisions. Furthermore, in matters of controversy, a knowledgeable proponent is better armed for the contest than those who lack information. A well-reasoned and well-documented argument may not only be persuasive but also a source of prestige. Minimally, it puts the opposition on the defensive.

Knowledge may come from two sources: expertise in a particular field and detailed intelligence about an organization. Executives are better endowed than boards with both.

Organizations requiring a high degree of technical expertise concede more influence to the expert. Thus the boards of hospitals play a lesser role in agency operations than the boards of welfare agencies since medicine requires more specialized skill. Concomitantly, medical professionals attain more control than the social agency executives because social work is viewed as a marginal profession, with an ill-defined body of knowledge and skill. Community work, seen as marginal to social work, is doubly disadvantaged. If the executive accepts this definition of the profession, or is personally uncertain of his own capability, he is even less likely to take the lead in decision making. Thus studies have indicated that "subjects who believed they possessed superior knowledge made more influence attempts, more frequently resisted [other's] suggestions, and displayed a high degree of assertiveness." [20]

Although less prestigious by comparison with other fields, profes-

[19] So, for example, a behavioral science symposium notes "the increasing tendency of action leaders in government, business, health, and education to turn to behavioral scientists for advice and guidance. Behavioral scientists are being wooed and won by the powers and principalities of the world." Kenneth D. Benne, "The Social Responsibilities of the Behavior Scientist," *Journal of Social Issues*, Vol. 21, No. 2 (April 1965), p. 6.

[20] Dorwin Cartwright, "Influence, Leadership, Control" in James G. March, ed., *Handbook of Organizations* (Chicago: Rand McNally, 1965), p. 6.

sional knowledge and the professional credential in community work
are nevertheless sources of executive influence. They constitute a
greater source of influence with sponsors who value professionalism,
that is, in agencies with a high percentage of professionally trained
workers, or which require training for the supervision of community
workers. In these settings, the function of staff as implementors of
program will be assiduously protected, and the distinctions between
policy and program will be defined in favor of broadening executive
discretion in regard to the latter. Sponsors with sociotherapeutic
objectives tend to fit this model better than others. Similarly, executives with inexperienced boards are likely to make greater use of
technical knowledge as a resource.

Because they are responsible for the internal operations of the
agency and devote full time to the task, executives are inevitably
more knowledgeable than their boards and must be relied on for the
information on which to base policy making. One need not be unduly
cynical to suggest that, however pure the motives of the executive,
information will be selected and shared differentially depending on
his interest and ideology.

Just as the availability of technical knowledge as a means to influence varies with the type of organization, so too does knowledge
about an organization (i.e., organizational intelligence). Differential
access to information between board and executive is greater in organizations which are larger, more complex, or geographically far-
flung. Since community work sponsors are, by and large, smaller and
less complex than other organizations, their boards have greater
knowledge, and therefore more influence, than other organizations.
Nevertheless, mammoth and complex bureaucracies also sponsor
community work, and their boards cannot possibly keep abreast of
the information necessary to make decisions about a wide variety of
policy issues, given the best of executive intentions. As a result,
they rely more on the executive, and administrative ascendency is increased. Similarly, the executive of a national organization with
widely dispersed affiliates will be more able to control his board, all
things being equal, than the executive of a centralized program. (Decentralization enhances the power of middle management since day-
to-day decisions are made at out-stations where middle management
is in charge.)

Location in the Communication Structure. The executive stands at the nerve center of the organization. The sheer quantity of his inter-action regarding issues of organizational moment is more than any other participant's. He meets with the board chairman to plan agenda, discuss committee appointments, and review agency prob-lems; he sits with board committees, prepares budgets for finance committee consideration, offers alternatives to the program commit-tee, and participates in nominating committee deliberations. The ex-ecutive is the only person in intimate and direct contact with all of these varied persons and groups. He serves, in addition, as the com-munications link between board and staff, interpreting the concerns of each to the other. His location in the agency's communication structure is his single most important resource; it allows him a con-siderable margin of control.

However, communication and power should not be considered synonomous, as they often are by workers or community groups who believe that change can be achieved simply by improving communi-cation with persons in power. Communication may solve problems which are caused by misunderstanding. Problems which stem from differing interests and ideologies, on the other hand, can be exacer-bated by increased communication since contentions may be height-ened by clarification. However, control of the means of communica-tion is one means of increasing power. When information is controlled, interests can be made to appear similar or dissimilar and the interaction may be discontinued or sustained as the party in con-trol desires. All of these possibilities lie in the executive's ability to control communication with his board.

Small group research on the relationship between communication and leadership has relevance for the executive. The studies have shown that by increasing interaction, interpersonal attraction is also increased; and, furthermore, that the greater the personal attraction, the more the power of the person to influence the other's decisions.[21] The tendency of persons with influence to initiate more communi-cation and to receive more messages is one of the most reliable phe-nomena reported in the small group literature.[22] Undoubtedly, life

[21] Barry E. Collins and Harold Guetzkow, *A Social Psychology of Group Processes for Decision-Making,* (New York: Wiley, 1964), pp. 124–26.
[22] *Ibid.,* p. 124, 155.

experience reflects these findings, and leads experts in administration to dryly counsel employees to establish good relations with the boss's secretary. She talks to him a lot.

There is a chicken-or-the-egg element to these findings. That is, it is not clear whether greater communication leads to greater influence, or whether greater communication results from influence already garnered. It is more likely that communication systems reflect rather than create power relations, and that interaction is merely the manifestation of influence. There is, too, probably a circular pattern between communication and influence in which one contributes to the other. In any event, if the location of the executive at the center of a communication system does not assure his ascendency, it at least provides him with the opportunity to maximize it.

Because they are employees, executives use their central location to enhance their personal attractiveness to board members, even if it is not primarily to achieve executive-oriented decision making. For the same reason, most will use the position to provide whatever favors are at their disposal, such as compliments, the passing of messages which bring approval to the messenger, and information to enhance the board member's ability to gain status with his fellows.(The wise executive will be mindful of the risk of excessively complimentary communication. If it is viewed as untrustworthy, it is of meager utility and is, in any case, subject to a law of diminishing returns.) Others will use their opportunities for extensive interaction to undercut nonsupporters on the board (e.g., "so-and-so has a conflict of interests," "he's not smart about these matters."). The executive ought to be mindful of the risk that such comments, made in excess or to the wrong party, may injure him because his judgment or integrity may be brought into question.

Even an executive with a powerful board may influence its decisions in his role as the initiator and definer of problem areas. Merton notes that values are, in part, determined by the very choice and definition of problems, since these influence the ways in which the issues are explored and, by extension, their outcomes.[23] Suppose, for example, the morale of black workers is low because of a preponder-

[23] Robert K. Merton, *Social Theory and Social Structure* (Rev. ed.; New York: Free Press, 1957), p. 216.

ance of white supervisors. One way of formulating the question is: How can we make white supervision more palatable to black workers? Another is: How can we increase the number of black supervisors? The definition of the problem and the framing of the question shape agency direction. Activities such as writing the agenda for meetings or preparing the budget, however much scrutiny it receives by a finance committee, permits the executive some latitude in raising and defining agency issues.

The executive's interaction with a great number of individuals and groups permits him to segregate audiences to affect decision making. Depending on whom he is talking to, whether they are likely to interact with one another, and the extent of the interaction, he can share information differentially or shift its emphasis.

An executive who was restive under an agency's integrative orientation provides an example of how leverage is attained by segregating audiences. The agency, a neighborhood council in a black ghetto, undertook to sponsor a conference on public education with the goal of increasing harmony between parents and school. A committee was organized composed of members of the agency's board, school officials, representatives of other community institutions, and low-income parents. The executive, who staffed the committee, felt that he could not move his cautious and conservative board to run a parent-dominated conference which would dramatize the educational disadvantages of their children. He successfully achieved this end, however, through his role as communicator with the various parties. Charged with inviting the committee's choice for conference chairman, he informed the latter that he had been chosen chairman by the parents on the committee, the people who were most interested in having the conference deal with the deficiencies of the schools. He encouraged parents—but not others—to attend planning meetings by contacting each personally. He privately informed community representatives that the conference chairman hoped for a parent-oriented program. And he aided a creative dramatics group which was to perform at the conference to highlight school problems. In short, by segregating his communication with the participants, his impact on the conference was potent.

The Group Nature of the Board. The group nature of board structure is another factor which increases the executive's ability to exercise influence. Since the board's authority rests with the collectivity, rather than with any individual member, control over the executive as an employee is diffused and his independence enhanced. Although he may be responsive to a single trustee for political or other reasons, the responsiveness does not extend to accountability. The distinction is fine but, nevertheless, it is a real one. It limits the trustee's sense of being an employer and, therefore, what he feels free to demand. It also allows the executive to put off some demands by introducing the reactions of another board member (e.g., "So-and-so might object if we did that") or of the board itself (e.g., "That may be a violation of policy").

The situation permits the maneuverability which comes from ambiguity. Thus an executive who disagrees with the edict of a board chairman might convince him of the necessity of bringing the matter to the board, where the position can be amended. Or, if the executive agrees with the chairman's policy decision, he might let it stand, allowing the chairman to bear the responsibility for deciding what might properly be a board matter.

The group nature of the board guarantees that there will be disagreements within the body. At times, executives may purposely engineer such controversy. The executive must be concerned with "conflict management," preventing it from reaching proportions disruptive to the sponsor's ability to "do business." But he might use disagreements to gain important substantive ends. For example, he might encourage steadfastness among proponents of his position, or seek out and proselytize the "neutrals," bolstering his case with facts and arguments. When the top influentials of powerful boards are divided, executives can have the greatest impact. For the executive, too many cooks may not spoil the broth; rather, they may allow for the executive to season the stew to his own tastes.

There are hazards in engendering controversy. If the executive's ascendency is not established and he is not able to expend his influence resources lavishly, he had better not lose too many arguments. There are a number of reasons for this. A group's decision represents its judgment about a matter; if an executive's position is too frequently contrary to the board's, it calls his judgment on these matters into question. It calls into question his political acumen as well, since it is assumed that in making a fight, one expects to win. Consistent losing also uses up the executive's reputation for influence, a precious commodity. In making use of the potential for group controversy within the board, then, the executive must be circumspect about his chances for a successful outcome. With a strong board, these chances exist only as the top influentials split on an issue.

The group character of the board also permits the executive to build a constituency among its members. An inherent aspect of the relationship between executive and board is their mutual dependency. As Kramer puts it, "The executive . . . requires the sanction and support of board members and the latter, in turn, gain prestige and a validation of their position as community leaders." [24] As we noted earlier, the executive's location in the structure allows him to put this mutual dependency to work. There is power in the informal social relationships which develop, and the opportunity to trade favors encourages the formation of coalitions. The executive can generally count on his friends or informal interest groups within the board to provide support for his positions.

We conclude this discussion of executive resources by noting that executive power is, in part, a function of the amount of time he has been the executive. Whether his influence stems from his greater knowledge, his location in the communication system, his potential for maneuver within the board group, or all three, these resources accumulate with increased tenure.

Over time, the executive will have influenced the selection of trustees through his participation in the nominating process.[25] In addition, newly appointed trustees are "trained" by the executive, and their proprietary interest in the agency, as it develops, *includes* him. Old timers among the trustees are more likely to see themselves as more "in the know" than a new executive, and to have stronger iden-

---

[24] Ralph M. Kramer, "Ideology, Status, and Power in Board-Executive Relationships," in Ralph M. Kramer and Harry Specht, eds., *Readings in Community Organization Practice* (Englewood Cliffs, N.J.: Prentice-Hall, 1969), p. 291.

[25] Social work administrative literature counsels against this, but we question whether such counsel is often heeded. See Ray Johns, *Executive Responsibility*.

tifications with the organization than he does. These conditions fix the bases from which the executive's relationship with his board evolves. Other things being equal, the long-tenured executive will have more influence, and can afford to be more risk taking.

Unfortunately, however, other things are not always equal, and those executives for whom risk-taking is most possible may be the very ones who take fewer risks. The need for risk taking is greater in innovative and social-change-oriented agencies. But these are the very agencies in which observation suggests there is greater executive turnover. Thus, of the 148 original executive directors of the City Demonstration Agencies (of Model Cities) 35 per cent had left their jobs by the end of two years.[26] Executives attracted to new and innovative programs are not only more prone to "get into trouble" because they dare to explore new fields but are also likely to move on as routinization takes hold.

The same may be said for staff as well. We turn, in the next chapter, to the cards held by the players in the lower ranks of the organizational game.

[26] Neil Gilbert and Harry Specht, Research in progress on Model Cities for Marshall Kaplan, Gans, and Kahn, San Francisco, 1972.

CHAPTER ELEVEN

THE STRAIN FOR ASCENDANCY: STAFF

STAFF INFLUENCE IN AN AGENCY is modest compared with the influence of board and executive. This is not to say that staff groups cannot have an agency at its mercy; some do. Circumstances sometimes permit staff to maximize the use of their modest resources and gain control. More usually, agency structure circumscribes staff ascendancy.

Community workers exert influence in two conceptually distinct but related ways. One is to create policy by their day-to-day activity, or to circumvent policies which already exist. This type of influencing does not require affirmative action by important organizational others; only their ignorance or inattention. The other way to influence the agency is by influencing the behavior of higher ranking participants, that is, educating, persuading, manipulating, or pressuring the decision makers. Although there is considerable overlap, the two types of influencing tend to call for different resources.

In this chapter we explore five features of the staff role which are related to the ability of staff to influence. They are: 1) degree of observability; (2) location within the agency's communication network, and interaction with the consumers of service; (3) professional norms; (4) knowledge and expertise; and (5) group composition. The first two features are most relevant to indirect influencing, although interaction with clients lends itself to assertive and direct attempts to influence as well. The first four features are available to individual staff members, as well as to the collectivity; although their potency is increased when they are widely applied, numbers are not a requisite for their use. To invoke the staff group as a resource, however, requires the involvement of many.

OBSERVABILITY

The ability of staff to prevent others from observing them permits them to circumvent authority and subvert policy. The opportunity is particularly available to social workers, since social work practice is less visible than that of other organizationally based workers. The caseworker and client ordinarily conduct their business in the privacy of an office. One of the unstated and sometimes unrecognized functions of social work supervision and written process records that detail client-worker interaction is to compensate for the worker's low visibility, that is, to increase accountability to the agency.

Community work practice is at once more visible and more private than casework. Although it takes place in the open forums of the community, where higher authorities may be present, this is usually only on ceremonial occasions. Surveillance of the worker's *informal* activities is another matter. The real business of community workers is less likely to occur within the physical domain of higher-ranking participants than the activities of other social workers. Thus the community worker has ample opportunity, if he wishes, to withhold or distort information.

Community workers have a greater incentive to withhold or distort than other social workers. Partly, the incentive springs from their ideology, their more prevalent anti-organizational bias, and their commitment to the achievement of a substantive end. It also results from their function within the sponsoring organization. Because they deal with issues of institutional moment, they function near the center of conflict. As such, the community worker must contend with agency resistance more than his colleagues in the other social work methods and, therefore, he has more incentive to avoid organizational surveillance. Since community work affects and is affected by the web of relationships developed by a sponsor with its environment, his work receives more attention and he will engage in more circumvention. The incentive to conceal their activities is greatest, of course, among change-oriented workers employed by agencies which pursue integrative and sociotherapeutic objectives.

Community workers in small agencies find it less possible to avoid observation since interaction among hierarchical levels and different constituencies is more extensive in those settings. But, on the positive side, because staff in the small agencies have greater access to its decision makers, they have a more direct impact on program. Heightened interaction also encourages cohesiveness among participants, reducing the need for secrecy.

If limited visibility permits staff to subvert agency policy, the ambiguity of the goals of community work provides them with the opportunity to create new policy. Daily practices repeated over time become common law and, in a sense, represent staff legislation. When the expectations of high-ranking participants are articulated with insufficient concreteness, tacit permission is given to the worker to "do his thing." Or his "thing" may be one thing to the agency and another thing to him even though subterfuge is unintended. For example, a worker who role plays with his group to prepare members to meet with officials may be perceived by the agency to be teaching members to cope, while the worker views himself as helping members to change systems. Even when the dissimilarity is obvious, both parties may wish to obfuscate the difference. Statements such as "We're really in agreement; it's just a matter of emphasis" serve this purpose.

Community work sponsors differ in regard to degree of formal structure. Agencies with integrative goals are the most highly structured, not only because they are usually large bureaucracies, but also because of their interest in harmony and organizational control. Intended or not, the desire for organizational control will be reflected in the development of a highly articulated structure of authority. Environmental-change-oriented sponsors tend to have less structure because they are usually smaller, often move from crisis-to-crisis, and because they are more frequently new agencies.

Whatever the sponsor's pattern, the community worker's tasks tend to be unstructured. A hospital may be interested in establishing co-operative relationships with its patients through the organization of a health council; a community mental health program may wish to engage residents in community issues for the presumed benefits to the mental health of the participants; or a welfare rights organization may organize a citywide council to support its militant action program. In none of these activities does the community worker offer a clearly delineated service, as do caseworkers and group workers. The description of practice in Part II of this volume offers testimony to the difficulties a sponsor confronts in defining a worker's job in small, concrete, and manageable units. Whereas casework interviews can be scheduled and group workers conduct meetings on some regular basis, the activities of community workers defy regulation and schedule. Much time is absorbed with informal telephone conversations, attending meetings in which they may have no formal role, talking with other professionals, and other difficult-to-specify activities.

Community work can be a source of misunderstanding and frustration in agency-worker relations, particularly when sponsored by highly formal agencies. Lack of structure, along with other factors inherent in community work practice, encourages a climate which is frequently not consonant with agency style. Thus, to highly structured sponsors in which community work is an ancillary function community work appears to be overinformal and community workers look like "free spirits."

Agencies attempt to control line workers by hiring those with value systems compatible with the agency's and by imbuing them with the appropriate sentiments once they are on the job. The aim is that even ambiguous decisions which workers make will reflect the agency's goals. Thus committing the worker to the agency and its values is a way to control him. Etzioni, in discussing organizational compliance systems, notes that normative organizations like community work agencies require the commitment of low-ranking participants to achieve their purposes.[1]

The agency pays for that commitment by limiting its use of

[1] Amatai Etzioni, *A Comparative Analysis of Complex Organizations* (New York: Free Press, 1961).

sanctions to those which will not hinder the development of commitment. Thus an administrator will weigh the costs of meeting worker requests against the consequences of rejecting them (i.e., the possible loss of worker commitment). Often, the executive will acquiesce in order to buy cooperation and to encourage identification with the organization.

The flexibility needed in community work necessitates discretion. Therefore, if the agency wants a staff member to make the "right" decision, he must be trained and trusted to make it. Surveillance is difficult or impossible when trust is the factor on which the agency relies for control.

The degree to which discretion is accorded varies with a number of other factors. We cite two: the size of the organization and the extent to which a program is critical to the community work agency.

Size affects worker discretion in two ways. First, the greater the number of hierarchical levels between line worker and administrator, the more that formalized roles and rules substitute for direct communication between upper and lower echelons. Variability and freedom of action are thereby inhibited. Rules in general, of course, are not necessarily inhibiting. Administrators do not usually expect that rules will always be enforced. They exist, rather, to provide *some* limit to their violation, for "full compliance with the rules at all times [is] probably dysfunctional for the organization . . . and complete and apathetic compliance may do everything but facilitate the achievement of organizational goals." [2] Gouldner suggests that rules are "the chips" to which organizations stake supervisors to play the organizational game. Having chips to cash in increases the supervisors' bargaining power with workers.[3] Second, the larger the agency, the more there is a specialization of staff function. When areas of staff responsibility are circumscribed and cover a narrow range, they permit more limited options to the worker.

The degree to which an issue is critical to an agency is another

[2] David Mechanic, "Sources of Power of Lower Participants in Complex Organizations," in William W. Cooper, Harold J. Leavitt, and Maynard W. Shelly II, eds., *New Perspectives in Organization Research,* (New York: Wiley, 1964), p. 148.

[3] Alvin W. Gouldner, *Patterns of Industrial Bureaucracy,* (New York: Free Press, 1954), p. 173.

factor which affects worker discretion. If a worker's activities impinge on the sponsor's relations with important interest groups, or if the latter are watching the program closely, more intense surveillance will result. This leads to something of a paradox in community work. Workers engaged in issues of importance to the sponsor have less latitude to do what may be necessary to achieve agency or worker objectives. On the other hand, workers engaged in programs of lesser significance to the agency may pursue their objectives with more freedom and flexibility. But organizational resources will not be forthcoming for issues of lesser importance to the agency, while they are more likely to be made available when the issue is of greater significance.[4] To dramatize the case we paraphrase Merton: he who is free to innovate is restrained by lack of resources; he who is *not* free to innovate will have the resources necessary to do so. Though overstated, this proposition identifies a major limitation on the worker's discretion to change policy and program.

STAFF AS LINKAGE BETWEEN
AGENCY AND CONSTITUENTS

The location of staff in an organization's communication network, particularly its position as the link between administration and service users, affects their ability to influence.

A study by McCleery of how guards impeded the reform of a prison is a striking example of the indirect power that line staff can exercise by controlling communication.[5] The humanitarian, treatment-oriented reforms instituted by a new warden moved disciplinary decision making up in the hierarchy and placed greater limits on the guards' discretion. The disruption this caused in the informal system

---

[4] In other words, resources are forthcoming for important issues that an agency wishes to pursue. And resources are not forthcoming for unimportant issues, unless the agency happens to want to pursue them. Readers are undoubtedly aware that many agencies choose to avoid issues of importance; and conversely, that many agencies expend considerable resources on essentially unimportant issues.

[5] Richard H. McCleery, *Policy Change in Prison Management* (East Lansing: Michigan State University Press, 1957).

by which prisoner leaders obtained privileges from guards for keeping prisoners "in line" moved both guards and prisoner leaders to subvert the humanitarian administration. Riots ensued.

Another example of the use of communication as a means of controlling is the failure of a state mental hospital to implement intended reforms because of opposition by hospital attendants.[6] Prior to instituting the reforms there had been an unstated agreement between ward physicians and attendants that attendants would assume some of the physician's responsibilities (e.g., record keeping and dealing with behavior problems) in return for their having increased power in decision making concerning patients. To resist the reforms, attendants withheld cooperation so that physicians had difficulty in making graceful entrances and departures from the ward, in handling necessary paper work, and in obtaining information needed to deal adequately with daily treatment. As a result, the physicians were forced to join the attendants in circumventing the proposed changes.

Both examples represent successful efforts by line staff to prevent agency change, rather than to create it. Most typically, the influence exercised by lower-ranking participants is based on their ability to subvert and resist change. The power to initiate change requires more in resources than they ordinarily command.

There are a number of factors which allow line workers to use their position as the link between agency and client to influence upper-level staff. In the mental hospital example, staff arrangements led to the dependence of upper echelon personnel on line workers. In other situations, the line worker can influence program and policy direction by defining constituent reactions to agency decision makers. Workers may, consciously or not, select from among numerous communications those they wish to report or underscore; and feeling tones may be purposely exaggerated to achieve an end (e.g., "the people are angry, so we had better. . . .").

Workers may also influence by interpreting agency authority to the consumers of the service. The guards in the McCleery study used the

---

[6] Thomas J. Scheff, "Control Over Policy by Attendants in a Mental Hospital," *Journal of Health and Human Behavior*, Vol. 2 (1961), pp. 93–105. This citation is drawn from Mechanic, "Sources of Power of Lower Participants." Our description represents a precis of Mechanic's summary.

prisoners to influence the agency in this way. There is wide variation in how workers can interpret agency policy ranging from rigorous enforcement to complete abandonment of rules. At the rigorous enforcement end, the worker identifies with the organization, enthusiastically supports its policies, and encourages constituents to endorse them too. At the other end, enforcement is lax or nonexistent, the worker is deeply dissatisfied with the policies and urges constituent resistance. Both subtly and directly, the latter was the stance of the prison guards.

Social workers are often counseled that "professional" responsibility requires their identification with their agency. The following comment by a leading casework theoretician is representative of this view:

> Every staff member in an agency speaks and acts for some part of the agency's function, and the case-worker represents the agency in its individualized problem solving help. . . . [In order to represent the agency, the worker] must be psychologically identified with it, at one with its purposes and policies.[7]

A closely related professional dictum makes it obligatory for the worker to try to change policies with which they disagree, but failing that, to interpret them faithfully to clients. One consequence of these principles is to close agency ranks against the client. This is rationalized as being in the clients' interests (i.e., it precludes their becoming confused), although the reality may be that it substitutes a collective responsibility for an individual one.

The faithful interpretation of policies about which the worker may have question results in a reduction of his influence, since in acceding to agency policy, he limits his ability to induce its change. Acceptance of these "professional principles" also serves to reduce the influence of constituents as well, since they may be pacified by interpretations of the rightness of policies which may not necessarily be in their best interests. On the other hand, constituents who are made aware of conflicting strains within the agency may become more assertive in advancing their grievances, or they may make their case with greater effectiveness.

[7] Helen Harris Perlman, *Social Casework* (Chicago: University of Chicago Press, 1958), p. 50.

We believe that the professional response to a questionable policy is for the worker to present the agency's basis for the policy honestly and fairly, and also to disclose his disagreements and his reasons for them. Nor does it violate professional ethics to identify the ill effects of pernicious policies for service users. The touchstone of professionalism is whether the worker is acting in his constituents' interests rather than his own.

Workers may use their role as communicators to engage constituents in attempts to revise sponsor policies. This occurs in two ways. First, when the service user feels aggrieved and asks for help, the worker explains the lines of authority and plans with the client(s) for the most effective means of proceeding. The second way to help clients redress grievances is much more difficult but cannot be dismissed out of hand. We refer here to situations where the worker takes the initiative in seeking out the constituents who will challenge an agency edict.[8]

The risk is great in either instance. Apart from the possibility of endangering one's job, there are other interpersonal and tactical difficulties. The worker who aids constituents to change agency practices or who organizes them in opposition to agency policies risks the fury that is reserved for renegades. If the discomfort of his colleagues' reaction to the violation of group norms is not enough to give a worker pause, the fact that he thereby sacrifices his current and/or future ability to influence them may be sufficient. At the least, the worker risks the trust and good will of agency decision makers, which may not be important in a specific instance, but it is tactically unwise over the long pull for those who wish to influence organizations from within.

Nevertheless, the hazards of a staff coalition with constituents do not apply in all circumstances, and occasions of sufficient moment may make the risk worth taking. It should be understood that the limitations are pragmatic and expedient. Morality does not preclude coalitions with clients. If anything, the reverse is true. In the matter of constituent-worker coalitions, the fear of unprofessionalism may be the straw man of straw bosses.

[8] A major risk, here, is that professionals may use constituents to further the political aspirations of the professionals under the guise of aiding their constituents.

PROFESSIONAL RULES OF THE GAME

"Rules of the game" in social work and community organization offer opportunities for, and constraints on, worker influence. Two norms in particular serve as a source of influence for staff to shape agency direction. Both rules refer to participation, one regarding staff, the other concerning clients.

The first might be termed "participatory management." The search for novel and creative solutions to problems is intense for a group which seeks professional sanction and status; the professional is at war with the follower of routine. The managerial revolution supports professional claims to self-direction and the generally accepted norm of social welfare administration that workers at all levels should be involved in agency decision making. The literature is replete with injunctions which support staff involvement in policy development. For example, Patti and Resnick point out that an ideal organization emerges from the literature of a social agency consisting of "several organically [cooperatively] related parts in which there is a continual flow of information and ideas between those who practice and those who ultimately make decisions. . . ." [9]

Although the norm prescribing that workers be included in decision making may be observed more in the breach than in practice, it is useful to workers. If agency authorities are committed to this norm and reluctant to violate it, staff is freer to press its prerogatives. An appeal to mutually shared sentiments, although ordinarily insufficient to resolve a major issue, can tip a noncritical decision in one direction or another.

The same is true in regard to the norm of client self-determination. However imprecise and rhetorical the notion, the concept is as esteemed by social workers as "academic freedom" is by university teachers. When their clients have "spoken," sponsors find it more difficult to prohibit their taking social action even though it may

[9] Rino Patti and Herman Resnick, "Toward the Formulation of an Organizational Change Methodology for Social Workers" (Seattle: University of Washington School of Social Work, 1970), p. 7. (Mimeographed)

threaten the sponsor's external relations. As we have noted, line workers define client attitudes to agency administrators and, therefore, the value of client participation is an important one to the worker.

The following statement of a worker who successfully organized a group of welfare clients under sponsorship which might have been expected to impose limitations is illustrative.

The social worker's Achilles' heel is that what the clients want to do is a sacrosanct thing. If a group of clients make a decision which is a group decision, then self-determination and democracy come in, and it becomes quite difficult for the agency to turn aside what the group wants to do. . . . The agency has real problems controlling the group, *especially if the worker wants to chart an independent course.* If in certain situations supervisory people said, "well, you can't do that," I could always point to the social work ideal and say, "Look, the group wants to do it, just ask them." . . . From the very beginning I tried to set up a situation where there was some kind of barrier between what the group wanted to do and a possible attempt on the part of the top people in the agency to stop something.[10] (Italics added)

One might be suspicious of a worker who had to add "just ask them" as he reported a group decision, and wonder if he had set it up. One may wonder, too, whether his remarks are excessively self-aggrandizing at the expense of agency administrators. However, the example illustrates how an aggressive worker can invoke the norm of self-determination.

KNOWLEDGE AND EXPERTISE

What we have said about the use of knowledge and expertise by the executive applies, with modifications, to staff. The disparity between the organizational intelligence available to board and executive in large, complex, or geographically dispersed agencies enhances the power of the executive vis-à-vis the board and the power of workers vis-à-vis their executives. That is, the workers are likely to have, and executives are likely to need, information about the agency.

[10] Mary Rabagliati and Ezra Birnbaum, "Organizations of Welfare Clients," in Harold H. Weissman, ed., *Community Development in the Mobilization for Youth Experience,* (New York: Association Press, 1969), pp. 120–21.

Knowledge is a more important resource when the professional function of the worker is central to the achievement of the sponsor's purposes. Workers whose specialization is related to primary agency goals have more influence than workers whose specialization fulfills only ancillary functions. A study of five correctional institutions revealed that psychiatric caseworkers were perceived as more influential in institutions with treatment goals than those with custodial goals.[11] Teachers were attributed a low amount of influence whether the institution was treatment or custodial, apparently because academic work was not central to the purposes of either institution.[12] This finding suggests that achievement of organizational purposes requires that participants whose specialization most represents the primary agency goal will be in the ascendancy. To cite another example: leaders who embody production or profit goals in a factory must be more influential than those who represent professional or artistic values. Similarly, in a normative organization (e.g., community work sponsor), the staff responsible for expressive activities should be superordinate to those performing managerial or financial tasks, since the former build up and sustain the value commitments required by the organization.[13]

When the worker's professional orientation closely corresponds to an agency's primary purpose, he becomes personally committed to the agency's ideology and, therefore, more reliable. This assumption follows from the proposition, advanced by Lazarsfeld and Thielens,[14] that ideology results from self-interest, selective perception, and processes of mutual reinforcement. A community worker or a comptroller are each more likely to emphasize the importance of their work (self-interest); they are each likely to have more interest in, and therefore greater knowledge about, program goals or money matters, respectively (selective perception); and each will have their beliefs and values reinforced by their tendency to interact selectively with others who are similarly involved (mutual reinforcement).

[11] Mayer N. Zald, "Organizational Control Structures in Five Correctional Institutions," in Mayer N. Zald, ed., *Social Welfare Institutions* (New York: Wiley, 1965), p. 462.

[12] *Ibid.*, p. 462.

[13] Etzioni, *A Comparative Analysis of Complex Organizations*, p. 106.

[14] Paul Lazarsfeld and Walter Thielens, *The Academic Mind* (New York: Free Press, 1958).

The research conducted at Mobilization for Youth (MFY), cited in the preceding chapter, supports this assumption. Staff responsible for program activities evidenced more commitment to the organization's goals than managerial personnel. On the index assessing "Commitment to MFY's Values and Goals," *none* of the managerial-caretaking staff were in the category of "most committed" compared to 30.9 per cent of the program staff.

The correlation between a staff member's influence and the degree to which his professional function is related to primary agency goals is advantageous to the agency. For one thing, if the worker whose professional function is related to primary goals is influential, it tends to insure that emphasis is put upon goal-related matters. This counters organizational tendencies toward goal displacement.[15] For another thing, these are the workers who develop the strongest commitments to agency ideology, and they can therefore be relied upon to make goal-relevant decisions "on-the-line."

Community workers tend to be generalists. They are expected to contribute the broad-gauged knowledge and skill which Wilensky ascribes to three different types of organizational expert: (1) the "contact man," such as lobbyists and public relations men, who supply political intelligence and mediate the relations of the organization with the outside world: (2) the "internal communications specialist," such as education directors and trainers, who transmit policies downward and deal with membership sentiment; and (3) the "facts and figures man," such as researchers and planning directors, who supply the technical knowledge required by the organization.[16] Community workers with special skill in any of these areas will be valued and influential, depending on which of these particular skills is required by the sponsor.

The worker with skill in changing attitudes through persuasion, who knows how to influence those who make decisions, provides a valuable resource to the sponsor engaged in controversy. "Secret" in-

[15] Etzioni notes that, for this reason, religious organizations tend to insist on the subordination of instrumental leaders (deacons) to expressive leaders (priests and bishops). Amatai Etzioni, "Organizational Control Structure," in James G. March, ed., *Handbook of Organizations* (Chicago: Rand McNally, 1965), p. 660.

[16] Harold L. Wilensky, *Organizational Intelligence* (New York: Basic Books, 1967). What follows is a summary of Wilensky's formulation, pp. 10–19.

formation about one's adversary enhances effectiveness. For example, the community worker employed by a welfare rights organization who has an "in" with, and is fed information by, workers in the welfare department, contributes importantly to the welfare rights effort. Environmental-change-oriented sponsors need workers whose "contact man" talents are well developed.

Frequently, when community action agencies feel the political heat generated by their social-change orientation, it is suggested that the programs would be better served with politicians in leadership positions rather than professionals. If the argument regarding the need for congruence between organizational goals and leadership structure is correct, however, this "solution" is clearly wrong, for political leadership would tend to divert the programs from their community change goals. What the projects do require to withstand the heat are program experts ("facts and figures" men) who also have political ("contact man") skills.

More than others, sociotherapeutic sponsors are likely to value, and therefore accord influence to, workers with internal communications skills since their goals tend to be directed inward to the growth and development of the service users. Integrative agencies may also rely on internal communications skills, although many engaged in community planning also value workers whose expertise lies in dealing with "facts and figures." This is particularly the case with politically weak organizations. Sponsors with a potent membership use their constituency to influence the environment for them, whereas those with limited access to a constituency must rely on research, professional knowledge, and effective arguments to win the day.

Shifting tides of conflict and reconciliation may revise the needs of the change-oriented sponsor for particular kinds of expertise to meet new contingencies. The fortunes of the Community Action Programs are a case in point. Dependent on government, and battered by charges of misusing funds, many found it necessary to devote greater resources to record keepers and accountants, often at a cost to the agencies' programs of action and service. These changes bring about concomitant changes in the relative degrees of influence of different groups of staff. Although staff cannot predict the shifting tides with accuracy, a continuing assessment of changing agency needs can inform staff of which elements of their expertise may be used as leverage to influence sponsor directions.

Information and expertise can also be put to use *against* the agency. A documented challenge to agency policy has internal utility that may be persuasive to the decision makers. If not, public exposure may be implied or threatened. The latter occurs, most typically in government operations, when staff "leaks" the information to the press. More direct than "leaking," workers may openly score the policies of the employing agency. This occurred when a group of professional planners employed by the New York City Planning Commission testified at a public hearing that the Commission had ignored the zoning recommendations of its own staff and yielded to real estate interests.

A frustrated and desperate staff appealing to the higher authority of the public in order to prevent agency calumny has a man-bites-dog news appeal. It dramatizes an issue, coming as it does from within the agency at the risk of the workers' positions. It cannot be dismissed as self-interest, and such testimony carries the mantle of intimate knowledge. The appeal has its disadvantages as well. Unless there is solid group support for the action, the worker risks the label of "dissident" and may find himself unemployed.

To conclude this section, we want to consider the possible uses of the collegiate relationships of staff members and executives, when both are professionals. In an agency hierarchy, much of staff's influence is exerted *through* the executive, directly if he is the decision maker, and a step removed if board sanction is required. In either case, the executive must be influenced to pursue staff-inspired directions. Careers bound in the same profession offer some degree of leverage in "collegiality."

Because of the differing locations, interests, and ideologies of its participants, community work involves mediating among many parties. The community worker must balance the needs of service users against the demands of sponsors. The executive, too, is a "marginal man;" he is *with* but not *of* the board; he is *with* but not *of* the staff group. The pull of the board and other powerful interests is strong, but staff too has its claims, one of which is based on the mutual obligations between colleagues.

In a study of school superintendents and their boards, Neal Gross found, that sharp differences were evidenced in the response to questions about who should hire teachers, and how superintendents should respond to unfair public pressures upon teachers. Superintendents' choices were markedly more supportive of teachers' rights than those of school boards.[17] The most plausible explanation for the difference is that the superintendent and the board are each responsive to different reference groups. The board's reference is to the community from which it springs; the superintendent, on the other hand, is a member of the professional fraternity.

It must be clear from the preceding pages that we are not of the "happy partnership" school of administrative thought which holds that when executive and staff share professional interests, all is harmonious. Rather, in our view there are inherent tensions and conflicts of interest built into these different roles. Each has a different focus of concern: the executive outward to the larger community; the staff inward to the client group. An executive's attention to external affairs often removes him from the agency, which workers sometimes define as lack of interest in matters of importance to them. The executive faces board pressure to maintain policies in the face of staff opposition. But because he is "boss," workers may perceive the executive to be a "free agent" no matter how fettered by the board in reality. Most importantly, there is inevitable strain between the professional's interest in functioning independently and the executive's need to manage the organization.

The strains notwithstanding, professional commonality can be a source of staff influence. Executives who seek the social approval and professional approbation of their professional colleagues are more amenable to worker influence. But in order for collegiate relations to work their influence, workers must allow executives to be perceived as "good professionals." Unless he believes it possible to achieve that status, an executive will not be stimulated to pay the necessary price. Staff must be mindful of "real life" administrative pressures and must attempt to view situations from the executive's political context. An executive is more likely to be influenced by staff members' opinions when he feels assured of their political acu-

[17] Neal Gross, *Who Runs Our Schools?* (New York: Wiley, 1958).

men and loyalty. If, from the executive's point of view, a course of action is impossible, the worker cannot press that course of action too strongly and too often. In effect, the worker must give something in exchange for the executive's understanding. Such "trading" constitutes an important dynamic of ongoing organizational relationships.

THE GROUP COMPOSITION
OF STAFF

The most potent resource that workers have is their collective composition. Although the group nature of the board limits its influence vis-à-vis the executive, the group nature of the staff limits executive power. Any group is stronger when there is solidarity and weaker when there is division. Groups with few other resources, such as staff, have the potential of solidarity as a source of impact. Groups, such as boards, which are well endowed with resources, on the other hand, do not need to be cohesive, and numbers are largely irrelevant as a resource to influence. This is why persons and organizations with access to material resources favor elitist strategies, and why the poor must organize.

The cohesion of groups is enhanced by the following social conditions: geographic proximity; common interests (e.g., wages and working conditions); a common target (e.g., management); homogeneity in background; and status congruency (i.e., a group of peers). A quick glance at the list indicates its applicability to workers as a group and explains the success of union organizing. Differences in cohesion and organization among work groups result from differences in these conditions from agency to agency.

Influence and dependency are related. A person who is dependent on another is subject to that other's influence. If that is so, then how much more dependent is an organization on a group of its workers than on any single individual? It belabors a point in a book devoted to collective activity by service recipients to argue that collectivities are a potential source of influence, but a first step for a worker who is dissatisfied with agency conditions is to find other persons with whom action can be effected.

Broadly speaking, there are two structural forms through which worker collectivities influence organizations: informal relations and formal organizations such as unions and professional associations. Informal relations create alliances and networks of communication which may or may not support organizational purposes. They develop morale or impede its development. They create and sustain worker attitudes and norms. They are a compelling force both in controlling the behavior of individual members and in influencing an organization's direction.

The research of Blau and Scott demonstrates that individual workers with a proclient bent were more apt than anticlient workers to offer services to welfare recipients rather than merely to check their eligibility. But regardless of the individual worker's orientation, he was significantly more likely to proffer services to clients if he was in a group where proclient values prevailed than if he was in a group in which an anticlient group climate predominated.[18] Thus work group climate affects behavior and attitudes of individual workers.

The formal organization of workers is a more forceful mechanism of organizational influence. This is so for many of the same reasons noted earlier in our discussion of institutional-relations organizations. It is "out front" and can self-consciously and assertively pursue its ends. It is task-oriented, rather than expressively oriented, and therefore is more efficiently structured for task achievement. Its existence as a formal entity encourages the search for an agenda, and thus formal organizations are likely to address a broader gamut of concerns.

But informal or formal, there is a risk for community work goals in the power of staff relations. As noted previously, there is no inherent rightness in the accrual of power by any of an organization's sets of members, apart from the purposes to which their influence is put. Groups tend to pursue the common interests of members to the exclusion of other concerns. They serve the "insider" (e.g., the staff) in a way which might be detrimental to the "outsider" (e.g., the client). As Blau and Scott indicate, staff relations can *dis*courage as well as *en*courage proclient attitudes.

Staff organizations often operate out of narrow professional self-

18 Peter M. Blau and W. Richard Scott, *Formal Organizations* (San Francisco: Chandler, 1962), p. 101.

interest. The central interest of unions is the improved working conditions of their members, and their survival as organizations depends on their ability to deliver benefits to members. Their means of doing this may well interfere with the interests of service users. The same may be said for professional associations. Although their source of influence is based on their power to direct the use of knowledge and skill, their primary interest is, like the union, the delivery of benefits to members. Here too, this may or may not coincide with what is beneficial to clients.

Fortunately, the change-oriented-service ideology of community work partially mitigates these tendencies. The central purpose of community organizing as articulated in this volume—to build the capacity of citizens to influence service-providing organizations—reduces the likelihood that organizers will completely overlook the interests of their constituency in favor of their own.

The historical emphasis in social work on worker self-awareness is another mitigating factor. This emphasis, stemming from clinical practice, suggests that a professional must be sufficiently self-aware to consciously use himself as a tool to maximize benefits to the client. Worker self-awareness obviates the risk that the worker's needs (e.g., for ascendency and love) will be imposed on the client. To the extent, then, that a worker is aware of his individual needs, *or his group self-interest,* the professional norm requires that these be minimized in practice.

The fact that community work ideology and professional norms may mitigate self-interest is suggested by a study based on a survey of 899 professional social workers conducted by Irwin Epstein.[19] The study explores the effects of organizational rank, specialization, and professionalization on social worker approval of militant strategies of social change. It was found that workers who score *low* on orientation to the profession tend to become more conservative as they move up the organizational hierarchy than those who score *high* on professional orientation. Community organizers and group workers start out more radical than their casework compeers, but only

[19] Irwin Epstein, "Organizational Careers, Professionalization, and Social Worker Radicalism," *Social Service Review,* Vol. 44, No. 2 (June 1970), pp. 123–31.

those who score high on professional orientation do not become more conservative with higher organizational status. Epstein concludes—contrary to common expectations about professions— that "professionalization *inhibits* the effects of conservatizing social forces for *all* social work segments." [20]

Nothing we have written about worker characteristics and resources or the desirability of enhancing worker influence is intended to deny the importance of the role of service users in decision making. Recipients of service ought not to count on sympathetic staff, even if they could. At the same time it would be simplistic to deny clients the allies they can have in a trained community worker staff. Sometimes, the staff will be followers, accountable to the community group, and sometimes it will be necessary for them to lead.

[20] *Ibid.,* p. 130. (Italics added)

Part IV

INFLUENCING TARGETS:
TACTICS FOR COMMUNITY CHANGE

CHAPTER TWELVE

A PERSPECTIVE ON TACTICS

THE CHARISMATIC LEADERS of social movements—those most effective of change agents—are all consummate tacticians. Gandhi's use of civil disobedience, for example, may be interpreted as a tactic resulting from the scarcity of other weapons. It thus represents an instance of turning weakness into strength. Riker notes that Gandhi's fasting was skillfully calibrated as an influence technique:

. . . The vast majority of his fasts were directed against caste Hindus . . . [who] were, of course, those persons most convinced of his saintliness and therefore the persons most likely to feel the force of this weapon. . . . . [With] a realism somewhat unexpected in a mystic, he fasted only when he could win. Never once did he expose his charisma to the humiliation of abandoning a fast in failure.[1]

A case has also been made regarding the tactical acumen of Jesus Christ. Jay Haley observes:

The innovations of Jesus as an organizer . . . have been overlooked. . . . Typically the credit for his achievements has been given to the Lord, which seems unfair, or to later followers like Paul, which seems more unfair. . . . The ideology of contemporary mass movement leaders differs . . . from that of Jesus, but . . . their basic strategy . . . was outlined in the New Testament and designed in Galilee by one man.[2]

[1] William H. Riker, *The Theory of Political Coalitions* (New Haven: Yale University Press, 1962), pp. 118–19.

[2] Jay Haley, *The Power Tactics of Jesus Christ* (New York: Grossman, 1969), pp. 20–21.

We are not, of course, so presumptuous as to suggest that community workers can assume the roles or wear the robes of such men, but only that there is much to learn about tactics from what, on its face, may seem an unlikely source. We cite the above to underscore the importance of tactical acumen in social change attempts, since it tends to be ignored or downgraded as a practice skill among social workers.[3]

In this chapter we discuss the different interventions which constitute the spectrum of tactical choices, choices which range from collaboration to disruption. We first explore how the perceptions of the actors, their resources for influence, and their relationships to each other are associated with particular types of tactics. In a final section, we deal with some of the practice principles the creative tactician must consider.

ISSUES, RESOURCES, AND RELATIONSHIPS

The tactics which organizers and community groups use to effect community change depend on three related factors: (1) the substance of the issue, or goal of the effort as *perceived* by the action and target systems; (2) the resources of the parties involved in the action; and (3) the relationship of action and target systems with one another. We explore each in turn.

Issues and Modes of Intervention. The association between different modes of intervention and different responses to issues has been described by Warren.[4] The range of responses to issues which he identifies are: (a) *issue consensus,* where there is a high possibility of agreement between the action and target systems; (b) *issue difference,* where for one or another reason the parties are not in complete

---

[3] In this chapter, we maintain the distinction between "strategy" and "tactics" which was made in chapter 6, i.e., "tactics" connote the short-range and specific behaviors of groups, whereas "strategy" refers to the long-range goals by which groups and organizations link problems with solutions.

[4] Roland L. Warren, "Types of Purposive Social Change at the Community Level," in Ralph M. Kramer and Harry Specht, *Readings in Community Organization Practice* (Englewood Cliffs, N.J.: Prentice-Hall, 1969), pp. 205–22.

agreement, but the possibility for agreement exists; and (c) *issue dissensus,* where these is no agreement on the issue between the parties.

Each response is associated with a particular mode of intervention. Thus, issue consensus yields to collaborative modes of intervention, such as problem solving and education. With issue difference, campaigns of a competitive or bargaining nature take place. Dissensus is associated with contests in which there is a high degree of conflict between the parties leading to confrontation and disruptive tactics.

What is it about issues that tends to elicit one or another response? Why do we find consensus in one instance, difference or dissensus in another? The response to an issue, whether rational or not, indicates how the issue is *perceived* by different parties.[5] Whatever the reality, the views of the different parties regarding what the action will mean for them is crucial in determining their response. The table below combines these elements but adds violence as a fourth mode of intervention based on a perception of change which aims at "reconstruction of the entire system" to which the response is "insurrection." [6]

WHEN THE GOAL IS PERCEIVED AS:	THE RESPONSE IS:	THE MODE OF INTERVENTION IS:
(a) Mutually enhancing adjustments; or rearrangement of resources	Consensus	Collaborative
(b) Redistribution of resources	Difference	Campaign
(c) Change in status relationships	Dissensus	Contest or disruption
(d) Reconstruction of entire system	Insurrection	Violence

There are some general remarks to be made about the typology. First, the range of responses has been simplified for the sake of clarity. In reality, there is no clear and definite cutting point for each of

[5] In his development of the typology of issue situations, Warren was working with a "value-interest" dimension rather than a perception dimension which, though related, is somewhat different.

[6] We hasten to note that violence is not a mode of intervention which is available to professional organizers, nor do we believe it should be. This is discussed further in chapter 16.

these sets of perceptions, responses, and modes of intervention. The typology should be conceived as consisting of several continua rather than of discrete categories. As one element changes, so too do the others. For example, the response to a rearrangement of resources may be either consensus or mild difference, in which case the mode of intervention will range from collaborative to mild campaign. Predicting change would be easier if we were able to scale and measure the perceptions, responses, and modes of intervention, and could then determine the conditions under which particular responses are reversible.

Second, all of the referents of these concepts are time limited, in the sense that they are subject to on-going social and legal redefinition. What is defined as redistribution today may be redefined as a rearrangement of resources tomorrow, and what is considered conflictual at one time may be merely competitive at another. The point at which a rearrangement of resources comes to be perceived as a redistribution is not easily predicted; and what one party views as a demand for change in status may be perceived as insurrection by another. Currently rent strikes and boycotts are examples of tactics which appear to hover between contest and campaign, depending on time, place, and specific application; similarly, disobedience and resistance may be responded to as insurrection or contest, depending on the social climate and the specific uses made of these tactics.

We note, finally, that within this schema conflict is viewed as an element that is present to some degree in all modes of intervention when change is involved, whether the intervention is collaborative, campaign, contest, or violence. Conflict is hardly involved in collaborative tactics with integrative goals (i.e., when the effort entails mutually enhancing adjustment of resources). In this instance, the change is ordinarily minor. In the discussion which follows, we ignore both extremes of the continuum of interventions—collaborative interventions when the goal is integrative, and violence to reconstruct the entire system—since the major work of organizers in the pursuit of community change falls among the other modes of intervention.

Perceptions, Responses, Interventions. The first mode of intervention—collaboration—is based on consensual responses to planned changes which are perceived as a rearrangement of resources. The parties to the change are in essential agreement about the coordination, or reorganization, of services. No one perceives that they stand to lose much money, power, or status by the change.

Redistribution of resources is a qualitatively different perception of a change. One or the other parties expects that he will end up with more or less of something—money, facilities, authority—but because it is perceived as remaining within the rules of the game (the institutionalized system of competition), the contending parties utilize campaign tactics to exert pressure, negotiate, and eventually compromise and agree.

Contest or disruption is generated by a challenge to existing status relationships. This view of a change creates an entirely different universe of discourse than either of the above. Contest or disruption is rooted in the competition for power in human relations. Status relationships refer to the social arrangements by which expectations, rights, and responsibilities are awarded, and these social arrangements always award more to some than to others. A threat to the system of relationships which give some people power over others is the basis for this kind of response, whether it involves parents and children, welfare workers and clients, students and teachers, or blacks and whites. When community issues are perceived by one party as eliminating or diminishing their power over others, the response may be predicted as dissensus, and contest or disruption the result.

Responses to a change effort—whether consensus, difference, or dissensus—are inevitably related to the parties' perception of the *scope* of the change attempt. In any specific instance, the greater the extent of a proposed rearrangement of resources, the more likely it is to be perceived as a redistribution. Similarly, the greater the redistribution, the more it will be perceived as status change. It might be argued, as a matter of fact, that real issues of change always involve alterations in status relationships, and that rearrangements and redistributions of resources are simply lesser degrees of status change.

Some Examples. The following examples will illustrate the interplay of the three elements—perceptions, responses, and modes of intervention.

Fluoridation, objectively, presents a good case for collaborative tactics. It is considered sensible, scientific, and is not only inexpensive but money saving. Perhaps because health officials and community organizers themselves viewed the issue as a mutually enhancing adjustment, and in planning their strategy ignored the perceptions of other actors, they have often approached the issue from a consensus framework, relying on educational modes of intervention. Yet the issue of flouridation has been the basis of harsh and vindictive social conflicts in hundreds of communities in the United States.[7]

There appear to be two major sets of reasons for the resistance. First, many people question the effectiveness of the proposed change and fear the possibility of flouride being poisonous. Interestingly, this line of resistance yields to collaborative modes of intervention.[8] But the second source of resistance, which is based on the belief that fluoridation infringes on the rights of individuals, and that "compulsory medication" usurps the rights of free men, does not respond to collaborative methods. Green's research supports the conclusion that indignation over the *presumed* violation of personal freedom was more fundamental, in the minds of informants, than the danger of poisoning; that the fear of poisoning symbolized a disposition to see fluoridation as an insidious attack by a vague constellation of impersonal social forces bent on usurping the powers of the common citizen; and the root cause of this feeling of being victimized, sensed by active opponents of fluoridation, was the increasing remoteness and impersonality of the sources of power and influence affecting the daily life of the individual.[9] In short, the issue of fluoridation becomes a contest when it is perceived to be a threat to status.

The civil rights movement provides another example of a shift over time from a major focus on rearrangement and redistribution of resources to a more focused concern with change in status. Of course, throughout its history, the demands made by the movement undoubtedly *required* a change in status for success. But there was increasing recognition that it was the power of whites over blacks

[7] "Trigger for Community Conflict," entire issue of the *Journal of Social Issues*, Vol. XVII, No. 4 (December 1961).

[8] Benjamin D. Paul, "Flouridation and the Social Scientist: A Review," *Ibid.*, p. 5.

[9] *Ibid.*, p. 7.

which was at issue. In the union organizing which preceded Martin Luther King, Jr.'s assassination in Memphis, the city was not confronting a question of redistribution of resources as they might in an ordinary labor dispute. That the striking workers perceived it as a question of status was evident in their signs which read "I Am a Man," for indeed it was their manhood that they saw at stake. That the mayor of Memphis perceived it the same way was clear in his statement that he would be damned if he would be the first southern mayor to bargain collectively with a black union.

Resources and Modes of Intervention. In our emphasis on the perceptions of the participants rather than the realities of the issues, we do not wish to leave the impression that we underestimate the importance of objective reality in shaping perception. This disclaimer is doubly necessary, since we wish now to suggest that perceptions of a change attempt are also importantly shaped by the resource requirements of action.

The Memphis strikers, alluded to above, are a case in point. The fact that a labor dispute became a symbol of racial injustice served the tactical interests of the striking union, since it greatly expanded the action system, increasing its sources of influence and the pressure it could bring to bear upon the target. In order to garner the resources for victory, the union had to redefine the effort and up the ideological ante.

Proponents also attempt to shape perceptions so that issues appear less threatening to potential targets. For example, the notion of participation by the poor in the poverty program was rationalized on the grounds of equity and as a means of developing their competence. Whether or not advocates of the program believed this to be the whole truth, the necessity for consensus and collaborative modes of intervention required that these perceptions be fostered. If the program had been perceived as promoting a change in status relationships (as happened later), it might have died aborning.

As these examples imply, our typology is not linear. That is, action efforts do not move inevitably from a particular perception (e.g., redistribution of resources) to its corresponding response (i.e., difference), and from there to the corresponding mode of intervention (i.e., campaign) as they do across the lines of the table. They might occur in reverse order. A tactic is chosen (only one mode may be available or valued), thereby creating a particular response and perception of the effort. Or, as we shall see later, the response itself may come first, as when consensual or conflictual relations between action and target systems are defined as necessary or desired.

Apart from the requirements of the community issue itself what determines the mode of intervention? Most important are the various resources which facilitate the exercise of power. Our earlier references to the resources of board, executive, and staff of sponsoring organization is relevant to the current discussion.[10] There is an extensive literature which examines the resources of power. Rossi, for example, lists wealth and other physical resources, control over interaction among prestigious groups, control of communications systems, control over values (as available to the church), threats to property, and the backing of solidary interest groups.[11] Dahl adds knowledge and expertise, popularity and charisma, legality and officiality.[12] Although the inventory is not complete, it is useful nonetheless. A cursory review suggests two factors of importance for our analysis: first, some resources are more advantageous, or necessary, in using certain tactics than others and, second, these resources are differentially distributed among community organizations which engage in community affairs.

The need to gain the interest and commitment of the poor encourages campaign and contest modes of intervention. Coleman has demonstrated that previously nonparticipating citizens are most likely to be drawn to community action when they have objections to register,[13] and that conflict in organizations and communities closely correlates with membership participation.[14] We do not cite these observations as a standard recipe for the would-be organizer, although

[10] See Part III, chapters 10 and 11.

[11] Peter H. Rossi, "Theory, Research and Practice in Community Organization," in Kramer and Specht, *Readings in Community Organization Practice,* pp. 51–52.

[12] Robert A. Dahl, "The Analysis of Influence in Local Communities," in Charles R. Adrian, ed., *Social Science and Community Action* (East Lansing: Michigan State University Press, 1960), p. 32.

[13] James S. Coleman, *Community Conflict* (Glencoe, Ill.: Free Press, 1957), p. 19.

[14] *Ibid.,* p. 3.

they are the basis of Alinsky's espousal of contest tactics. Whatever one's stance regarding the latter, it is important to understand that one of the few resources available to the poor requires perceptions of difference or dissensus—and, therefore, campaign or contest types of intervention are likely to be the tactics of choice.

The only other item on the list of resources which is readily at the disposal of the poor is the threat of disruption and threats to property. (Rossi and Dahl omit threats to life, as in guerrilla warfare which, though a resource, may be ignored for our purposes.) To threaten property is, by definition, to engage in contest or disruption. In short, two of the resources which the poor can significantly muster are resources which are bound to generate competition and conflict.

To be real, collaborative modes of intervention, such as problem solving, education, and persuasion, require that an issue entails more than a rearrangement of resources and reflect a commonality of interest. Although there are undoubtedly commonalities of interest between the poor and some target systems, this is less often the case than the widespread use of collaborative tactics would suggest. Its use might best be explained as a consequence of the unequal power of service users in relation to officials. When the reach of the poor is modest, it is, by and large, because their less potent resources require less strident behaviors. In other words, the fact that collaboration is the only mode of intervention available often determines the definitions of community issues rather than the other way around.

To collaborate because there are common interests—or because one has no other alternative—or to *appear* to collaborate for political advantage is reasonable. But to prescribe collaborative means as preferential, if not exclusive, methods, as do many professionals, is another matter. It is, we suspect, making a virtue of necessity.

Our discussion of the association between resources and tactics has, until now, assumed the poor *acting on their own*. Often this is not the case. Action systems may be composed of the poor and the nonpoor. But since the resources available to the poor and those available to influentials are different, the two tend to use tactics which are contradictory. Thus an action system which, owing to the access of its influentials, has established relations with public officials cannot easily maintain those relations, seek favors, persuade, and at the same time subject the officials to virulent public pressure. These contradictions require delicate balancing, and may require that the poor choose to go their route for a time alone.

Relationships and Modes of Intervention. The composition of action and target systems affects the perceptions of the parties regarding the action effort. By no stretch of the imagination, for example, can a breakfast program for ghetto children, an activity of the Black Panthers, be defined as, on the face of it, leading to a change in status relations. When a program is conducted by a revolutionary group such as the Black Panthers, however, it is so perceived.

There are a number of reasons why the character of the parties, rather than the issues, shape the perceptions of an action effort. Issues often serve as a means to long-range ends which are vastly different from short-range ones. Another reason is that organizations devote considerable attention to creating images of themselves and develop reputations which condition perceptions of their activities. Banfield makes this point in regard to civic associations in Chicago:

Each association created for itself a corporate personality and aura. It has made itself both the custodian and the symbol, as well as the spokesman, of certain values. . . . The association's influence with the political heads and with prospective contributors, members, and supporters depends in part upon what it "represents" or symbolizes. Projecting the right image of itself is therefore essential to its maintainence as a going concern.[15]

Perceptions of issues and the tactics used are also shaped by past relationships between the parties. Having engaged in prior interaction leads each party to have expectations regarding the positions and behaviors of the other. As noted by Deutsch, the number and strength of cooperative bonds (e.g., superordinate goals, mutually facilitating interests, common allegiances and values, linkages to a common community) enhance present cooperation, while "experiences of failure and disillusionment in attempts to cooperate make it unlikely." [16]

The relationships of action and target systems are influenced by

[15] Edward C. Banfield, *Political Influence* (New York: Free Press, 1961), p. 273.

[16] Morton Deutsch, "Conflicts: Productive and Destructive," *Journal of Social Issues,* Vol. XXV, No. 1 (January 1969), p. 27.

their respective structures.[17] Often action and target systems are the same entity. The worker trying to change an agency policy, or the community group engaged in influencing its sponsor, constitute action and target systems operating within the same structure. Even when action and target systems are separate entities, individuals or groups within each structure may overlap or have intimate connections to relevant third parties. The Community Action Agency or groups which it supports (action system) engaged in modifying school practices (target) exemplifies overlapping entities, since school personnel may be on the CAA board, or actors from both systems may be related to relevant third parties, such as city officials. Finally, there are instances in which action and target systems are structurally discrete entities, as when independently organized community groups (action systems) press for changes in a welfare department (target system).

By and large, these structural relationships define the modes of intervention that can be invoked, as follows:

WHEN ACTION AND TARGET SYSTEMS ARE:	THE MODE OF INTERVENTION IS:
Part of same system	Collaborative (education, persuasion)
	Mild campaign (political maneuver)
Overlapping systems	Collaborative
	Campaign (mild coercion, bargaining)
Discrete systems	Collaborative
	Campaign
	Contest and disruptive tactics.

The more intimate the relations between action and target systems (i.e., when they are the same entity) and the less powerful the action system, the more likely it will be bound by consensual means. It is easier within a single structure—and, to a lesser degree, among overlap-

[17] For a sophisticated discussion of the connections between the structure of bureaucratic organizations and primary groups, the extent of social distance between them, and the varied ways in which this affects how they interact and influence one another, the reader is referred to the work of Eugene Litwak and his colleagues. One such discussion is Eugene Litwak and Henry J. Meyer, "A Balance Theory of Coordination between Bureaucratic Organizations and Community Primary Group," in Edwin Thomas, ed., *Behavioral Science for Social Workers* (New York: Free Press, 1967), pp. 246–62.

ping entities as well—for the more powerful party (the target system) to invoke sanctions than when relations with the action system are more distant. Furthermore, the closer the relationship, the more visible the action; and the greater its visibility, the more it can be controlled.

TACTICAL CREATIVITY:
SOME PRACTICE CONCERNS

In this section, we discuss some of the practice principles applicable to the modes of intervention which we have identified. Each mode (collaborative, campaign, and contest) constitutes a set or category of tactics, as indicated in the list below:[18]

MODE OF INTERVENTION	TACTICS
Collaborative	Problem solving
	Education
	Joint action
	Persuasion
Campaign	Political maneuvering
	Bargaining
	Negotiation
	Mild coercion
Contest or disruption	Clash of position within accepted social norms
	Violation of normative behavior
	Violation of legal norms

There are significant interrelations and overlap among these sets of tactics that make for difficulty in coherently exploring practice principles. Some technical concerns apply primarily to only one tactic on the list; others apply to a few of them; and there are practice principles which apply equally to all interventions. We deal only with the latter in this section as we discuss the following technical concerns: the development of a tactical game plan; research to be done

[18] We have omitted violence from our list of interventions (e.g., deliberate attempts to harm, guerrilla warfare, and attempts to take over the government by force), because these tactics are unavailable to professional organizers.

on the target; the uses of empathizing with the target; image management; and some elements in timing the action.

Game Plan. An organizer and group ought to have a good idea of what they plan to do before they set out to do it. They need to identify the essential players and, as in a game, anticipate as many of the moves as possible. Some factors to be addressed in the tactical plan have already been suggested: how an issue is likely to be perceived by the various actors; the resources available to the action system; the congruence of its resources with particular tactical choices; the target's relationship with the action system.

We wish to call attention to two other factors in game planning. The first is who is to be influenced by the action; and the second is the dynamics that are inherent in any attempt to exert influence.

The question of who is to be influenced is more complex than appears on the surface. The controversy between the advocates of black power and coalition politics is based, in part, on their respective views of whether black ghetto residents or white sympathizers of black causes ought to be appealed to. In this instance, the differing goals —to seek a black power base in the hope of long-range impact or to exact immediate and modest benefits for blacks—identify the respective targets of the appeal. Too often, however, goals are either poorly specified or they fail to clearly identify the appropriate target.

Frequently, community leaders must influence disparate groups simultaneously. Lipsky suggests that the problem of powerless groups is "to activate 'third parties' to enter the . . . bargaining arena in ways favorable to [them]. This is one of the few ways in which they can 'create' bargaining resources." [19] At the same time, the cohesion of the community group must be maintained and concessions won from institutional officials. In effect, leaders have to appeal to their constituents, third parties, and target institutions all at once. Each may be responsive to different types of messages and actions.

There are a number of ways in which leaders handle the problem of different audiences. One is to decide that one or another audience has primacy at a particular moment, so that appeals may be shifted from one to the other as circumstances warrant. A second is to segre-

[19] Michael Lipsky, "Protest as a Political Resource," *American Political Science Review,* Vol. XXV, No. 1 (January 1968), p. 1145.

gate the audiences, altering at least the tonal quality if not the content of the message as he speaks to each separately. Union negotiators have been known, for example, to emphasize one aspect of an issue when reporting to their membership and another in private conversation with management. Another means is to balance the message, so as to maximize the payoffs with one audience while minimizing the risks with another.

Another important factor which is often overlooked is the dynamic nature of attempts to exert influence. Whether educating, bargaining, or disrupting, community workers and groups must assess what response or retaliation is possible from the target as they plan their course of action. The proper use of influence must thus be judged on more than its utility as a reward or punishment; account must be taken of the counterresources the other may bring to bear. A community worker may, for example, help his group take an action which challenges the sponsor's policy, but the sponsor can fire him. The sponsor must, in turn, consider the consequences of firing the worker.

Provoking a reaction from the target is often necessary to the success of a community effort. The civil rights marches in the early 1960's did less to galvanize the conscience of the nation than the "overkill" of the sheriffs' firehoses and police dogs. Sometimes, preventing a target reaction is a condition of effectiveness. Raising the level of intensity of a community issue is unwise if it mobilizes a potent but hitherto dormant opposition.

Awareness of this dynamic is reflected in choice of target. Targets are selected on the basis of their power, or lack of power, to retaliate against the action system. The settlement house—which, for a time, was the *bête noire* of Alinsky's contest tactics—was an easy mark. It did not have the power to retaliate, and if it did, it could not have been repressive because of its value system. This is the reason why relatively benign institutions become the focus of virulent change attempts. Their norms prescribe a moderate rather than a coercive response.

Obviously, attempts to predict the responses of another party are highly uncertain. It is possible in developing a game plan, however, to estimate possible target responses, to assess the effect of each response on one's goal, and to be ready with alternative reactions to the response. To neglect the development of such a tactical balance sheet is to endanger not only the success of the effort but also the worker and the community group.

Researching the Target. The efficacy of a tactical game plan depends on the accuracy of the information about the target system it incorporates. Bureaucratic officials, recognizing the importance of information, tend to shield their operations from scrutiny, particularly from scrutiny of those who threaten their authority. Welfare officials, for example, have refused to allow client groups access to the regulations of their department, information which is routinely made available to social agencies.

In researching the target, the answer to three questions are almost always of major significance: Who makes the decision regarding the desired change? What rewards or punishments will impel the decision makers to make the change? What is the basis, or sanction, of the current policy?

Organizers and community groups frequently run a maze in trying to determine who makes the decisions in particular instances. The tactic of targets in denying their authority is particularly effective because it is so often true—although it is frequently the case that when sufficient pressure is brought to bear, authority to act is found. In any case, organizers must identify the structure of authority in an organizational or community chain of command and the legal or political constraints on the target. The choice of issue on which to take action might be contingent on the decision-making jurisdiction. Thus welfare groups initially chose issues which local administrators had the discretion to act on. Their demands were for the enforcement of the law, rather than its change—demands which were more likely to be won because of local jurisdiction and the accessibility of the decision makers.

A second matter for community action intelligence is to identify actions to which the target group's response will be positive and those it will want to avoid; in effect, to identify one's leverage. Leverage implies the use or threatened use of an action where acquiescence is in the target's self-interest. Organizers must identify "what's in it" for the other, so that they may call forth the desired response.

There are a number of leverage points generally available to community groups. One is the potential damage to a target's public image when the complainant's case has strong public appeal. Another is the response that can be elicited from the target's superordinates. High-ranking officials will pay some price to keep their agencies "out of the public eye." Thus they value administrators who are adept at soothing troubled waters, since they are aware that regardless of the merit of a complaint, some part of the public will sympathize with the complainants, whether it is justified or not.

An ill-considered complaint can backfire, however. When high-ranking officials and disinterested third parties have been prodded into action in response to protest, they become attentive to the evidence which supports a group's accusations. If charges are not sustained, an undesired outcome might result. For example, in an extreme case, the administrator who let the situation "get out of hand" might be replaced by one who uses repressive measures against the dissenters.

Another leverage point is the self-image of the target agency's officials. If they are professionals, internalized professional norms may require that they view themselves as client focused. However much their practice violates a client orientation, there is likely to be some tension between this professional standard and their willingness to enact a restrictive organizational policy. Appeals to their personal or professional sense of justice may therefore be effective. Such an appeal can maximize any divisiveness within the target institution and strengthen the hand of supporters within the target system.

Leverage points may be difficult to discern, and their discovery is often part of the change process. Important to such an assessment is the understanding, as implied above, that target groups are not monolithic. Organizations are essentially "a coming together of different interests, a 'political' coalition of subunits." [20] The task of the action system, then, is to ferret out those individuals or subunits of the target which might be most amenable to its arguments—either because the individual or unit is friendly to the action system's viewpoint, or vulnerable to its pressure.

[20] Edward Harvey and Russell Mills, "Patterns of Organizational Adaptation: A Political Perspective," in Mayer N. Zald, ed., *Power in Organizations* (Nashville: Vanderbilt University Press, 1970), p. 186.

Knowledge about the sanction or standing of the target agency's policies is an important element of intelligence. Bureaucracies abound in rules. Some regulations circumvent other regulations; some, like laws, remain in disuse or are differentially applied depending on whether it is in someone's interest to do so. In contentious situations, the actor who knows the rule, its applicability in particular instances, its "common law," administrative, or legal basis, is decidedly advantaged over the actor who does not. Unless the action system knows the specifics of the regulation it is trying to change—its basis and whether contradictory rules exist—it will have to depend for these matters on definitions given by the target. What may seem to be the facts of a case may be, in reality, only an interpretation. Even if it were not the target's intention to "double-talk," it would inevitably perceive facts from the perspective of its own self-interest. Wisdom would suggest independent investigation by the action system.[21]

Seaver indicates the importance of knowing the regulations when contending with the welfare department:

When the local welfare department realizes it is faced with a knowledgeable clientele, the whole atmosphere improves—particularly if the feeling can be generated . . . that the county is crawling with self-taught welfare experts. The most helpful regulations in terms of pressuring the welfare department are the federal regulations requiring a maximum 30 days for a notice of disposition.[22]

It is important, in assessing a target system, to separate one's feelings about the target from cognitive tactical judgments. Camus wrote: "My greatest wish: to remain lucid in ecstacy." [23] And that, in effect, is the task of the professional organizer. In addition to the emotional commitment he brings to organizing, the worker must be sufficiently

[21] A caution ought be noted. In collaborative ventures there is a risk in independent investigation, since it implies a lack of trust in the target. The action system would thus have to weigh whether the trust of the target was more or less important than surety regarding the facts of the policy in any particular situation.

[22] Ted Seaver, "The Care and Feeding of Southern Welfare Departments," in Paul A. Kurzman, ed., The Mississippi Experience (New York: Association Press, 1971), p. 54.

[23] Quoted in Edgar H. Schein and Warren G. Bennis, Personal and Organizational Change through Group Methods: The Laboratory Approach (New York: Wiley, 1966), p. 46.

objective to judge the intentions and interests of the target with clarity and predict the range of its potential responses. The standard is, of course, not easy to meet. One study has shown, for example, that interviewers with strong political attitudes did not accurately record interviewees' responses, and that the direction of error was consistent with the direction of the interviewer's political bias.[24] Similarly, studies indicate that outside groups are undervalued in comparison to one's own, and that in competitive situations they are undervalued even more.[25] What can be asked of the professional, however, is sufficient self-consciousness so that while he cannot reach the unreachable, he can attempt to approach it.

Empathizing with the Target. A related expectation of the organizer is that he empathize with the target. To observe, hear, and understand the target permits more informed tactical judgments and increased tactical options.

Unfortunately, in their anti-establishment ethos, organizers sometimes lose sight of the fact that target systems are composed of people. Indeed, some organizers may be "turned off" by the very notion of empathy for the target. The strategic usefulness of empathy for the target varies with circumstances and modes of intervention. It may be most important to collaborative action, since shared understanding is required in a collaborative process. Empathy is also more necessary for workers who act from within a target system than from outside of it,[26] since sustained interaction requires that the organizer approach the other as a person rather than as an object.

However, empathy for the target is also useful in campaign and contest tactics. If nothing else, identifying with the other's problems can suggest where pressure may be applied most tellingly. Objective political judgment is increased when a worker can separate a person from his social role and limit his predisposition to blame. But this

[24] Herbert Fisher, "Interviewer Bias in the Recording Operation," *International Journal of Opinion and Attitude Research,* Vol. 4 (Spring 1950), p. 393, as quoted in Raymond L. Gorden, *Interviewing* (Homewood, Ill.: Dorsey Press, 1969), p. 135.

[25] Bernard M. Bass and George Dunteman, "Biases in the Evaluation of One's Own Group, Its Allies and Opponents," *The Journal of Conflict Resolution,* Vol. VII, No. 1 (March 1963).

[26] It should be kept in mind that action and target systems may be subsystems of a larger entity, or may even have overlapping membership.

understanding has its limit. It must not extend to acting as if the worker *is* the other. It is one thing to understand the pressures faced by an actor in the political arena, but quite another to be unwilling to exert pressure oneself because of that understanding.

Image Management. However much spontaneity and free expression are prized in social interaction, it must be recognized that individuals say and do things to influence the perceptions of others toward themselves. Goffman has argued that the basic underlying theme of all interaction is the desire of each participant to guide and control the responses made by the others present.[27] The attempt to influence impressions about ourselves, and to control the definitions of situations in which we're involved, may often be unconscious and ingrained in one's "life-style." But there are many occasions when it is intentional and conscious.

Image management does not necessarily mean giving a false impression. A group may wish to replace a stereotype with a more accurate definition. For example, a professional organizer, meeting with a union official who saw social workers as well-intentioned ladies, decided to appear rough hewn to revise the false image. Sometimes, on the other hand, impression management entails projecting ambiguous images to obscure what is real. Sometimes, too, a picture may be embroidered out of whole cloth.

Unlike persons, organizations are only conceptions based on agreements and commitments among people. And, also unlike persons, the conception of an organization can only be transmitted as an *image*. No one can *see* an organization, but they can hear of its size, read its literature, meet its members, learn about its activities—all of which constitute an organization's image. In considerable measure, the success of a leader rests on his ability to manage that image. Those who overdo it appear to others as so much "sounding brass and tinkling cymbals;" those who fail to fully develop the organization's image are squandering a useful resource.

The desired image varies with the tactics selected. In educating and persuading, trust is emphasized and difference deemphasized. The intent is to promote a sense of confidence, of command over

[27] Erving Goffman, *The Presentation of Self in Everyday Life* (New York: Doubleday, Anchor Books, 1959), pp. 3–4.

material, and possession of knowledge and expertise. At the other extreme, in contest interventions, actors play a different role. Objectives tend to be overstated. "Demands" replace "requests," since "demands" imply determination and resolve, whereas "requests" suggest reasonableness and subordination. The aim is to connote anger, righteousness, and a groundswell of support for change.

A useful tactic, as a matter of fact, is to obscure the very tactic one is pursuing. In other words, there is a political advantage in seeming to be nonpolitical (as every expert knows). For example, one may ask for information under the guise of collaborating, when the actual intent of the request is to monitor the other so that the information seeker may intervene to prevent action.

However, one must not be seen as image making. Blau's counsel to individuals in social interaction is applicable more broadly:

> To make a good impression, a person must infer which of his qualities would do so in a given group and adapt his conduct accordingly. Self-conscious concern with impressing others, however, can easily become self-defeating. . . . If others suspect him of deliberately putting up a front, he will have made an unfavorable impression. Creating a good first impression is a subtle form of bragging, but its success depends on its being so natural that it does not appear to be bragging at all.[28]

Timing the Action. The order and pace of any process shape its outcome. Timing is a tactical consideration of community workers and groups, whatever the mode of intervention.

It is in the interests of those engaged in community work to effectuate an action as early in a process as possible. In the field of intergroup relations, one maneuver of this sort is known as the *fait accompli,* whereby change is initiated swiftly and unequivocally. The integration of Southern public schools proceeded most successfully, for example, in cities where officials acted quickly and firmly. Allport suggests one reason for such an outcome: "Clear-cut administrative decisions that brook no further argument are accepted when such decisions are in keeping with the voice of conscience."[29] Actions which reflect prevailing values are more likely to gain acceptance

[28] Peter M. Blau, *Exchange and Power in Social Life* (New York: Wiley, 1964), p. 39.

[29] Gordon W. Allport, *The Nature of Prejudice* (New York: Doubleday, Anchor Books, 1958), p. 471.

through the *fait accompli*. Slavin indicates another reason for its effi-cacy. He notes that "Where feelings run deep . . . the *fait accompli* attempts to set action . . . before opposing forces have time to mobi-lize their resources and develop momentum for counterattack." [30] He suggests that this point is generally recognized in such instances as armies which are committed before war is declared, political deals which are made before legislation is proposed, and social agency pol-icies which are implemented before they are announced. Ordinarily, of course, the *fait accompli* is more often used *against* rather than *by* community groups.

The earlier one engages in any decision-making process, the greater the impact on the decision itself. In making an early move, one usurps "the power of definition," and as a decision progresses, it becomes harder to modify. The point is suggestive in two ways. Workers and community groups must, in the first instance, seek to enter any development process early in the game. Their impact on planning community housing is less, for example, when they are asked to react to plans which have already been drawn. Conversely, they must try to prevent too early intrusion of the target system into their own planning.

Furthermore, an action taken in the early stages of a process can later be invested with meaning which was not fully understood or ex-plicit in the initial action. A first step can thus be defined retrospec-tively as a moral commitment to a fuller action, thereby making it more difficult for the target to turn back. For example, a group may achieve recognition as the bargaining agent for a constituency when the issue around which they seek to bargain is an appealing one to the target. Only later need they raise more contentious matters.

Time may be a neutral or critical factor in any intervention. When a situation is in flux, timing is ordinarily critical. If, for example, a policy decision is pending, immediate action might determine its shape or delay might foreclose its outcome by default. Under these circumstances, a community organization could move before it was "ready," become "ready" more quickly, or face a more difficult situa-tion at some later point. On the other hand, in less dynamic situa-

---

[30] Simon Slavin, "Concepts of Social Conflict: Use in Social Work Curricu-lum," *Journal of Education for Social Work,* Vol. 5, No. 1 (Fall 1969), p. 57.

tions, neither the target nor community events are likely to be altered significantly by the passage of time, and it makes little difference when an action is begun in such time-neutral circumstances. Victories may be won or lost by discriminating accurately between these two aspects of time. Thus a tactical game plan should include, in addition to what a group expects to do, a rough estimate of when it will do it, and what circumstances might require that it slow down or speed up the process.

An action system which desires third party support must appear reasonable and responsible to that party. Or it must, at the least, be able to present an effective public case to explain its unreasonableness. One means of accomplishing this is through attention to the sequence of its tactical behaviors. To justify its actions, it must avoid "jumping" the process which a third party considers to be correct. Protocol prescribes that certain moves must precede others, and that when actions escalate, the escalation be in response to the target's recalcitrance rather than a reflection of the action system's immoderation. An agency staff member, for example, must exhaust lower-echelon channels before he can appeal to the executive. Or if he skirts the channels, he must not appear to be doing so. A community group pressing for school change must seek to meet with school officials prior to taking to the streets—even if they believe that nothing will come of the meetings.

There are risks in this position. A major one is that the target system can deplete the community group of strength and energy through its own "moderate" response. It can dispense symbolic or token rewards in place of real ones, and it can postpone action through such a ubiquitous device as a committee to study the problem. Since community groups are inherently unstable, token satisfactions and postponements further strain their cohesiveness and staying power. The solution is to expose the target's "moderation" for what it really is when the group finds it necessary to escalate its tactics rather than to ignore the niceties of process. This is particularly important when the issue is one which makes the target publicly vulnerable. When a target system is on uncertain ground regarding the substance of a disagreement, it will inevitably decry the process which is used and challenge the tactics of its adversaries.

We have, in this chapter, discussed the tactics of community work, the association of tactics with perceptions about community issues, the resources of the actors, and the relationship of action and target systems. We have also explored some of the technical concerns of organizers and community groups which are applicable to all tactics. We turn, in the following chapter, to some of the ethical issues with which the tactician is confronted.

CHAPTER THIRTEEN

POLITICAL MANEUVER:
THE ETHICS OF TACTICS

FOR MANY SOCIAL WORKERS, the use of the words "strategy" and "tactics" rather than "long-range goal" and "method" is discomfiting. Whether this is due to the military antecedents of the words, or because they suggest grand design and nefarious measures, is not immediately apparent. What is clear is that it is not possible to discuss tactics in community work without raising questions of morality.

Such questions arise particularly when tactics require the worker or group to be political. "Political maneuver," by which we mean maneuvering for position or manipulating others, is listed in chapter 12 as a campaign tactic, but we discuss it now for two reasons. For one thing, it refers to behaviors which are often present in the use of *any* tactic. Most collaborative efforts contain *some* political maneuvering and, in the final analysis, all power tactics involve some degree of manipulation of others. More important, since the words conjure up pictures of dishonest dealings in back rooms—an activity not ordinarily esteemed by professionals—the tactic lends itself to a discussion of ethics.

We wish, in using the words "maneuvering and manipulation" to connote artfulness in inducing a desired attitudinal or behavioral outcome in others. This includes, but is not limited to, the covert exercise of influence. Parties engage in maneuver and manipulation when they have insufficient resources to resolve differences in their favor by other means, or when it is believed that an overt display of power will have undue negative side effects.

This chapter has two sections. In the first, we discuss professional ethics in regard to maneuver and manipulation. Since values influence, and are influenced by, matters of effectiveness and expediency, in the second section we consider the pragmatic factors which lead to the use or avoidance of manipulation.

THE MORALITY OF
MANIPULATIVE BEHAVIOR

Covert influence—or manipulation—has long been considered out of professional bounds. There are, in our judgment, good reasons for this tenet. By and large, the methods and value constructs of professions deal with worker-client relationships, rather than the interaction of the worker with other systems which impinge on clients. A regulative code of professional ethics insures the client that he will not be tricked or cheated, and fosters the client trust which is essential to the helping relationship, for this trust is violated when the worker engages in manipulative acts. Furthermore, a contract in which one person is the helped, the other the helper, implies a disparity of influence. Clients who are dependent on the professional to begin with ought not to be subject to the double jeopardy of worker guile.

There are particular complexities, however, in defining the client of the community organizer. The term "client" usually refers to one who engages the services of a professional, and in this sense, social workers do not ordinarily have clients. In social work usage the term connotes those whose interests are served. This has been taken to mean persons in interaction with the professional. In community organizing, however, contact is often with the providers, rather than the recipients, of service. Defining the client system to mean those who are intended to benefit from the worker's activity, rather than those with whom he is in direct contact, alters one's professional perspective. Prescriptions are different when the beneficiaries of a committee's process, and therefore the primary concern of the professional, are not the participants. His activity may then be evaluated by how well he represents the absent client rather than how well he services the committee member.

Generalizing from worker-client interaction to all of the worker's relationships in community organization oversimplifies the issue in any case. Organizers function at the fulcrum of a field of interacting interests: community elites, agents of government, organization officials from their own and other service agencies, colleagues, and the like. To act in his constituency's interests, the organizer must walk a tightrope between the conflicting demands of all these actors. Thus operating within a political arena, he faces the dilemma of being "ethical" on the one hand, and fulfilling his obligation to his constituents as effectively as possible, on the other.

It is not facetious to suggest that when other means are available, manipulation ought be avoided. The fact is, however, that organizers and their constituents are hardly in a commanding position. The constituents are themselves often the objects of manipulation by important others. They are least likely to be involved in community decision-making processes or, when involved, to be influential participants. Nor is the social worker a powerful figure in our society. His authority is weak and his resources for influencing community affairs are sharply circumscribed. Fear of abusing his power through its untrammeled application is, in this context, unrelated to reality. For the social worker, who serves as a role model, to eschew manipulative behavior, or to counsel his constituents to avoid it, even indirectly, is to diminish even further the ability of the disadvantaged to obtain a redistribution of resources. Thus professional purity may be most costly to the victims of social problems.

Professional purity is, in any case, impossible. If, as we believe, manipulation is an unavoidable component of professional behavior, it is well to recognize it. Only by being aware that it cannot be avoided can it be handled, limited, or resisted.

In studies of manipulation, Richard Christie developed a scale which was based on statements from Machiavelli's writings concerning the ways in which people view one another and their means of influencing the behavior of others. The scale, intended to measure the respondent's acceptance of manipulation or use of guile in interpersonal relations, appears to have predictive validity: academicians who were identified by their colleagues as "smooth operators" scored higher than others.[1] In laboratory experiments involving a series of three-person games, those who scored high on the scale were consistently and dramatically the victors.[2]

Unfortunately, there have been no samples of social workers in these experiments. Although a related professional group, the social psychologists, score consistently high as a group compared to other professionals, studies of the medical profession are most interesting. Physicians' scores vary by their medical specialization. The scores in descending order were as follows: psychiatry, pediatrics, internal medicine, obstetrics, and surgery.[3] These findings are reported not to indicate that psychiatrists are less principled than their fellow physicians or the rest of us, but to point up Christie's interpretation that the degree of interpersonal manipulation required by professional role is the most salient factor in explaining his test responses. Persons in social roles that require influencing others, Christie notes, are more in agreement with Machiavelli than persons oriented primarily to the manipulation of things or pure ideas.[4] Manipulative behavior, then, may be an inevitable concomitant of job roles and tasks.

Since community organizers fill roles and perform tasks that require influencing others, they can be expected to use guile. A study of the role of neighborhood coordinators in Pittsburgh's antipoverty program is illustrative. A survey of citizens and welfare department staff regarding the coordinators' performances reveals that a coordinator's role and loyalty were perceived differentially by the two groups. Operating in a context in which there were conflicting pressures, a coordinator apparently maintained his position by presenting a different face to different groups.[5]

[1] Richard Christie, "The Prevalence of Machiavellian Orientations," paper presented at the annual meeting of the American Psychological Association, Los Angeles, September 1964. (Mimeographed)

[2] Florence Geis, "Machiavellianism and the Manipulation of One's Fellow Man," paper presented at the annual meeting of the American Psychological Association, Los Angeles, September 1964. (Mimeographed)

[3] Christie, "The Prevalence of Machiavellian Orientations," pp. 12–13.

[4] *Ibid.*, p. 14.

[5] Neil Gilbert, "Neighborhood Coordinator: Advocate or Middleman?" *Social Service Review*, Vol. 43, No. 2 (June 1969), pp. 136–44.

Although we have argued that political maneuvering is at times desirable and may be inevitable, we do not by any means propose a moratorium on morality. Rather, it is necessary for professional guidelines to be imposed on the use of manipulative methods, that is, to consider the circumstances under which they are professionally justified or appropriate, in regard to whom, and within what limits.

Each circumstance must be assessed on the basis of its gestalt. Broadly, standards used to guide the worker relate to: (1) who benefits and who loses; (2) the object of the activity; (3) the substance of the issue; and (4) the nature of the act.

Who benefits and Who Loses. The service ideal of professionals requires that the end of manipulative behavior must not be the interest of the professional himself. Although this rule is often breached in reality, unconsciously and otherwise, such behavior should not be condoned. The justification for violation of a value must be its inherent conflict with some other value of equal or greater import. It follows, then, that manipulation should be eschewed *except* when it clearly supports another, overriding, value. The magnitude of the need, the powerlessness of the constituent, and the rules of the game as played by adversaries dictate the conclusion that manipulation is sometimes justified.

It is not justified to further the professional's self-interest. At one end of the continuum in our scale of values is the disadvantaged and powerless constituent; at the other, the professional himself. Midway between the two are the interests of other constituents and one's agency.

Certain cautions must be introduced before manuevering or manipulation may be counseled, even in the "best interests" of the constituent. One has to do with risk. For example, a strategy may be pursued that is in the long-term interest of the client but that risks losses to him in the short run. Thus a worker advocating a rent strike to improve tenement housing may, ethically, try to convince tenants to withhold rents no matter what the cost. But he must neither impose nor manipulate the acceptance of his opinion. Instead, he must make clear to them what their choices are and the dangers that might be involved, however this may inhibit the success of the effort. We have said elsewhere in this volume that one objective of community organization is to maximize constituency choice and competence. When the worker decides that the outcome of the process must be as he ordains it *despite* his constituency's outlook or the risk to them, he has violated their trust.

The Object of the Activity. Manipulation by the worker occurs most understandably when he is dealing with target systems, next so when the manipulation is of action systems (including his agency), and least understandable in dealing with constituents. Four considerations which determine these differences are: (1) the similarity of objectives between the worker and others, (2) the quality of their interaction, (3) their relative influence, and (4) the rules by which the game is played.

When there is similarity of both objectives and interaction that permits shared understanding, as is the case with professionals in their dealings with most constituents and many action systems, manipulative behavior violates a trust. On the other hand, as disparity of influence widens between parties and interaction is reduced, political maneuvering becomes more understandable and more justifiable. And if the structure of an action group is such that it inhibits or forecloses decision making by or interaction with constituents, manipulative behavior may be the only feasible response.

As organizers have become involved in arenas other than social services, the rules of the game tend to shift. To play by one's own rules without cognizance of the other's may be to suffer severe disadvantage (although again, perhaps, only to constituents). One sharp illustration would be when a government official lies in his dealings with social workers. For example, when Mobilization for Youth was under attack, it was discovered that New York City's deputy mayor was feeding false information to the press. When confronted by agency officials, the deputy mayor categorically denied, contrary to all evidence, that he had made the statements. Since he was in a position to further harm the agency and its constituents, it could hardly be expected that agency officials would feel bound to be candid in their dealings with him.

The Substance of the Issue. A third important standard in evaluating the appropriateness of manipulation relates to the values inherent in the substantive issue. Risks to life and limb, deprivations which deny the meeting of basic physical needs, and violation of legal rights are areas that justify political intervention more so than others. Thus manipulation by, or on behalf of, the victims in a case of clear social injustice might be appropriate, for example, on behalf of clients who, through deception or threat, are unable to register a grievance when they are denied welfare benefits. Similarly, one could condone a lie, even to a client, to entice a potential suicide off a ledge, although one might be highly critical of such behavior in other instances.

The Nature of the Act. The nature of the act is a fourth factor in evaluating the ethic of worker maneuvering. Manipulative acts vary in their degree of concealment; some are barely so, while others are clearly meant to deceive. In the next chapter, for example, we note how moderate and extreme messages are variously used to convince message recipients. The worker who self-consciously adjusts the intensity level of his message in order to be persuasive may be telling the whole truth, but he is nonetheless attempting to influence, albeit covertly. Yet this is of a different order of morality from the invention of a message out of whole cloth.

Manipulative behavior may include truth arranged for effect, withheld information, exaggeration, distortion, or an outright lie. The supervisor who counsels a graduate student worker not to indicate his student status to his constituency is encouraging the withholding of information. The worker who overstates his client's strength because it is "helpful" to the client to be supported is an example of exaggeration. These may be professional stretchings-of-the-point, but they do not violate professional sensibilities. There are, in other words, different orders of morality depending on the nature of the manipulative act. In our view, the appropriateness of such behavior can only be evaluated by weighing the nature of the act itself in balance with the other standards that have been suggested.

The Worker's Sanction. Ordinarily, sanction stems from the organization which hires the professional. If, however, as we have suggested, the worker's agency is the target of his manipulation, the question of sanction must be addressed. In such a case, from where does his social license stem? There are three considerations: the client; the profession; and the purposes of the program.

One source of social license stems from the client; in other words, the worker's accountability in meeting client needs and following client dictates. This is not an issue in professions in which the practitioner is paid directly by the client. In social work, the social agency constitutes a powerful intermediary between practitioner and client which, although it creates strain, does not inherently affect the moral question. Sanction stems from client needs and wishes nevertheless.

Although sanction stems from the client, it does *not* stem from the worker's conception of the client's "best interests," apart from the latter's involvement. The professional organizer may attempt to convince his constituency to pursue particular ends in particular ways (sometimes he has a responsibility to do so), but unless his constituency is in accord, the client does not provide sanction. However fervent his ideology, his reforming zeal, or his identification with the poor, none of these offer social license to the worker *in his professional capacity.*

A second source of sanction stems from the standards of behavior established by the profession. Criteria are "soft" in all professions, perhaps more so in social work than others. The Code of Ethics of the National Association of Social Workers is general, but provisions such as the following are suggestive:

I regard as my primary obligation the welfare of the individual or the group served, which includes action to improve social conditions.[6]

The NASW Ad Hoc Committee on Advocacy which studied these questions commented as follows on the above passage:

It is implicit, but clear, in this prescript that the obligation to the client takes primacy over the obligation to the employer, where the two interests compete with one another.[7]

Essentially, however, such statements have limited value, and standards stem from consensual, often implicit, norms which are widely held. Although the ideals and objectives of social work support the ends to which political maneuvering may be put, the behavior itself

[6] NASW Ad Hoc Committee on Advocacy, "The Social Worker as Advocate: Champion of Social Victims," *Social Work,* Vol. 14, No. 2 (April 1969), p. 18.

[7] *Ibid.,* p. 18.

receives scant justification. Only some of the professional "young turks" ordinarily assert it is justified.

A third consideration in regard to worker sanction is the *stated* purpose of the program. The professional may, justifiably, be guided by the explicit intentions of the legislation, the organization's charter, or the specific program proposal under which he operates. Is it ethical, one must ask, for a professional to accept an agency's distortion of a program's purpose which stems from agency needs to maintain itself, but violates the legal, moral, or philosophical purposes of the program? Or is it more ethical to circumvent such program distortion through manipulation if the latter is necessary? A typical example is the hospital which obtained money to develop a viable health council, but which subsequently ensured, through its policies and procedures, that consumers would play no active role in shaping health policy. The worker's moral responsibility, then, is to the program rather than the organization. Such a situation justifies the worker's leaking information secretly to the funding source when other efforts to reverse the situation have proved fruitless.

However much one might wish for simple rules to guide professional behavior, the day-to-day practice of organizing is replete with moral dilemmas. In regard to maneuvering and manipulating, the dilemmas are mitigated somewhat when factors of effectiveness or expediency are taken into account. Although we have thus far limited our discussion to value issues, these are not separable from pragmatic concerns.

MANEUVERING: SOME PRAGMATIC CONCERNS

Relationships with other actors and the nature of the situation in which the organizer finds himself influence his decision to be manipulative. In this section we first consider the matter of relationships, particularly as relationships inhibit or increase the risk in maneuvering politically. Following this, we identify two components of political maneuver which are part of the organizer's armamentarium: manipulative communication and putting norms and rules to political use.

The Nature of the Relationship. The potential costs of political maneuver must be assessed against the potential gains. Organizers must take care not to use up their moral currency too quickly, as happens when a worker develops a reputation for guile. If his motives are suspect, if he is perceived as always carrying hidden agenda, and if his word is of dubious value, he can hardly practice effectively. In the long run, a professional's reputation for integrity may be more valuable than an immediate victory. Indeed, the very people in whose interests he dissembles may wonder about the reliability of the dissembler even as they accept the benefit of the deception.

Individuals and groups are differentially tolerant of being the target of manipulation. The value prescriptions mentioned earlier are relevant in this regard. People are more likely to be charitable toward guile exercised on behalf of disadvantaged clients concerning a significant issue than toward guile exercised in a professional's self-interest or concerning a matter of small moment. Expectations regarding appropriate behavior shape judgments about that behavior, and thus the potential risk of engaging in it. In community work, three types of relationships or situations minimize or maximize the hazards of manipulative behavior.

In adversary situations there is considerable margin for political maneuver; both parties ordinarily expect it, and discovery would cause little further disruption. Target systems are thus safer candidates. The welfare worker whom the organizer is flattering, cajoling, disputing, intimidating, or threatening on behalf of his constituents questions the organizer's information, quietly assesses his strength, and is not shocked at the thought that he is somewhat lacking in candor.

The matter is circular, however. Although adversary relationships allow for guile, guile shapes relationships as well. If the welfare worker were friendly, the organizer's dissembling could create an adversary where none might otherwise have existed. The organizer must thus distinguish between opponents and friends—which is simple enough in concept, but not always obvious in practice. When potential friends in target organizations are indiscriminately defined as "the enemy," they are likely to live up to the expectation. When opponents have been correctly defined, however, the organizer's risk in being manipulative is limited.

Situations short of conflict, in which there are differences of interest clear to both parties, allow a smaller margin of safety. The prospective employer hardly expects complete openness from the job applicant. The professor is likely to expect to be, in some measure, "conned" by the student. The behavior becomes problematic only when it is done without grace, is the student's predominant way of relating, or takes place after a significant relationship has developed between them.

In an ongoing collaborative relationship the dangers of manipulation are significant. Here, trust is expected between the parties and discovery may seriously damage the attainment of immediate objectives. More important, it may damage the relationship. Manipulation in an on-going relationship which contravenes the rules understood by both parties is not only of dubious morality but fraught with risk. Thus are questions of values and questions of expedience interfaced.

Manipulative Communication. Manipulating the flow of information is a means of avoiding influence or exercising it. Communications which regulate the flow of information is a vast subject, much beyond our scope. We wish only to identify three of the techniques which communicators use in political situations to consciously control information with the intention of making-things-seem-what-they-are-not: ambiguity and "sounding out," content selectivity, and attention diversion.

The organizational uses of planned ambiguity have already been discussed.[8] "Sounding out," a process which Thompson describes, is a form of ambiguity often employed in trading when one party wishes to estimate the willingness of the other to enter into or change the relationship, without at the same time revealing his own position.[9] Thompson illustrates the process with the boss who has designs on his secretary, must determine her willingness, but at the same time, do so without rebuff, since the latter would be costly. He "sounds her

[8] See chapter 6.

[9] James D. Thompson and William J. McEwen, "Organizational Goals and Environment: Goal-Setting as an Interaction Process," in Mayer N. Zald, ed., *Social Welfare Institutions* (New York: Wiley, 1965), pp. 416–17.

out" ambiguously, so that she can either ignore the proposal or indicate receptiveness. A form of double talk is often employed. The parties employ euphemisms, refer to hypothetical situations, or transmit messages through a third party. In this way, neither party manifestly carries the responsibility for initiating or rejecting the exchange.

"Sounding out" has important uses in community bargaining, as does the indirect or implied threat. Both allow one to communicate without taking responsibility for the content of the communication. If a bluff is involved, it is a bluff which cannot be called since, on the face of it, the bluff was never made. It lets one deny the intent of the communication when conditions so require.

Selecting a content to omit from a communication is another means of manipulating information. To be successfully executed, however, it must *appear* that all of the salient information has been shared. Budget-setters typically use this gambit. They present a total budget in which the categories are so contrived that important or controversial aspects of the budget are eliminated or obscured. We may suspect too that social agency recording carries its fair share of such consciously selected-out information.

A third technique of manipulative communication is to divert attention from the relevant information in order to "cover oneself" from the accusation of having withheld data while, in effect, the data are withheld. It may be achieved by burying the information in a mass of irrelevancy, or by drawing attention to other aspects of the communication through emphasis or interest-arousing language. The former tactic was employed by a social work student placed in a welfare department which dropped AFDC mothers from the rolls if they were known to cohabitate. On a home visit, she surprised her client in a compromising circumstance and, shaken by the discovery, she agonized about whether to include it in the record she was required to write for her field instructor. She decided to make reference to the matter to protect herself, but only in passing and embedded in a mass of other verbiage. At their conference, her field instructor made no reference to the matter. The supervisor may not have noticed the detail but, more probably, her silence occurred because the student's maneuver allowed the supervisor to cover herself. She could assert, if necessary, that the item had escaped her notice. In effect, then, diverting attention from salient information in a communication also allows superordinates the option of ignoring the data if they wish to.

Manipulative communication finds its flowering in a worker's desire to circumvent agency policy. It is perhaps fitting to conclude this section with the advice of a government official on the art of writing memorandums. He suggests that when a superior must be implicated, but hopefully not informed about an impending action, a memorandum should be thoughtfully constructed as follows:

Make it long and dull. Make the subject sound highly technical. Send a faint carbon or a bad xerox. See that it is delivered late Friday afternoon.[10]

The Use of Rules and Norms. Management of relationships requires planning one's actions and shaping one's words in ways attentive to existing belief systems and putting accepted rules and norms to work on behalf of one's objectives. It is a form of manipulative behavior which involves little risk.

In a cogent analysis of community power, Bachrach and Baratz observe that political systems develop "a set of predominant values, beliefs, rituals, and institutional procedures ('rules of the game') that operate systematically and consistently to the benefit of certain persons and groups at the expense of others."[11] They note that, as a result, challenges to the elite definers of these predominant values are thwarted by invoking the existing bias of the system. Thus "a demand for change may be denied legitimacy by being branded socialistic, unpatriotic, immoral, or in violation of an established rule or procedure."[12]

One tactic by which to counter this sort of offensive is to redefine existent values and beliefs. Essentially, this is an objective of women's liberation and other such movements. The aim of direct action may frequently be less to win a concession from an opponent than to "turn around" the minds of a larger audience, or at least to get them thinking.

[10] Joseph Porter Clerk, Jr., "The Culture of Bureaucracy: The Art of the Memorandum," *Washington Monthly* (March 1969), p. 61.

[11] Peter Bachrach and Morton S. Baratz, *Power and Poverty* (New York: Oxford University Press, 1970), p. 44.

[12] *Ibid.*, p. 45.

Another countermove is to use existent values in the service of one's own cause. This may take three forms. One is to argue in the context of values which are preached but not practiced, such as appealing to the collective conscience in citing equal rights as justification for a change attempt. A second form of using extant values is to join two widely esteemed values in the service of one of them, (e.g., peace is patriotic). Finally, there is a form of behavior in which the tactician *assumes* that thing are as-they-ought-to-be. An example is the community group which does not petition for its demands, but takes for granted that the demands have been (or will be) met. Instead of demanding seats on the policy-making board, the group asserts that "since the poor are supposed to constitute a majority on the board, the action taken is illegal." All discussion is pressed into the framework of the assumption, and participants act "as if" it were so. At some later point a formal agreement has to be made on what it was the group assumed, but the terms of the settlement may have been "upped" by the ploy. The tactic constitutes an attempt to construct a "self-fulfilling" prophecy and requires a high degree of audaciousness, discipline, and effective organization.

When a group has limited power, or wishes not to arouse potential opposition, its political stance may be to cast as wide a value net as possible, perhaps framing its demand for innovation as though it consists of no change at all. An example of Jesus' artfulness in this regard is cited by Haley:

Throughout his public life Jesus managed to call attention to himself as an authority who was presenting new ideas. At the same time, he defined what he said as proper orthodoxy. He achieved this feat in two ways: first, he insisted that he was not suggesting a change and then called for a change, and second he insisted that the ideas he was presenting were not deviations from the established religion but a more true expression of the ideas of that religion.[13]

A more recent example is provided by the Henry Street Settlement in New York. In radically altering its program, the Settlement developed a policy statement which read in part as follows: "The statement is fully in accord with the history of Henry Street. It selects from that history a particular emphasis and highlights it as a central

[13] Jay Haley, *The Power Tactics of Jesus Christ* (New York: Grossman, 1969), p. 23.

purpose." [14] We suspect that the words are as much a bid for the support of Henry Street "old-timers" as a reflection of historical fact. Apparently, there are occasions when change viewed as no-change is the most feasible way to attain change.

Applied to organizations, the tactic is to form the action effort in the context of the organization's existent values and maintenance needs (i.e., morality and self-interest are a potent combination). Artfulness in doing this requires that one observes the organizational amenities whenever possible. An example is a worker "touching base" by informing interested parties what he is about, to avoid the accusation of by-passing authority, or needlessly creating opponents by ruffling sensitivities. Amenities may be stretched when a worker understands the range of the permissible, such as the thin line between informing a supervisor and asking permission. Politically sensitive workers know when and where to locate themselves in relation to that line.

Organizational policies may be put to the service of nonorganizational ends. Rules are devised to meet finite circumstances, to apply to conditions which may have subsequently changed. They are also used to promote a particular organizational image. Rule A, which was intended to apply to situation X, may be invoked to meet the requirements of situation Y. Thus, bureaucratic "war horses" know how to use one set of rules to justify an action, and another set to prevent it, depending on their preference. If an organization's rules were applied to the letter of the law, it might prove, at best, administratively burdensome, and at worst, threatening to the organizational system. Thus, Alinsky counsels as one rule of gamesmanship: "Make the enemy live up to their own book of rules. You can kill them with this, for they can no more obey their own rules than the Christian church can live up to Christianity." [15]

In discussing the ethics of tactics, we have argued, by implication, that the age-old query, "Do the ends justify the means?" poses, if not a false dichotomy, an insufficient one. Salutary goals may, of course,

[14] National Federation of Settlements and Neighborhood Centers, *Making Democracy Work* (New York: NFSNC, 1968), p. 14.

[15] Saul Alinsky, *Rules for Radicals* (New York: Random House, 1971), p. 128.

be sought through immoral means—but morally pure measures can also lead inexorably to impure outcomes.[16] Ends and means are, in our view, mutually determining, and one cannot be evaluated, morally or otherwise, without reference to the other.

We have tried to suggest some guidelines for the tactical dilemmas which face the organizer: who benefits and who loses from worker manipulation; who is the object of the political behavior; the principle that is at issue; and the nature of the act itself. Fortunately, the organizer's stance is not dependent on values alone, but is mediated by questions of effectiveness and expediency. Maneuver and manipulation require a high order of skill, but some situations are more fraught with risk than others. Tactically adept organizers must be clear about the value issues, know the limits of their ability, have the acumen to assess risks accurately, and the dedication to take a chance.

[16] For a fictional example, see Frederick Duerrenmatt, *The Visit,* which portrays the execution of an innocent man in a Swiss town, following a process which was exemplary, including a town meeting in which all members of the community participated.

CHAPTER FOURTEEN

COLLABORATIVE TACTICS:
PERSUASION

COLLABORATIVE TACTICS include problem solving, education, joint action, and persuasion. In problem solving and education, information is assembled, alternatives examined, and mutually satisfying solutions are devised. Joint action entails the pooling of resources to attain joint goals; and persuasion involves some change of mind by the target to bring it into greater conformity with the action system. These interventions are useful under three circumstances: (a) when there are shared objectives between action and target systems; (b) when misunderstandings can be mediated rather than exacerbated by improved communication; and (c) when disagreements are sufficiently modest to be modified by reference to common interest.

We devote this chapter to a discussion of persuasion, because, of the collaborative interventions, it has been most neglected in the social work literature.[1] Yet, changing minds and shaping attitudes are major tasks in social-change-oriented practice, and skill in persuasion is an important skill in community work.

---

[1] One might choose almost any book at random which deals with social work methodology and find material on problem solving, education, and joint action. For some community organization examples, see William W. Biddle et al., *The Community Development Process* (New York: Holt, Rinehart and Winston, 1965); Arthur Dunham, *The New Community Organization* (New York: Thomas Y. Crowell, 1970); Murray Ross, *Community Organization:*

There are, of course, other ways than by direct face-to-face interaction to alter attitudes. These might be called "structural persuaders," since they rely on the use of changes in social arrangements to change beliefs. Underlying the use of structural persuasion is the implicit belief that structural change may precede and determine changes in attitudes and feelings. For example, a promotion from worker to supervisor, or a move from the lower to middle class, may induce the behavioral requirements of these new roles and attitudes supportive of the new behavior.

Co-optation is an example of structural persuasion. In bringing dissident elements into an organization, it is intended that their participation will revise their attitudes toward the organization. Legislation provides another example that, as Katz notes, may influence attitudes powerfully. This occurs when the law is directed against behavior rather than attitudes (e.g., against discriminatory practices rather prejudice), the behavior is regarded as in the public rather than the private domain, and when the legal authority is accepted (i.e., when vigorous and consistent application of the law supports its legitimacy).[2]

That changes in social arrangements may result in changes in attitudes is of profound importance for community work. In community development, for example, one of the major goals is community integration, the development of a "sense of neighborhood." The means to achieve this end is ordinarily an interactional process, for example, bringing people together, organizing neighborhood groups, and providing the opportunity for mutual self-help. Although the interactional aspects of the process merit attention, some of the technical aspects (e.g., goal development and program) are frequently overlooked. Consequently, particular means by which communality may be fostered are neglected. To mention only a few: the physical structure and location of dwellings; employment opportunities within the neighborhood; the political structure; the types of shopping available;

Theory and Principles (New York: Harper and Row, 1955). See also Ronald Lippett et al., *The Dynamics of Planned Change* (New York: Harcourt Brace, 1958).

[2] Daniel Katz, "The Functional Approach to the Study of Attitudes," in Otto Lerbinger and Albert J. Sullivan, eds., *Information Influence and Communication* (New York: Basic Books, 1965), p. 302.

policies which encourage one or another population mix in the public schools, and so on. Each may influence the sense of neighborhood more powerfully than the interactional process of a neighborhood council.

Our primary interest in this chapter, however, is in the means by which changes of mind occur from an interactional process, from a communicator imparting a message to a receiver. We draw on the considerable body of knowledge from social psychology, adapting it to community work. We have organized this chapter in the way many social psychologists deal with the subject by examining, in turn, each of the three elements of a persuasive attempt: the communicator, the message, and the audience.

One qualification is necessary before we begin. Persuasion is practiced in a wide range of situations without regard to the relationship of the communicator and message recipient. Persuasive techniques may be used with many audiences, such as constituents, other members of an action system, or targets. The appropriateness and effectiveness of the techniques vary with the extent of the interaction, and whether the contacts are on-going, limited, or one-time occasions. We shall not make these distinctions, however, since they will be contextually apparent.

THE COMMUNICATOR

The prestige, attractiveness, and credibility of the communicator to his audience, and the congruity of their values, influence the success of attempts to persuade.

Prestige and Attractiveness. It is obvious that prestige and attractiveness enhance persuasiveness. A prestigious speaker is convincing because his audience has faith in him, for example, in his knowledge, judgment, past successes, or good intentions. An attractive speaker is persuasive because his audience wants to please him. The former uses his reputation; the latter serves as a role model. Prestige and attractiveness are characteristics which community workers would do well to cultivate and husband against future needs to be convincing.

Prestige and attractiveness inhere in both personal attributes and social role, and are often beyond any organizer's ability to control. Two factors are manipulatable, however, one having to do with his own position, the other with his choice of channels for persuasive communications.

Role influences sentiment and, to a considerable degree, group position defines the regard in which one is held. The boss, for example, is a prestigious figure to his workers. Role and group memberships also impose behavioral expectations on incumbents. These expectations are often imprecise; role partners differ regarding appropriate role performance; and actual role behavior varies because of personal differences among incumbents. Nevertheless, although some variability is permissible, there are prescribed, if implicit, expectations. So, for example, *how* good or bad a boss is perceived to be depends on how well or poorly he meets worker's expectations in performing that role.

Workers may not be able to choose the positions they fill in groups and organizations. Once in a role, however, they can be sensitive to the expectations which inhere in that role. And although sensitivity to role expectations will not by itself ensure prestige or attractiveness, insensitivity may destroy both. The point is important in ongoing contacts, particularly when the worker is attempting to influence his own agency.

He must, in other words, take positions and frame arguments in the context of his role, however constraining this may be. An executive who wishes to influence his board may press a point of view vigorously, but he must stay within the range of the board's definition of appropriate administrative argument. A faculty member may argue a student-held position, but to maintain persuasiveness among his colleagues, he must argue it *as a faculty member* and without violating the norms of appropriate faculty discourse.[3]

A worker who is expected to advocate the interests of his clients within an agency is also expected to frame his advocacy as an agency "representative," and in the context of agency identification. He will

[3] This point assumes, of course, that he wishes to persuade faculty, not mobilize students, make himself attractive to them, or pursue some other strategy. There are many reasons why one might violate role expectations, but one would rarely do so to persuade role partners, which is what we are discussing here.

thus have to weigh how often and how energetically he may press his client's case without being defined as a dissident or malcontent, and so lose the ability to be persuasive. The worker must have some sense of priority, measure his capital, and not squander it unnecessarily. At the same time, his expenditure of "goodwill" must not be so frugal that he avoids risk whatever the justification. Finding the critical point on the fulcrum is an essential aspect of a worker's art.

In an earlier chapter we noted that the unique function of a community organizer lies in his knowledge of the requisite roles to be filled in community action groups and in his skill in helping constituencies fill them. We suggested too that he frequently fills a "missing role" himself. It is pertinent to add now that the role the worker selects will, to some extent, prescribe certain behaviors and proscribe others. Some roles, of course, are compatible. Thus the "enabler" and the "compromiser" are mutually supporting. Other roles produce strain but, with skill and in certain circumstances, may be bridged. A "mediator" may, for example, also be an "advocate," but he must be circumspect about the ways in which he frames his advocacy. But some roles cannot be carried by the same organizer—for example, an "agitator" can hardly function credibly as a "neutral third party." As organizations and circumstances change, a skillful worker will make commensurate changes in his role behavior. But even so, he must be sensitive to the effects of these changes on the perceptions of persons in complementary roles.

The prestige and attractiveness of others may be put to use in attempts to persuade. Before an issue is decided by a group, prestigious persons may be "lined up" through private consultation. At the least, important members can be neutralized by individual attention. At best, they may be induced to introduce or champion the desired position. Consideration to the prestige and attractiveness of who is to initiate any proposal, and who is to argue for its adoption, should be part of any action scheme.

A corollary point to consider in making use of prestigious persons for filling roles is that actors must be rewarded for performing their roles well. Prestigious persons who are "lined up" to support a plan must not be duped into doing something that they did not intend, or learn too late that they had lost more than they had bargained for in supporting a position. In the case of blatant subterfuge, the actor may withdraw his support, with possibly devastating consequences. And miscalculation, even though unintentional, may make it difficult or impossible to garner aid in the future.

Convergence of Values. Likeness between the communicator and the message recipient increases the latter's persuasibility. Studies suggest that the opinion leader, "the person who occupies a position of influence in the word-of-mouth communication system . . . is seen as 'one of us' by the persons whom he influences." [4] The point extends to similarities of values, according to opinion research. Establishing agreement with an audience on one topic promotes its acceptance of a speaker's other positions.[5] Thus, convincing teachers about the value of open classrooms would be more likely if the speaker were to start his talk by calling for higher teacher salaries.

Community workers may thus disarm a potentially negative audience or sway a neutral one by finding an area of agreement before making a persuasive attempt. Although the point is somewhat mechanistic, it is useful in practice. In the give-and-take of discussion, the worker must seek and find convergent values and ideas with those with whom he has on-going interaction. This is particularly important when the worker and the other have basic ideological differences, as in the instance of organizers working with prejudiced whites. Only as he can find some similarity between his and their values can his viewpoint influence the process.

Goodenough was making another point in a different context, but the following anecdote is illustrative:

In our own experience, we have encountered a missionary in New Guinea who [achieved] considerable success from the standpoint of his objectives. There had been a strong cargo cult in his area. . . . The missionary's predecessor had openly resisted and preached sternly against it. For his pains, he was seized and tortured [though ultimately rescued]. . . . [Cult] disciples came to the present missionary . . . showed him the new myth, which they had written down, and asked him what he thought

[4] David Krech, Richard S. Crutchfield, and Egerton L. Ballachey, *Individual in Society* (New York: McGraw-Hill, 1962), p. 232.

[5] W. Weiss, "Opinion Congruence with a Negative Source on One Issue as a Factor Influencing Agreement on Another Issue," *Journal of Abnormal and Social Psychology,* Vol. 54 (1957), pp. 180–86.

of it. He did not sneer, but expressed approval of its obvious Biblical content, of the aspirations it revealed, and what it was they were trying to conceptualize within the outwardly fantastic myth. Finding that he was not hostile, they asked him if he could show them the road by which they might achieve their aspirations. . . . He succeeded, accordingly, in getting the several villages in the movement to revise a number of their marriage and family customs in the direction endorsed by his religious denomination . . .[6]

Acceptance of particular arguments varies, depending on whether one is a peer or an expert. As common sense suggests and studies attest, a peer is most effective in value-related areas. When an appeal is to the facts of a case, however, the expert is more likely to be listened to.[7] The distinctions between peer and expert, and values and facts, are often blurred in practice, but the concepts are useful nonetheless. For example, one organizer successfully set up an initial tenant's meeting by having a community person make an "inspirational" statement about the benefits derived when people stick together, followed by the worker's review of actions open to the group in dealing with their landlord.

Credibility. In a classic experiment, Hovland and Weiss demonstrated that more attitude change takes place when a message is attributed to a high-credibility source than to a low-credibility one. As the perceived trustworthiness of a communicator increases, his ability to convince his audience also increases.[8] Some determinants of credibility transcend the person and include the content of the message and the mind set of the audience. There are, however, factors relating to the communicator himself which have particular salience for community work.

First, we may logically assume that credibility decreases as a communicator is perceived to be arguing in his own self-interest. When he is so perceived, the audience is more likely to expect selective in-

[6] Ward Hunt Goodenough, *Cooperation in Change: An Anthropological Approach to Community Development* (New York: Russell Sage Foundation, 1963), pp. 314–15.

[7] Edward E. Jones and Harold B. Gerrard, *Foundations of Social Psychology* (New York: Wiley, 1967), p. 436.

[8] C. I. Hovland and W. Weiss, "The Influence of Source Credibility on Communication Effectiveness," *Public Opinion Quarterly,* Vol. 15 (1951), pp. 635–50.

terpretations and less than total candor. Unless a communicator has built up a store of trust, his arguments will be taken with a grain of salt. In community work, organizational (and subsystem) self-interest creates as potent a source of low credibility as personal benefit. As close observers of interorganizational meetings know, agency representatives' reactions are finely tuned to furthering their organization's advantage, and thus they are open to suspicion and imputations of subjectivity.

Sensitivity to the ascription of self-interest can sometimes help to close the "credibility gap." If a worker is arguing in his organization's interest, but there are other cogent reasons for the argument, he might say just this. Like George Washington and the mythical cherry tree, when there is no choice but complete candor, candor may help and can't hurt. Less cynically, when one's audience is unsympathetic or suspicious (or if it is knowledgeable about the issue under discussion), the communicator must carefully and self-evidently transmit unbiased messages. If, on the other hand, the worker's argument *appears* to be, but is not, in his organization's interest, that point should be clarified. Finally, if a position is *against* his personal or his organization's interest, much should be made of the fact, since credibility is increased if he is arguing against his own interest.[9]

Stereotypical positions are also likely to decrease credibility, since a "line" suggests bias. Workers with fixed ideological and political positions are prone to use stereotyped arguments. Investigators report that when people expect unfamiliar arguments, the communication will be more persuasive than when they expect the known, no matter how similar the messages.[10]

Finally, the most convincing communicator does not appear to try to convince at all. Apparently, his presumed lack of stake in the out-

[9] So, for example, in one experiment, the statement that "generally speaking, the number of U.S. casualties in the Vietnamese conflict has far exceeded that reported in the U.S. press" was judged more credible when attributed to General Westmoreland, a "hawk" on the Vietnam war, than when presented anonymously. The experiment is reported in Marvin Karlins and Herbert I. Abelson, *Persuasion* (2d ed.; New York: Springer, 1970), pp. 116–17.

[10] D. Sears and J. Freedman, "Effects of Expected Familiarity with Arguments upon Opinion Change and Selective Exposure," *Journal of Personality and Social Psychology*, Vol. 2 (1965), pp. 420–26.

come enhances his trustworthiness. Furthermore, the audience is disarmed. Not having to resist an assault on its beliefs, it is more open to hearing the message.

A conversation "overheard" accidentially is more persuasive than one intended to convince the hearer. In an experiment, college students were permitted to listen to a conversation in an adjoining room regarding supposed misconceptions about a causal relationship between smoking and lung cancer. One group of students were led to believe that the speaker knew they were listening; the second group of students believed they were eavesdropping. The results confirmed the hypothesis. Responding to a health survey a week later, the students who "eavesdropped" indicated greater skepticism about the causal relationship. Replication of the experiment with other issues produced similar results.[11]

Thus, when credibility is the important value, a worker should illuminate issues rather than intensify arguments. He should use the "soft" rather than the "hard" sell or, better still, no sell at all. He might use, or advise the use of, exhortation in order to mobilize the committed, frighten the opposition, or for other reasons, but not to add credibility to the message. Furthermore, it may be possible to reconstruct the "eavesdrop" condition. For example, a community group might "leak" a story to the press or print a story in its paper, ostensibly for membership but really intended for the target system; or a leader might "unintentionally" reveal something to a second party expecting that it will thereby reach a third party's ears.

THE MESSAGE

The framing of the message is another factor which determines the effectiveness of attempts to persuade. Phrasing and organizing communications are wide-ranging topics, which cannot be dealt with adequately in a single chapter section. We limit ourselves to a few important techniques: shaping the message to deal with underlying factors; steering between moderate and extreme appeals; and using messages to generate fear.

[11] The experiment, conducted by Walster and Festinger, is reported in Jones and Gerrard, *Foundations of Social Psychology,* pp. 444–45.

Dealing with Underlying Factors. Persuasiveness will be increased by knowing what is behind an attitude-to-be-changed. Messages can be tailored to the audience when the communicator knows what function an attitude serves for its holder. An official may support a policy because he is unaware of its negative effect on clients, in which case his mind may be changed by new information. Or his endorsement of the policy may stem from its utility to his organization. In that case, additional information about clients will not sway him, although arguments about its ill effects on the agency might. On the other hand, if his position stems from personal need (for example, fear of or anger at clients), neither of the above messages would be persuasive and might even reinforce his earlier conviction.

According to the functional approach to attitudes developed by Katz, the attitude of the official in the first instance illustrates the *knowledge* function of beliefs (i.e., they provide a frame of reference for understanding one's environment). The second is an example of an *instrumental* or adjustment function (i.e., the official's attitude is a means for reaching a desired goal or avoiding an undesirable one). In the case of his fear of clients, the attitude may serve an *ego-defensive* function, in which there is denial or distortion in order to protect oneself against internal conflicts or external "dangers." [12] The varying functions served by the attitude should shape the approach to the message.

Attitudes which are instrumental are more subject to modification by changes in conditions (e.g., additional money is available for a new program, a policy impels client counterattack) than by verbal appeals. Verbal expression can, however, highlight the unsatisfying aspects of current conditions, the potential ill consequences should circumstances remain the same, and the superiority of proposed solutions.

Research in regard to attitudes which pose a threat to the ego has focused largely on minority group prejudice, and Katz suggests three basic ingredients. The first is to remove the threat through an objective, matter-of-fact approach or the use of humor (which is not directed against the audience or the problem). Second, catharsis or the ventilation of feelings can release energy and bring the nature of the conflict to the surface. (He cautions, however, that a gripe session

[12] Katz, "Functional Approach to the Study of Attitudes," pp. 279–84.

can reinforce negative reactions unless there are positive forces in the group, or time is allowed for less querulous voices to come to the fore.) The third ingredient is self-insight achieved by discussion which reveals, in as nonthreatening a way as possible, the underlying bases for ego-defensive positions. The effects of insightful materials was demonstrated in one experiment in which the subjects were exposed to the psychodynamics of prejudice through a case history of a person similar enough to the subjects to gain their sympathy. A major finding was that the prejudicial attitudes of subjects of low or moderate defensiveness (but not those of high defensiveness) were significantly modified by the gain in insight.[13]

However ill-used it may be, motivational research is a technique which similarly taps the emotional and unconscious aspects of self. For example, when the appeal to patriotism in a Red Cross blood drive resulted in failure, the organization turned to another means:

Using the . . . techniques of motivation research, it was determined that giving blood arouses many unconscious anxieties, especially with men, by whom it is equated with giving away part of their virility and strength. . . . Information about the rapid regeneration of blood, or references to national emergencies will not be heard by the anxious individual. Even if he acknowledges the truth of the facts, they will only raise the level of anxious conflict . . . and leave unchanged his unconscious tendency to avoid the threatening act. To get a man to give blood, then, it is vital to make him feel more masculine. . . .[14]

A Red Cross campaign, based on the above premise, resulted in a dramatic increase in blood donations.

Moderate or Extreme Messages. Some organizers and community leaders appear to believe that by raising the decibel level of their rhetoric, they can prevail over the unbeliever. In this view, the more extreme or one-sided the argument, the more convincing it will be. The truth may seem so obvious to them that they have little doubt it will bring light to the unlearned if only it can be articulated strongly enough. Or, their frustration is such that self-expression requires the sacrifice of their "cool." Both explanations are understandable, but they do not necessarily lead to effective persuasion.

[13] *Ibid.,* pp. 288–89.
[14] Phillip Zimbardo and Ebbe B. Ebbeson, *Influencing Attitudes and Changing Behavior* (Reading, Mass.: Addison-Wesley, 1969), pp. 109–10.

Extreme and one-sided communications *do* work, but only under certain conditions. The research is equivocal in this regard, so that much must be inferred and remain tentative. One problem is that "moderate" and "extreme" are designations that shift with time. Thus ideas are moderate or not in relation to competing notions and the general ideological climate. Extreme arguments may appear to be less radical as they become familiar. One important function of extreme ideas is that they make relatively radical notions seem mild by comparison. So, for example, in the movement of blacks for social justice in the 1960's, the ideas of Martin Luther King, Jr., sweeping and absolute in themselves, seemed moderate to the white middle class in comparison to the positions of black leaders like Stokely Carmichael.

Extreme arguments tend to be more or less effective depending on the communicator, the audience, and the issue. Communications which advocate a great degree of change in the recipient's current position tend to produce greater opinion change than communications which are closer to views already held by the audience,[15] provided that the audience views the communicator as trustworthy. The rub is that the extremity of the change which is asked for may affect the credibility of the communicator, and *low* credibility communicators are more successful when they request moderate rather than extreme opinion change.[16] Some investigators hold that appeals for sweeping opinion change are more successful when the issue has low salience for the audience or is not ego-involving. Appeals on issues on high involvement are more effective when made moderately.[17] In short, if a worker is trying to persuade (and we are not discussing pressure or other tactics here), he will choose moderate or extreme arguments depending on his relationship with his audience and how meaningful the issue is to them.

[15] C. Hovland and H. Pritzker, "Extent of Opinion Change as a Function of Amount of Change Advocated," *Journal of Abnormal and Social Psychology*, Vol. 54 (1957), pp. 257–61. This study and the two which immediately follow are reported in Karlins and Abelson, *Persuasion*.

[16] E. Aronson, J. Turner, and J. Carlsmith, "Communicator Credibility and Communication Discrepancy as Determinents of Opinion Change," *Journal of Abnormal and Social Psychology*, Vol. 67 (1963), pp. 31–36.

[17] J. Whittaker, "Attitude Change and Communication-Attitude Discrepancy," *Journal of Social Psychology*, Vol. 65 (1965), pp. 141–47.

How extreme an argument seems depends on whether it contains opposing points of view. One-sided communications—those which omit opposing arguments—are most effective with audiences predisposed to agreement. Two-sided communications, in which the speaker apprises his audience of alternative arguments, are more convincing to those with less favorable initial attitudes.[18]

The educational level of the message recipient is an additional factor. Two-sided arguments are more effective as the educational level of the audience rises, and this occurs regardless of their initial disposition. One-sided communications are overwhelmingly more effective for those with less education and an initial predisposition to respond favorably. Much, then, depends on the initial attitude and education of the audience to which the message is directed. To expand support in low-income communities, extreme arguments are likely to be effective, because of the probable receptivity of low-income persons to self-interest arguments, as well as because of their limited educational attainment. If the appeal is to a broader middle-class public who are more educated and less convinced about social injustice, a moderate two-sided argument will be more persuasive. The latter point may, at least in part, explain the failure of socially committed college students to persuade their fellows on social issues with arguments that do not credit an opposing view.

The proper use of these techniques—manipulating the level of intensity, choosing between moderate and extreme messages, and presenting one or two sides of an argument—requires that they change as groups move through the organizing process. In the earlier stages of a change attempt, messages might be framed in an intense, extreme, and one-sided fashion. Later on, when negotiations are underway, tactics might become more subdued and balanced because, having got an adversary to the conference table, he ought not to be offered a frivolous excuse to leave it.

Fear Arousal. The community leader proclaims that unless people organize, they face dire consequences from the landlord, the principal, or the welfare official. He also threatens the official with com-

[18] The pioneering work in this area is C. I. Hovland, I. L. Janis, and H. H. Kelley, *Experiments on Mass Communication* (Princeton: Princeton University Press, 1949).

munity ire and disruption unless his demands are met. In both instances, he is using fear arousal to change an opinion or to prod to action. And he is quite right to assume that fear, when it is credible, is persuasive. Ordinarily, however, he does not ask whether the appeal to fear should be mild or strong, or under what circumstances it will be most effective. A number of studies shed some light on these questions.

Surprisingly, mild fear arousal is generally more effective than a strong appeal to fear. Thus smokers, exposed to low, medium, and high fear conditions regarding the relationship between cigarette smoking and lung cancer, were significantly more likely to indicate intentions to stop smoking when subjected to *low* fear arousal.[19] Similarly, children prohibited from playing with a toy judged the toy less attractive when the threatened punishment was milder than more severe.[20] There is also evidence to suggest that the greater the subject's involvement in the message (e.g., the smoker and the lung cancer communication), the more likely will mild rather than strong fear arousal be persuasive.[21] Apparently, the stronger the message and the more important it is to the audience, the more the audience will respond defensively and discount it.

Generally, there are two ways in which a person can react to fear. One is to contend with the threat and try to overcome the circumstances which induce it. A second is to withdraw, avoid the stimulus, or deny the danger. Community workers are, by trade, people who cope with adverse circumstances, and they are prone to respond to a strong fear appeal by taking action. They tend to assume, accordingly, that others do likewise, and in the face of resistance, may even intensify their appeal. But many of their constituents have been socialized to accept if not withdraw from threat, and officials too may tune out fear-arousing messages whose potency is too great.

Whether the appeal to fear is mild or strong, however, the message which includes concrete steps for immediate action is always more effective.[22] The order of presentation of the fear appeal and the in-

[19] The experiment, conducted by Leventhal and Niles, is reported in Jones and Gerrard, *Foundations of Social Psychology*, p. 463.

[20] Aronson and Carlsmith, as reported in *ibid.*, p. 463.   [21] *Ibid.*, p. 466.

[22] H. Leventhal, "Fear: For Your Health," *Psychology Today*, Vol. 1 (1967), pp. 54–58.

structions for action are important too. Prescriptions for action should follow fear arousal, in part because they help to reduce the threat and assuage the fear.

We conclude this section with the counsel that organizers will be more likely to persuade to the extent that they believe in their message and demonstrate confidence in its merit. Investigation of the process of influencing has shown that "persuaders tended to use words expressing confidence, while persuadees used words expressing doubt." [23] The investigators suggest that this is a function of the communication *per se*. The use of words or phrases such as "I am convinced that" builds confidence in the message.

THE AUDIENCE

Audiences avoid, misconstrue, and distort messages, as well as listen to, hear, and understand them. Obviously, the effect of a persuasive attempt depends on the audience at whom it is directed. In the concluding section of this chapter, we focus on some technical considerations in dealing with audiences: forewarning an audience about the speaker's views; inoculating against counterargument; and participation in the persuasion process.

Forewarning the Audience. People tend to expose themselves to communications with which they already agree. Partisans of political candidates, for example, usually listen to the man they support rather than to his opponent. (One of the tasks of the persuader is, in fact, to get his target-audience's attention, by no means an easy feat. Gaining the attention of nonsupporters is sometimes the intention of community groups which take dramatic actions or make unexpected statements.) The phenomenon of "selective exposure" has been cited to support Festinger's theory of "cognitive dissonance." [24] Festinger holds that people reduce inconsistency (or "dissonance") between two beliefs, or between a belief and an action, in three ways: by avoiding or minimizing the importance of a dissonant idea;

[23] Harvey London, Philip J. Meldman, and A. Van C. Lanckton, "The Jury Method: How the Persuader Persuades," *Public Opinion Quarterly,* Vol. XXXIV, No. 2 (Summer 1970), p. 173.

[24] Karlins and Abelson, *Persuasion,* p. 84.

by acquiring new information to buttress existing consonance; and by changing those attitudes or behavior which are involved in the dissonance.[25]

The theory suggests that if people avoid dissonant ideas, the speaker who gives notice of potential disagreement in advance (for example, "You may not totally agree with me, but . . .") may lose his audience through "selective listening." The fact is that forewarning about disagreement does increase listener resistance to a persuasive attempt. Thus high school seniors, forewarned that they would hear a talk on the dangers of teen-age driving, were less likely to change their position on increasing the age of driver eligibility than other seniors who heard exactly the same talk with no forewarning.[26]

Dissonance theory suggests two other possible audience reactions. In disagreement with a speaker, an audience can reduce dissonance (a) by adopting a view which is closer to the speaker's, or (b) by discrediting the speaker. There is evidence which suggests that the second is the usual outcome, and that when an audience expects to disagree with a speaker, it silently prepares itself for counterargument.[27] Studies also indicate that distractions (primarily moderate and pleasant) during an argument increase the effectiveness of a persuasive attempt.[28] Presumably, one of the reasons for this outcome is that the audience is distracted from mustering its silent rebuttal. A joke or a poignant anecdote may have such an effect. The presentation of pictures, slides, and guests may also serve to both warm and distract the audience to its persuader's advantage.

Inoculating against Counterargument. There is an advantage to a speaker in *weakly* presenting opposing arguments to audiences that are thoroughly convinced of his position. This point is related to our earlier discussion of one- and two-sided arguments. McGuire sug-

[25] Leon Festinger, Henry W. Riecken, and Stanley Schachter, "When Prophecy Fails," in Eleanor E. Maccoby, Theodore M. Newcomb, and Eugene L. Hartley, eds., *Readings in Social Psychology* (3d ed.; New York: Henry Holt, 1958), p. 158.

[26] The experiment, conducted by Allyn and Festinger, is reported in Jones and Gerrard, *Foundations of Social Psychology,* p. 475.

[27] *Ibid.,* p. 475.

[28] Karlins and Abelson, *Persuasion,* p. 16.

gests something similar to "germ theory" operates in regard to attitudes. That is, just as the body can be immunized by small doses of a germ in diluted form, so too can people's attitudes be protected from counter argument if they are prepared by mild doses of the opposing view. According to McGuire, attitudes are especially vulnerable when they have not been previously challenged. The defense, then, is to challenge them sufficiently to motivate the listener's thinking about refutations.[29]

Community workers who assist groups in negotiations with officials are often unaware of the need to inoculate against counterargument. The following excerpt from a worker's report of his neighborhood committee's meeting with a police official is perhaps all too typical:

I had the feeling that all five members were nervous. They are not used to making demands on public officials and had probably never been inside a police precinct. I indicated that we were well within our rights as citizens to be here to complain. We then reviewed what was to be presented to Captain Jones. Each one of us was to speak about the problems which we personally had had. Our purpose, we agreed, was to present our specific grievances, and to demand more police protection.

. . . Mrs. Arnold was first to speak. She told how she had needed a policeman in an emergency and was not able to find one. Unfortunately, she rambled on with irrelevant material, and when at one point she made reference to parents, Captain Jones picked this up and spoke about parental irresponsibility. He used this argument to shift blame from the Police Department to the people themselves. I felt I had to make the point that Mrs. Arnold had lost, namely, that in an emergency she had been unable to find a policeman.

Mrs. Korn then spoke about the lack of safety on her block, and noted that the children were unruly and undisciplined. Captain Jones again made reference to parents' lack of control. Everytime he did something like this, I had to respond by saying. . . .

Although the committee had prepared for the meeting, they had not anticipated the official's counterreactions. Clearly, the group foundered, and without refutations to his arguments, they had to rely increasingly on the worker.

In a refutational defense, an audience is provided arguments (in

[29] McGuire's formulations and experiments are discussed in Jones and Gerrard, *Foundations of Social Psychology*, pp. 480–85.

small doses, to be sure) which threaten its and the speaker's position, followed by the answers to these arguments. A supportive defense, on the other hand, builds resistance by reinforcing the arguments in favor of the held beliefs. If there is merit to the "germ theory," one would expect a refutational defense to be more generally effective than a supportive one. This is, in fact, the case. Most effective of all are the two together.

Active and Passive Participation. Generations of social workers have been weaned on Kurt Lewin's studies which demonstrated that discussion is superior to the lecture method as a means of teaching (or persuading). Although some of Lewin's findings have been challenged by more recent research, it is nevertheless true that active participation increases receptivity to opinion change more than passive participation. When effort is required to hear a communication (e.g., traveling a long distance, or making complex arrangements to attend a meeting), an audience will be more influenced than when little expenditure of energy is required. And even an audience's expectation of having to expend effort increases its persuasibility.[30]

Role play—a form of active participation—is highly effective as a persuasive technique. It is ordinarily used as a persuader when the goal is to induce "subtle modifications of a person's perception and evaluation of another, usually someone he dislikes . . . [or] to make the person more tolerant of a given contrary position by having him publicly espouse a set of opinions with which he . . . disagrees." [31] It is employed in conflict situations to get opposing parties to see things from each others' perspective.

The advantage of active participation is a point which need not be belabored here, however, and we wish only to deal with one aspect of the matter: the consequence of taking a public stand. One of the questions about the Lewin studies is whether the housewives in his group changed their food-buying practices because of the discussion method or because they were asked to make a public commitment through a show of hands at the discussion's end. Subsequent studies have shown that public avowal of a position increases adherence to

[30] Karlins and Abelson, *Persuasion*, pp. 20–21.
[31] Zimbardo and Ebbeson, *Influencing Attitudes and Changing Behavior*, pp. 55–56.

the position, thereby immunizing against counterargument. People are apparently more committed to behavior when they have given public witness.[32]

The consequences of public position taking are significant for community work. A chairman should know, for example, that it is unwise to call for audience avowal until there is some indication that the audience has got the message. Until this is indicated, the stance may need to be to "have more discussion of these ideas" or to "hear from all sides on the matter." In persuading someone who is hesitant or mildly opposed to his position, a communicator should seek to avoid an early expression of the other's attitude, for once the other has declared himself, he becomes that much harder to convince.

On the other hand, if a leader is seeking to "fix" a position, or to ensure that an action is taken, he would want the members of his audience to make their stand publicly. If there has been sufficient support to assure a group decision, he might then ask silent members if they agree, and thus commit them to the group's judgment. Or if the decision requires further action (e.g., attendance at a meeting or demonstration), members might be asked to indicate by a show of hands whether they will participate. Tasks are also likely to be performed more conscientiously when members have found it necessary to commit themselves in front of others. There is a risk in forcing such commitment: embarrassment to the silent member; feelings of entrapment or imposition; or even anger. The decision to press for public avowal often rests on the grace with which it can be elicited on the one hand, and the importance of guaranteeing the action on the other.

Our concern in this chapter has been with persuasion. Having indicated some of the factors affecting the three components (communicator, message and audience), we wish to underscore one point. The advice to workers and leaders which we have proffered relates only to attempts to persuade, and may not be applicable to other modes of intervention. For example, communicator attractiveness or a similarity of values between communicator and audience are important in persuasion, but may be of no consequence or even contraindicated when there is a high degree of disagreement between the

[32] Karlins and Abelson, *Persuasion,* pp. 59–61.

parties, and other tactics may be called for, such as political pressure or disruption. Perhaps it would be well to close the chapter with the admonition that opened it. Collaborative tactics, including persuasion, are useful when objectives are shared or disagreements are modest. If this is not the case, then one may wish to give the *appearance* of collaboration, but then the tactic might better be characterized as a political maneuver.

CHAPTER FIFTEEN

CAMPAIGN TACTICS: BARGAINING *

CAMPAIGN TACTICS include political maneuvering, bargaining and negotiation, and mild coercion. These tactics are often intertwined with collaboration and contest tactics. For example, problem solving and education contain some elements of bargaining, and inherent in bargaining is the threat of coercion. Because of this, much of our earlier discussion of persuasion, and our exploration of direct action in chapter 16, is relevant to campaign interventions.

The aims and outcomes of campaign tactics are middle range. For example, in their study of eighteen racial disputes that led to negotiations between the disputants, Chalmers and Cormick conclude that the resultant changes "represent modifications in outputs and procedures. They are unlikely to include any real reallocation of power or redefinition of organizational purposes." [1] Laue draws a similar conclusion:

It is clear that negotiations . . . are [an] appropriate mechanism if the parties are mutually seeking a middle-range of goals—resources redistribution, grievance machinery, tension reduction or return to the status-quo. . . . They are inappropriate—in fact, they get in the way—if the

* This chapter is drawn, in large part, from an article published by *Social Work* and written in collaboration with Valerie Jorrin.

[1] W. Ellison Chalmers and Gerald W. Cormick, *Racial Negotiations: Potentials and Limitations,* a Research Report to the Ford Foundation (Ann Arbor: Institute of Labor and Industrial Relations, University of Michigan—Wayne State University, October 1970), p. 1.

goal of the dominant group is repression. And they are least appropriate if the goal of the subordinate group is revolution or the establishment of identity or peoplehood, free of outside dominance.[2]

We focus in this chapter on bargaining and negotiation. Bargaining refers to an exchange between two parties, the intent of which is to reach an accommodation regarding some issue. It ordinarily takes place through offering demands, arguments, and concessions. Although our primary interest is in its explicit manifestation, bargaining may also be implicit, and a word on implicit trading is in order.

Attempts to influence involve exchange; that is, each party gives something to get something. Long, in an analysis of how territorial systems function, refers to the interlocking nature of various community games (i.e., the banking game, the civic organization game, the newspaper game, etc.). He notes that "the players in one game make use of the players in another. . . . Each is a piece of the chess game of the other, sometimes a willing piece, but to the extent that the games are different, with a different end in view." [3] As part of an interlocking system, they are required to trade when they cannot coerce and, in the exchange, they try to get as much as possible for as little as possible. They seek, in short, to strike the best bargain they can.

Sometimes trading is a matter of extending credit. So, for example, X performs a service for Y, for which no current payment is exacted. At some future time, Y is expected to return the favor. This is the *quid pro quo* which every politician knows. From the practice point of view, it suggests that workers seek opportunities to be helpful to those whom they would hope to influence through trading. And conversely, that they themselves try to avoid too great indebtedness. Thus, in politics, it *is* more blessed to give than to receive.

Trading is sometimes covert, and does not appear to be bargaining at all. Thus one party offers a "favor" to another, aware that the

[2] James H. Laue, "Urban Conflict—What Role for Negotiations and Mediation?" Prepared for a seminar on community disputes settlement at the Center for Mediation and Conflict Resolution, Automation House, New York, June 1971, pp. 19–20. (Mimeographed)

[3] Norton E. Long, "The Local Community as an Ecology of Games," in Mayer N. Zald, ed., *Social Welfare Institutions* (New York: Wiley, 1965), p. 254.

favor is in fact a trade, since the other is enjoined to reciprocate. These implicit bargains constitute an important dynamic in influencing organizations from below. The services which lower-ranking participants supply to higher-ranking ones accrue equity for lower-ranking members and redress some of the inequalities in their formal status. The point suggests that a worker who brings competence to the achievement of agency purposes will increase his influence. As his value to the organization grows, so too does his latitude and ability to take organizationally deviant positions.

Explicit bargaining, which is formally expressed in negotiations, ordinarily takes place when there is a perceived parity in power between the parties. Sometimes parties seek negotiations as a tactic to increase their power. They hope, through bargaining, to establish recognition of their right to speak for a constituency and to legitimize their voice in institutional decision making. But by and large, bargaining and negotiations are more likely to reflect power relationships then to significantly alter them. More than any other single factor, the shape and outcome of bargaining are determined by the power resources of the bargainers. This point should be kept in mind as we explore some of the practice concerns in each phase of bargaining in this chapter.

PRENEGOTIATION

Bargaining moves through phases. The first is prenegotiation. In this phase, groups with minimal resources establish themselves as serious contenders. Often, the group must engage in direct action to demonstrate its ability to invoke sanctions. Bargaining that eventuates from public confrontation between groups and officials carries the implicit or explicit threat of further conflict should an impasse develop. A second phase is the mutual decision to bargain and the negotiation itself. There is then, finally, settlement and implementation. Or perhaps, not finally, since the whole process may be recycled as power relations continue to change.

Throughout the process, bargainers must assess the rewards they have to grant that their adversaries want, or the punishments they can inflict. To miscalculate by underestimating one's resources may result in gaining less than might otherwise be obtained. To miscalculate by overestimating can lead to defeat and group disarray. The point applies as much to the question of when to settle as to when to begin. Since each community action is unique, some of the considerations of the prenegotiation phase can only be suggested generally.

The bargainer, whether it is a contending neighborhood group or a community agency that wishes to wrest concessions from some other organization, must weigh its strength in comparison to its opponent's before it moves to the bargaining table. A community group is "ready" only when it has something to trade, when it has demonstrated by action or implication that it can apply sanctions. (Unless this is the case, the group is involved in a process of persuasion rather than bargaining). Newly formed groups or those with insufficient resources must rely particularly on negative sanctions such as the threat of public embarrassment or disruption. The efficacy of the threat depends on whether the group can actually "pull it off," as well as whether the price it demands is less costly to its opponent than invoking the sanction would be.

All bargainers, even those who are rich in resources—money, prestige, authority, control over values, etc.—must make a cost-benefit assessment of their resources. Possession of a resource is a necessary but insufficient condition for "clout" in bargaining. The bargainer who is attuned to the market will consider several other questions: Does the other party to the trade *recognize* the need for the resources which the bargainer has to "sell?" If not, the resources are obviously insufficient to influence the transaction. If the need is recognized, is it sufficient to exact the payment which is required? Black nationalist groups, for example, were unwilling to pay the ideological price required to maintain their access to white contributions. Can the resources be transformed by means of a three-way exchange or otherwise, in order to make them more compelling in the present instance? For example, can community support that is insufficient to compel an exchange be transformed into the intercession of prestigious figures and thus win the day? Are alternate suppliers available? If the other party can choose from among potential givers, one's own price must be scaled down. Indeed, can the resource actually be withheld?

The last question appears to have gone unasked in some public ef-

forts to induce community change. Or if asked, not answered satis-
factorily. When an agency hopes to influence a target institution by
providing a carrot (something the latter needs), it must be able to
hold it at a distance, so that the target must move towards it. If the
refusal to give the carrot costs the giver more than contributing it, it
is not likely to be able to exact payment. This can be illustrated in
the relations of some poverty agencies to the public school system.
One of the tactics commonly used to influence the educational system
was to grant funds to the schools through the Community Action
Agencies. The funds, it was expected, would obligate the schools to
the experimental approach of the poverty agency. The fact that this
tactic did not work was due to a number of fallacies, not the least
being that no actual sanction could be invoked when the schools
spent the money in traditional ways. CAA's, as government-sponsored
programs requiring municipal approval and with school officials on
their board of directors, found that the withdrawal of funds from
schools was so costly to their own well-being as to be inconceivable.

When resources are insufficient to achieve ends, a community
group or organization must augment its sources of influence as it enters the bargaining arena. One means of doing this is by appealing to
a wider public. This requires hard-headed consideration of the points
at issue before negotiations take place. The issues chosen determine
the extent to which the group is able to generate community support
and commitment (as well as the resistance it will encounter). If issues
are ill-defined, and if the community group is more interested in expressing anger than winning points, form will take precedence over
substance in bargaining. In such an instance, the group may win the
battle but lose the war.[4]

A community group must "get itself together" before it moves to
the bargaining table. It must have sufficient organization to act as a

---

[4] We refer throughout this chapter to serious rather than spurious bargaining. Spurious bargaining occurs when the objective is to prevent actual bargaining from taking place. As is often the case in competitive interaction,
form may be used to obscure function. Bargaining may be promoted by both
sides to obfuscate their unwillingness to accommodate or trade, as much as to
obtain agreement. For officials as well as neighborhood groups, it may constitute a delaying tactic, or it may be a means of "exposing" the venality or in-
tractability of the other side.

cohesive entity and be prepared for the exigencies of the transaction. It is of particular importance in this regard to work out the relationship of the negotiating committee to its constituency in advance. To maintain unity and integrity, arrangements must be made for members and negotiators to be in constant contact, for developments to be reported as they occur, and for broad guidelines to be agreed on and revised as necessary.

Since negotiations are often undertaken by the entire membership of community groups (because the number of bodies present may be their mark of power), the relationships of individual negotiators must be defined before the process begins. Officials are no less aware than community organizers of the advantages of dividing opponents, and they act accordingly. New and ad hoc groups are especially vulnerable to factionalism because of the fluidity of group structure. A cardinal principle once bargaining has begun, then, is that differences must be aired privately and cooled publicly. Frequent caucuses during negotiation sessions can serve this purpose if procedures have been worked out in advance.

Although a community group must "get itself together" if it is to strike the best bargain, it must begin bargaining before its power has peaked. Although, as is true in any dynamic situation, it is difficult to predict whether influence is rising or declining, this is the single most important indicator of when to move to the bargaining table. A group's chance of success is greatest when it (and its opponent) knows that it can escalate its effort if necessary. Conversely, however vicious the group's bite may have been in the past, the important question to the target is, "What can you do to me lately?"

Once the decision to bargain is made, adequate preparation is required. Group members, rather than the professional, should carry as much of the interaction as possible in sessions with officials. Therefore, the demands, lines of argument and defense, and potential concessions need to be rehearsed. Who will pursue what arguments and assume which roles must be decided in advance. Whether the group's stance will be militant or moderate, or who among the members will be one or the other, ought to be agreed on. Inexperienced groups need help to anticipate the responses of officials and to fortify themselves against spurious counterarguments. They should analyze the actors with whom they are dealing to assess who is most vulnerable and who might be a sympathizer. Depending on the circumstances, they must understand that compromise is essential in bargaining and that not all of their demands will be met.

NEGOTIATIONS

The complexities of negotiation cannot be treated adequately in a single section. Therefore, we highlight only three practice concerns that are particularly relevant to the community bargainer in this section. These are: the formulation of demands; the regulation of threat; and the use of reasonableness vs. intransigence.

Formulating Demands. It has been suggested that skill in negotiating may be the ability "to set the stage in such a way as to give prominence to some particular outcome that would be favorable." [5] In this view, the outcome of bargaining is determined by the way in which demands are formulated rather than by the merits of the case or by the pressures applied during bargaining.

How extensive or extreme should demands be? The ritual form of labor-management bargaining is suggestive in this regard. The union offers an extensive and grandiose series of demands that neither it nor management take seriously. The company, in turn, makes a grudging counteroffer that is also not serious. So common a ritual must have functional uses; we propose three.

Extreme demands lessen the disadvantage inherent in being the initiator. The initiator of a proposal may reveal information about his eagerness for a settlement and risk divulging too much too soon. Making unrealistic demands offsets this disadvantage, since they can hardly be taken as a proposal at all. Management, which becomes the de facto initiator, responds in kind.

Extreme demands allow parties to test points of "give" and "firmness" in each others' positions. In foreign diplomatic exchanges as well as in labor-management disputes, what is *not* said may be as important as what *is* said. Throughout negotiations, each party attempts

[5] Thomas C. Shelling, *The Strategy of Conflict* (Cambridge: Harvard University Press, 1963), p. 68.

to assess the intention of the adversary and the point at which he may be more willing to settle than to incur sanctions. Clues are derived by questioning the meaning of a demand or proposal, noting the degree of interest in discussing one or another item, the points at which the talk gets heated, and identifying those demands which call forth extensive argument in contrast to those which are passed over. Although tactical considerations require that each party at first oppose all offers put forth, assessment and testing have in effect been taking place.

Demands also define the limits of trading. Extreme demands expand the perimeters of the situation, so that the ultimate compromise may be more advantageous than the proposer anticipated, while it appears to be a victory for the other party. Extreme demands allow the negotiator to return to his constituency with the claim that he forced the other to make concessions.

Since community bargaining is not an institutionalized practice, as is collective bargaining in labor-management disputes, extreme demands may often unnecessarily harden official resistance to any bargaining at all. Indeed, extreme demands may allow officials to walk away from the negotiations altogether. These are important considerations for community groups to whom an image of responsibility is advantageous, or who, because of their limited power resources, cannot otherwise compel responsiveness. Most critical, however, may be the effect of extreme demands on the public case of community groups. Bringing important others to the bargaining table as silent partners may determine the success of some negotiations, and newly developing community groups may wish to demonstrate their reasonableness in contrast to their "hard-nosed" opponents. A public case and public support may be the major access to influencing officials, particularly for groups with limited resources.[6]

What about the content of demands? Should low-income groups limit themselves to identifying problems, or should their demands include program remedies as well? Is it sufficient for them to dramatize

[6] The discussion on moderate and extreme messages in chapter 14 is relevant here, i.e., extreme or moderate demands will have differential impacts depending on the educational level of the audience and its initial disposition.

the existence of decayed slum housing, or should they propose solutions? If they do both, how specific and comprehensive must the solutions be? Housing proposals, for example, might run the gamut from altering the tax structure to adding building inspectors.

The issue stirs controversy among organizer-planners. In the first chapter of this volume, we discussed the inherent strain among the values of participation, leadership, and expertise which operate in all organizations. The bias of "rational" planners favors the "white paper" approach: extensive investigation of the problem and a well-reasoned solution. Political activists, on the other hand, are impatient with what seems to be an academic exercise, since in the final analysis, power will decide. In part, the debate is analogous to a dialectic in social change movements. That is, there is a tension between an emphasis on technically sound programs and an emphasis on social action. Oppenheimer suggests that the struggle between the two should be welcomed: "It insures that the program will be real and at the same time that [action] will not simply be based on momentary whim or opportunity. . . . Too much emphasis on the immediate, on (action), and the goals are lost sight of. . . . Too much emphasis on program and the movement becomes isolated, sectarian . . . and profoundly elitist. . . ." [7]

Arguments can be advanced on both sides of the question in community bargaining. Groups that limit themselves to identifying problems are less likely to be deflected from a focus on change-oriented action. Program development activities tend to absorb time, energy, and attention that might otherwise be directed to building support or intensifying pressure. Social action directed *against* a policy does not require substitute program proposals. On the other hand, a group that engages in planning alternate programs demonstrates its seriousness of purpose. If the long-range intent of the group is to play a continuing role in decision making, program planning moves it in that direction. The knowledge acquired in planning is necessary for consistent involvement in decision making.

Ultimately, the interest, capacity, and location of the group should guide whether its demands emphasize identification of problems or

[7] Martin Oppenheimer, *The Urban Guerrilla* (Chicago: Quadrangle Books, 1969), pp. 58–59.

program solutions. For example, a mothers' group, concerned about the quality of their children's education in an inner city school, was composed of a core of ten Puerto Rican women with perhaps fifty others who could be called on to participate in specific events. The group did not have the experience or sophistication to deal with the complexities of educational policy. Nor was this their concern. The mothers did know at first hand, however, of the lack of respect with which they and their children were treated and they limited their demands to wanting "something" to be done about this problem.[8] Encouraging the members to devote attention to wider ranging educational issues at that point in the group's life might have resulted in the dissolution of the group, or its transformation from an action to a study focus.

To ask an ad hoc, inexperienced, or volatile group to map a course through the shoals of institutional program or policy is to place a great burden on its membership. On the other hand, groups located *within* the institutional system, groups with sophistication in programming and politics, groups which are relatively well organized and have developed a tradition are more likely candidates for planning.

Regulating Threat. Negotiation is an art, say Bakke and Kerr, "composed of almost equal parts of bluffing and bulldozing," [9] and the effective regulation of threat is a major element of bargaining skill.

Threats may be communicated with varying degrees of firmness. Walton and McKersie suggest three ways in which an unyielding stance may be transmitted.[10] One is the degree of finality with which a demand is communicated: for example, "We *must* have such-and-such." Another is the level of specificity; the more specific the demand, the more ignoring it poses a threat: for example, "Three black

---

[8] "I know it's not popular to say this," a school principal told the group, "but you're culturally deprived. You hardly understand what I'm saying, so how can you expect your children to understand the teachers?" Case record, Mobilization for Youth, New York, N.Y., February 1964.

[9] E. Wight Bakke and Clark Kerr, *Unions, Management, and the Public* (New York: Harcourt, Brace, 1948), p. 353.

[10] Richard E. Walton and Robert B. McKersie, *A Behavioral Theory of Labor Negotiations* (New York: McGraw-Hill, 1965), pp. 93–95.

staff members" is more threatening than "More blacks." The third relates to the consequences of not meeting a demand: for example, "We'll boycott the agency." The three together constitute the most determined threat: for example, "We must have three more black staff members or we'll boycott the agency" would thus be most threatening.

Threats of sanction that are disproportionate to an issue or its tactical requirements are not likely to be believed. They are likely to be seen as weakness, or more "bluff" than "bulldoze." Groups which have strength can afford to be less blatantly menacing, since strength itself is a threat. Furthermore, disproportionate threats leave little room for escalation as negotiations continue. When a target is predisposed to make concessions, strong threats may raise the hackles of resistance.

Threats are often more effective than actually invoking them. To illustrate: a group of slum tenants who wished to force their landlord to make repairs scheduled a picket line demonstration at his suburban home. Wiser persons advised the group to postpone the demonstration, so that news of its imminence might be "leaked" to the landlord. The threat brought the landlord to the bargaining table and, ultimately, he was persuaded to make the repairs. The *anticipation* of embarrassment before his neighbors was the significant factor, whereas the demonstration, by accomplishing the embarrassment, would have provided little incentive for settlement. If the threat had not worked, the group would have had to hold the demonstration in order to protect its credibility. But the single action might have been ineffective, and an ongoing series of actions to raise the embarrassment quotient would then have been required.

Threats, to be effective, must be credible. Rhetoric without resources—particularly as there is a steady din but little doing—is ordinarily dismissed. An insufficient but necessary condition for maximizing a threat's credibility is the demonstrated ability and readiness to carry it out, such as engaging in planning required for its implementation and having access to the necessary resources. (This is one reason why unions take early strike votes.) Another means of increasing credibility is to act on minor threats, suggesting the ability to also deliver in the "showdown."

Another aspect of credibility is the cost of fulfilling the threat. If to act on it would cause the group great pain or damage, the threat is not likely to be believed. In these and other instances, two of the ways in which plausibility may be increased is through irrevocable commitment and "irrationality."

Schelling refers to the ability to "bind oneself," that is, to make so firm a commitment that retraction is virtually impossible.[11] The irrevocable commitment may refer to either a threatened action in the event of official intransigence or to the terms under negotiation (e.g., a *real* "non-negotiable" demand). A dramatic example was the position of a group of railroad workers striking for better wages who chained themselves to the tracks in order to halt railroad operations. That they threw away the keys so they could not escape even if they wished to was the critical action.[12] This is a more literal example of binding oneself than is ordinarily practiced, of course, but there is a range of actions that can make group commitment to a fixed position difficult to retract and, therefore, more persuasive to an adversary. This is one reason why leaders stir the passions of their constituencies and thereby limit their options for flexibility. When reputation is important to a person or group, public commitment to take a threatened action puts one's reputation on the line and thus makes the threat more credible.

Threats of action that would cause pain or damage to the threateners are more likely to be believed when the threatener is perceived to be irrational. Schelling calls this "the political uses of madness," and notes:

[A] self-destructive attitude toward injury—"I'll cut a vein in my arm if you don't let me" . . . can be a genuine strategic advantage; so can a cultivated inability to hear or comprehend, or a reputation for frequent lapses of self-control that make punitive threats ineffectual as deterrents.[13]

One need not go all the way to madness. Similar advantages accrue to the bargainer who exudes an excess of anger, is erratic, regards compromise as defeat, or has little to lose. The leaders of low-income organizations frequently put the (usually irrational) fears

[11] Shelling, *Strategy of Conflict*, pp. 22–28.
[12] Alan McSurely, *How to Negotiate* (Louisville, Ky.: Southern Conference Educational Fund, 1967), p. 2.
[13] Schelling, *Strategy of Conflict*, p. 17.

which opponents have of their constituents to good effect in negotiating: "I see your predicament but some members of my group are mean. I'm not sure I can control them if you delay; some are just itching for blood." Irrationality is by no means necessarily unproductive in community bargaining.

   Reasonableness vs. Obstinacy. There are advantages and disadvantages in both reasonableness and obstinacy, in "hard" and "soft sells." Reasonableness suggests that a settlement is possible; obstinacy implies that real concessions must be made. This is why negotiating teams sometimes embody both approaches in different team members. Seaver, describing the process of bargaining with southern welfare departments, refers to two roles—the "Mau Mau" and the "Moderate."

The job of the Mau Mau is to raise the maximum amount of hell in the most militant and annoying way possible. . . . The Moderate comes onto the scene later after the uproar has subsided, dripping with sweet reason and terms like "the breakdown of communications" and "what can we do constructively." . . . The Moderate takes the attitude that the Welfare Department is trying to help, and that he is there to help them help.[14]

This example represents an effort to press a number of leverage points simultaneously.

   A polite but firm stance by a negotiating team is another way of balancing the advantages and disadvantages of reasonableness and obstinacy. The indirect or implicit threat also serves this purpose, and another one as well. It permits the person who is threatened to save face. He may, if he wishes, appear to concede on the merits of the case, rather than as a consequence of pressure which, because it is implicit, can be ignored.

SETTLEMENT

It has been suggested that bargaining is "an exercise in graceful retreat—retreating without seeming to retreat." [15] To help one's op-

[14] Ted Seaver, "The Care and Feeding of Southern Welfare Departments," in Paul A. Kurzman, ed., *The Mississippi Experience* (New York: Association Press, 1971), p. 56.

[15] Bakke and Kerr, *Unions, Management, and the Public*, p. 353.

in bargaining, we wish to conclude with a point that transcends methodology. The effective involvement of the consumers of service in community decision making ultimately requires the institutionalization of bargaining mechanisms, just as collective bargaining arrangements have come to be the normal practice in labor-management relations. In a complex and highly bureaucratized society, solutions to institutional problems need to be formalized. Consumer-oriented bureaucratic mechanisms, organized to challenge and counteract other formal organizations, are one means by which individuals may be protected from official inequity. Institutionalized bargaining can thus be regarded as a major step toward the democratization of social welfare services.

ponent to do so through face-saving, and to relate one's own intere:
to an adversary's is important in bargaining. Throughout, bargain(
must search for goal convergence, and must support their demar
not only by reference to the merits of the case, but also by argui
that a concession to them is in their adversary's best interests. In s
tling, if an adversary has bound himself to a position from which
wishes to withdraw, his ability to justify withdrawal may determ
his willingness to concede at all. When his opponent can help him
tionalize his change of position, settlement becomes more possil

Community mediators report the concern of institutions to ma
tain a pretense of not responding to pressure, often resulting
"imaginative efforts to achieve agreements without appearing to
so." A number have been cited: a letter to the third party medi:
describing the *unilateral* actions the institution is prepared to ta
an announcement by the officials of actions taken which are resp
sive to demands but do not grow out of the negotiation.[16] Pre
gious third parties also offer a face-saving mechanism. They pe:
one of the contenders to concede to the prestige figure rather t
seeming to succumb to the challenger. Thus, in a conflict between
students and administration of Columbia University, the then-Pi
dent Kirk acceded to the "request" of New York City's mayor to
construction of a gymnasium to which sitting-in students objecte

Community bargaining is inherently unstable, since it is respor
to shifting power relations. Thus the Center for Mediation and (
flict Resolution reports, "Should a community group suffer a
crease in power, an established organization might decide that
unnecessary to fulfill all or part of the agreement. Should the con
nity group increase its relative power, it might then press fo:
creased gains." [18] Or in other words, the end of bargaining may
stitute a beginning.

Although our focus in this chapter has been on practice con(

---

[16] Ronald W. Haughton, D'Jaris H. Watson, and Gerald W. Cormick,
diators in Community Disputes," a paper presented to a conference spor
by the Center for Mediation and Conflict Resolution, New York, June
pp. 51–53. (Mimeographed)

[17] *New York Times,* April 25, 1968.

[18] Haughton, Watson, and Cormick, "Mediators in Community Disp
p. 44.

CHAPTER SIXTEEN

CONTEST TACTICS:
DIRECT ACTION AND DISRUPTION

IT IS FITTING to conclude this book, as well as our discussion of tactics, with a consideration of contest interventions. Direct action and disruption entail conflict, and conflict is an inevitable concomitant of social change attempts, since those who benefit from existing allocations of power and resources can be expected to resent and resist the challenge to them. Social change and conflict are reciprocal—neither can exist without the other.[1]

Conflict may be positive or negative, constructive or destructive, and functional or dysfunctional to the wider society and to varying subsystems. However, since social work professionals have tended to prefer cooperation, no matter how spurious, to conflict, no matter how necessary, we wish to note some of the important functions of social conflict. Coser has described conflict as a way of establishing relations between people where none existed before, or of establishing a new relationship.[2] It is sometimes a means of increasing the productive interaction between groups since the absence of conflict does not necessarily indicate that positive ties exist; stability may re-

---

[1] This point is made and developed further by Simon Slavin, "Concepts of Social Conflict: Use in Social Work Curriculum," *Education for Social Work,* Vol. 5, No. 1 (Fall 1969), pp. 47–60.

[2] Lewis Coser, *The Functions of Social Conflict* (New York: Free Press, 1956), p. 121.

sult from the repression of hostility.[3] On the other hand, when conflict between groups is expressed rather than repressed, anger does not accumulate, and relationships exhibit neither ambivalence nor tension.[4] For example, Rose found that among union members, those with the most stable bonds to union organization were the *most* likely to engage in conflict with the leadership of the union.[5]

Coser also points out that the revelation of strengths of contending groups is an effective deterrent to conflict, but, paradoxically, "since power can often be appraised only in its actual exercise, accommodation may . . . be reached only after the contenders have measured their actual strength in conflict." [6] In other words, conflict may be an inevitable function of groups' taking each others' measure.

But it is not only because conflict and social change are reciprocal that a discussion of contest interventions provides an apt conclusion to this volume. There are compelling methodological reasons as well. Contest interventions are, at once, more visible and more virulent than other tactics. They are difficult to mount and maintain, and are liable to call forth reprisals. Thus they require mastery of many aspects of community work at once. For example, an effective campaign requires a cohesive and "representative" community group, and calls on the knowledge and skill in dealing with process, program, and group structure discussed in Part II. Even in its most benign manifestations, direct action demands worker sensitivity to its impact on sponsoring agencies—a subject which was addressed in Part III of this volume. The successful use of contest tactics requires, finally, that an organizer employ all the other modes of intervention to which our attention has been directed: problem solving, persuasion, political maneuvering, and negotiation. In short, to engage in contest interventions effectively requires an organized constituency, the support (or neutrality) of significant interest groups, such as the sponsor, and tactical acumen.

This chapter, then, is intended to fill in some of the pieces which

[3] James S. Coleman, *Community Conflict* (New York: Free Press, 1957), p. 81.

[4] *Ibid.,* p. 83.

[5] Arnold Rose, *Union Solidarity* (Minneapolis: University of Minnesota Press, 1952), pp. 51–54.

[6] Lewis Coser, *Functions of Social Conflict,* pp. 133–34.

are still missing. We first look at the objectives and forms of contest intervention, after which we shall identify some of the practice principles which guide the use of direct action and disruption. We conclude the chapter with a brief comment about violence.

THE OBJECTIVES AND FORMS
OF CONTEST TACTICS

The philosophy of nonviolence, as exemplified in contest tactics, owes much to the elaborate system developed by Gandhi called *satyagraha* ("search for truth"). *Satyagraha* is a difficult term to define because it embraces both a philosophy of life and a methodology of social action. It is a refined technique for social and political change which transcends the simple concepts of civil disobedience, nonviolence, or disruptive behavior. Although we shall not, here, describe the system in detail, we will draw on some of its ideas.

Clash-of-position is one of the tactics in the Gandhian scheme. It is used within accepted social norms and essentially involves actions like debate, legal disputes, and public manifestoes. In the Gandhian view, clash of position comes at a quite advanced stage in dealing with an issue, and a number of other steps are necessary before a *satyagrahi* properly makes use of this tactic, such as reasoning and negotiation, to win over the opponent. Civil disobedience is one of the final stages of this system of action.[7]

In analyzing the process by which the oppressed become revolutionaries, Oglesby describes clash of position as the tactic of "mass-based secular prayer." This appeal to a higher power, he says, sometimes results in change. Often, however, it shows the victim-petitioner that change is more difficult to achieve than he imagined, and this may become "the spiritual low point of the emergent revolutionary's education," for he learns from this that "the enemy is not a few men, but a whole system." [8]

[7] Joan V. Bondurant, *Conquest of Violence* (Berkeley: University of California Press, 1965), pp. 40–41.

[8] Carl Oglesby and Richard Shaull, *Containment and Change* (New York: Macmillan, 1967), p. 145.

A second tactic is the *violation of normative behavior*. It refers to action which might be viewed as moving out of the bounds of what is considered "proper" behavior or good manners. These "violations" are protest activities; examples are marches, demonstrations, rent strikes, haunting (i.e., a technique of following one's opponent around for long periods), and *hartals* (having large masses of people stay at home; a spiritual variation of a general strike).

More than other contest interventions, this tactic demonstrates the effects of changing social and legal definitions of behavior. Rent strikes and boycotts, for example, lie in a gray area between violation of normative and violation of legal rules. Increased citizen protest over the last decade has elevated demonstrations and marches to tactics that are more like a clash-of-position than anything else.

The violation of legal norms are tactics which include civil disobedience and noncooperation. Carried to its final stages in *satyagraha,* law violation incorporates the usurping of functions of government and setting up of parallel government. Civil disobedience presupposes that there is an absence of, or inadequacy in, established law that morally justifies its violation.

Community work, conducted with funds from established sources, may engage in protest activity which violates normative behavior, although this is sometimes difficult and often impossible. But the violation of legal norms (except in ambiguous situations, e.g., when the law is unclear) is inevitably out of bounds. Community groups and workers who are independent of "establishment" funding, however, must adress the value questions of civil disobedience and determine whether they can find it morally correct to disobey an unjust law in order to protest its injustice, or to disobey a morally just law to protest another injustice.

Based on a philosophical anarchism and a conception of "natural rights," these acts have an honorable tradition in American life.[9] This tradition is based on the recognition that our system of law has and will always have imperfections, that the majority whose wishes the law (at least theoretically) is supposed to reflect is itself imper-

[9] Vernon Louis Parrington, *Main Currents in American Thought,* Vol. II, Book III, "The Mind of New England" (New York: Harcourt, Brace and World, 1930), pp. 271–460.

fect, and that all moral values have not been and will never be enacted into law.

There are particular requirements for actions which are classified as nonviolent civil disobedience. They are utilized only after all other remedies have been exhausted; they are used openly and selflessly (that is, the actions have a public character carried out with public explanations of the reasons for the action in the name of some higher morality); and they are utilized with foresight of the potential consequences for the participants.[10] Those who have committed themselves to nonviolent civil disobedience express faith in the value of the existing legal-political system. It is the absence of this faith which distinguishes insurrection from nonviolent disobedience. Although rebellion may claim *moral* justification, it aims at the overthrow of the social order, whereas the goal of civil disobedience is change and reconciliation. This separation between the legality and the morality of the social order was precisely the distinction which Socrates made in recognizing the right of his judges to condemn him to death.

OBJECTIVES OF CONTEST TACTICS

Each of these tactics—clash-of-position, violation of normative behavior, and violation of legal norms—may be employed for the same ends. Three types of objective may be cited: first, goals which relate to the effect of protest action on the participants; second, those relating to the education of a wider public; and third, ends which threaten some opponent.

Contest actions may stir far-reaching reactions in the participants. They may rouse discontent, heighten a sense of injustice, and energize demands for change. They may change consciousness, foster pride, and develop feelings of moral superiority over an opponent and a sense of identity with others. When the demonstration is successful, they engender confidence and feelings of strength. They also serve to generate support from others in similar circumstances; as a study on racial negotiations notes, "By a wide range of appeals, including peaceful demonstrations, black leaders and constituents . . .

---

[10] John de J. Pemberton, Jr., "Is There a Moral Right to Violate the Law?" *The Social Welfare Forum* (New York: Columbia University Press, 1965), pp. 194–95.

strengthen the determination of undecided black potential constituents to support the black demands. . . ." [11] On the small group level, public confrontation serves as program activity, which promotes membership involvement and provides the social glue necessary for community group development.

It should be recognized, however, that direct action may exhaust a group or produce internal conflict. More important, the use of demonstration and disruption puts increasingly fewer limits on the "oppressor," freeing him to utilize disruptive or violent tactics which he might otherwise have been constrained to avoid. Both Gandhi and Martin Luther King, Jr., consciously sought to use nonviolent techniques as a rein on the violent capacities of the established ruling class, a method "to keep the conversation open and the switchblade closed," [12] and the correctness of their views is borne out by the fact that there were fewer deaths in ten years of nonviolent direct action in the south than in ten days of northern riots.

One may suspect that radical action groups seek a middle-range response from authorities, that is, to be attacked with sufficient force to garner sympathy and to demonstrate their status as serious contenders, but not so forcefully as to frighten off supporters or destroy their movement. Officials, for their part, may be guided by Machiavelli, who wrote, "One has to remark that men ought either to be well-treated or crushed, because they can avenge themselves of lighter injuries, of more serious ones they cannot. . . ." [13]

Another set of objectives of contest interventions has to do with winning a wider audience. As Rainwater observes, "Systems of deprivation and exclusion depend for their smooth operation on a good deal of selective inattention to the effects of this exclusion. . . . Low communication [between the disadvantaged and the rest of society] is maintained by mutually ignoring what goes on 'on the other side of the tracks,' and by the development of elaborate etiquettes that mask

[11] W. Ellison Chalmers and Gerald W. Cormick, *Racial Negotiations: Potentials and Limitations,* a research report to the Ford Foundation (Ann Arbor: Institute of Labor and Industrial Relations, University of Michigan— Wayne State University, 1970), p. 14. (Mimeographed)

[12] Oglesby and Shaull, *Containment and Change,* p. 149.

[13] As cited in Antony Jay, *Management and Machiavelli* (New York: Holt, Rinehart, and Winston, Bantam Books, 1969), p. 16.

and conceal the actual facts of exploitation." [14] Direct action breaks through this silence to place issues on a community agenda. The dramatization of discontent forces political leaders, harried by divergent pressures, to seek answers to problems they would otherwise choose to ignore.

Direct action is also intended to create bargaining power for community groups by activating potential allies, some of whom may be considerably more powerful than the protesters. (It should be noted, though, that this is a short-term solution for powerless groups; ultimately, they must develop their own political resources which are available for exchange in the political marketplace.) To achieve this objective often depends on the communications media. Lipsky notes that media coverage of protest activities not only influences potential allies but the protesters themselves. He argues that "Conformity to the standards of newsworthiness in political style, and knowledge of the prejudice and desires of individuals who determine media coverage . . . represent crucial determinants of leadership effectiveness." [15]

The third set of objectives is to compel a target's compliance to protesters' demands. This may be accomplished through the massing of large numbers to demonstrate pervasive political support, or by halting the normal operations of the target. Strikes and sit-ins are frequently used examples; squatters who move into housing slated for demolition are another. The *threat* of violence is inherent in these actions, and is sometimes subtly suggested to induce concessions.

In whatever ways the target may be threatened, the ultimate aim is some redress of power imbalance. In the Gandhian use of disruptive techniques, the major question asked of the *satyagrahi* is whether he has engaged the opponent in a manner designed to transform the complexity of relationships so that new patterns emerge.[16]

[14] Lee Rainwater, "Neighborhood Action and Lower-Class Life-Style," in John B. Turner, ed., *Neighborhood Organization for Community Action* (New York: National Association of Social Workers, 1968), p. 37.

[15] Michael Lipsky, "Protest as a Political Resource," *American Political Science Review*, Vol. XXV, No. 1 (January 1968), p. 1151.

[16] Bondurant, *Conquest of Violence*, p. viii.

The forms of contest intervention have been identified as falling within three categories: (1) *protest or demonstration,* (2) *noncooperation,* and (3) *intervention.*[17] Protest or demonstration serves primarily to dramatize a point of view, while noncooperation indicates the withdrawal of participation from expected activity, and intervention connotes physical obstruction or interference with routine procedures. One expert lists thirty-six kinds of protest, seventy-two forms of noncooperation, and sixteen methods of intervention.[18] Undoubtedly new forms of contest are created every day, so we shall identify only a few of them.[19]

Protest or demonstration includes door-to-door canvassing, leafleting, petitioning, picketing, and marching. Meetings of various kinds, such as street corner rallies or the teach-ins of the anti-war movement, constitute other forms of protest. Vigils, a type of picketing that suggests spirituality, are used to bear moral witness, and put religious sentiment to the service of social change. The renunciation of honors, another protest technique, was effectively demonstrated by the nation's response to the Vietnam war veterans who, during a 1971 Washington demonstration, discarded their medals at the White House.

Fraternization and harassment are related techniques. In the first, demonstrators attempt to win over the guardians of the law and other "enemies" by soft words and persuasiveness, as some marchers on the Pentagon did with the troops who guarded its portals. In the second, epithets and obscenities are hurled in hopes (usually vain) of isolating one's opponents. Oppenheimer makes a cogent point in this regard:

[17] See, for example, Martin Oppenheimer, *The Urban Guerrilla* (Chicago: Quadrangle Books, 1969).

[18] American Friends Service Committee, *In Place of War: An Inquiry into Nonviolent National Defense* (New York, Grossman, 1967), p. 61. As noted in *ibid.,* p. 141.

[19] Readers interested in the specifics of organizing direct action campaigns ought to refer to the O.M. Collective, *The Organizers Manual* (New York: Bantam Books, 1971) and Martin Oppenheimer and George Lakey, *A Manual for Direct Action* (Chicago: Quadrangle Books, 1964, 1965).

Confrontation name-calling, or "shock therapy," can be effective only with opponents who think they are something they are not. Police do not generally suffer from this ailment; moderates do. For example, when a black nationalist calls a policeman a "pig" he may be building his own morale, but he only confirms the policeman's attitudes toward blacks. On the other hand, when he calls a white liberal a "white racist snake," he may force some real introspection in him. . . .[20]

Noncooperation may extend from malingering to absenteeism to strikes. The last may be intended actually to halt normal operations or to serve symbolic purposes: for example, the call to blacks to stay away from work on "Black Solidarity Day" was to symbolize the importance of their labor and demonstrate black unity. Boycotts are another form of noncooperation that is often potent. The boycott of the buses in Montgomery, Alabama, which heralded the civil rights movement, and the grape boycott which won union recognition for Chavez' United Farm Workers, are two examples, one local, the other national, of the successful use of this form of noncooperation. A more threatening form of noncompliance than strikes and boycotts, since the latter are ordinarily within the law, is the resistance to government mandate, as in tax refusal and draft resistance. Perhaps nothing arouses greater anxiety and outrage on the part of officialdom than actions such as these, which not only challenge the legitimacy of government but also can halt its functioning if there is sufficient participation.

As the above implies, noncooperation must be widely supported to be effective. This is not necessarily the case with protest because relatively small numbers can dramatize an issue; nor does it apply to intervention, since a few strategically located people can tie up a city. To withdraw cooperation makes no mark except as it is noticeable in the mass.

Intervention usually entails law violation, although "milling" is one form which does not. An example of milling is to have large numbers of protesters go shopping, hang around, tie up store counters, all with the ostensible purpose of making a purchase, but the real intent of disrupting normal business activity. Although there are many creative variations on this theme, intervention is by

[20] Oppenheimer, *Urban Guerrilla,* p. 98.

and large physically threatening and law violating, and therefore most dangerous to the participants. It is ethically untenable unless those who take part in it are aware of the risks to themselves in advance.

The sit-in is a classic form of intervention, used widely in the civil rights movement and subsequently by protesting university students. From this form has evolved such other innovations as the stand-in, wade-in, phone-in, lie-in, and so on. Physical obstruction of various kinds, such as placing onself between another person and his work, is a technique of intervention which carries, for many, an undertone of violence. Yet, it has been a popular tactic with pacifist anti-war protesters. They have, for example, tied canoes to troopships, boarded destroyers, chained themselves to AWOL soldiers, and destroyed draft files.[21] We note, finally, one other form of intervention: the reverse strike, in which the protesters do work which is outside the scope of their responsibility. The construction of a "People's Park" in Berkeley in 1969, for example, was a reverse strike which ended with the calling of the national guard, replete with helicopters and tear gas, by the Governor of California. The issue—who would have the power to determine the uses of public property—had been brought to the point of a military confrontation by the tree-planting, sod-loving tactics of the demonstrators which made a dramatic pastoral contrast to the Governor's violence.

CONTEST INTERVENTIONS:
SOME PRACTICE PRINCIPLES

The form and substance of protest, noncooperation, and intervention are shaped by its objectives—whether the action is intended primarily to mobilize constituents, appeal to a wider public, or threaten some target. Although these goals are not mutually exclusive, there are inherent tensions among them, for example, to threaten some target may offend some public. As in all aspects of practice, the organizer and community leader do well to clarify what it is they hope

[21] Jerome H. Skolnick et al., *The Politics of Protest: A Report to the National Commission on the Causes and Prevention of Violence* (New York: Ballantine Books, 1969), p. 70.

to accomplish, with what priorities, and with regard to whom. Direct action requires that leaders concern themselves with matters of leadership (i.e., bringing their constituents along) as they attempt to develop negotiable power (e.g., securing widespread support or posing a credible threat). We wish to consider briefly some elements in regard to each of the important actors: constituents, public, and target.

Constituents. Obviously, the extent of constituent commitment has relevance for the type of action chosen. The greater his commitment, the more risk a person will take, and the more energy he will expend. Law-violating behavior requires the most committed group, and engaging in a clash-of-position the least. Similarly, noncooperation, when it is legal, requires somewhat less commitment than protest, and significantly less than intervention.

Unless a community leader is calling on dedicated participants or veterans of other protest actions, he must start with low-risk, minimal-energy activities. These must be structured to provide as much support as possible. The soundest actions are those which are neither so foreign to the experience of the participants nor so difficult that they are not enjoyable; at the least, they should not be onerous. Hopefully, from these low-risk and limited-energy activities, solidarity grows and ideology develops.

Group style is another important variable. It is well to note, in this context, that tactics are *patterned* group behaviors. Styles of action differ among action systems, depending on such group and organizational variables as social class, ideology, and resources. This point is illustrated in a report to the National Commission on the Causes and Prevention of Violence, as follows:

Insofar as movement tactics court exposure to police billy clubs, blacks cannot work up the requisite enthusiasm. Unlike the alienated middle-class whites, they already know what it means to be dealing with antagonistic police on a daily basis, and they find it difficult to appreciate the value of getting publicly clubbed so as to expose the system's latent violence.[22]

This is not to say, however, that direct actions are not contagious. Within limits, the use of similar tactics may spread from one group to another.

We have already suggested that the power of any collectivity is

[22] *Ibid.*, p. 62.

half myth and half real, and that the organizer must be concerned as much with the appearance of representativeness and commitment as with its fact. Alinsky, whose major contribution is as a tactician in conflict situations, makes the point as follows: a vast constituency should be seen, that is, paraded openly and visibly. With a smaller group, numbers ought to be concealed, and noise maximized; and when constituents are too few in number even to make a decent sound, the organization should "stink up the place." [23]

Somewhat less flamboyantly, one organizer reports how he re-trieved a poor situation through his recognition of this principle when a demonstration to protest the relocation policies of a city housing agency did not come off as planned:

Since we had only been able to mobilize 30 of our 300 site tenants, we could not go downtown as a mass demonstration. We would only appear weak and foolish. As some of the participants questioned whether we should go at all, I pointed out that our failure to act would not only de-stroy our credibility in the eyes of housing agency officials (who expected our demonstration), but it would also undermine our credibility in the neighborhood. I proposed we go as a "delegation." After all, the deputy commissioner had said he wanted to sit down and talk with a group of us —OK, we'd sit down and talk first. We had called off our demonstration this time, but if we received no satisfaction of our demands at this meet-ing, we could call out the whole community. The bluff seemed to work. We gained a written guarantee of our first two demands, and the agree-ment to negotiate the third demand for more low-income housing.[24]

It is not always possible to retrieve a failed demonstration as spon-taneously and successfully as this organizer did. Because direct ac-tions are highly visible ceremonies, they can reveal either weakness or strength. For this reason, as well as the fact that protest actions are volatile, it is well to develop a contingency scenario which antici-pates unplanned events such as a smaller or larger number of protes-ters than expected and police behavior.

Direct action campaigns require a finely tuned sense of process. To bring one's constituents along, leaders may start with a less ambi-tious program (this will, at the least, tell them where their constitu-

[23] Saul D. Alinsky, *Rules for Radicals* (New York: Random House, 1971), p. 127.
[24] Student paper, Columbia University School of Social Work, 1969.

ents are), and build momentum to more ambitious actions. One wonders, for example, why, in the demonstration described above, so few of the constituents who were expected turned out. Was the "communitywide" demonstration planned as the beginning of the effort or its culmination? If the former, what made the organizers think the residents were ready to march downtown? If the latter, what led to the miscalculation? Perhaps the leaders planned the event as spontaneously as they shifted its focus, without sufficient consideration of what had gone before or what might come after.

There is an inevitable ebb and flow in contest tactics. Momentum, once generated, tends to peak, and then diminish. The heat which conflict activity generates is too intense to be sustained, and enthusiasm for the fray (except among the most committed) tends to dissipate. Periods of regeneration are necessary. Furthermore, militant groups are usually insufficiently stable to maintain pressure for extended periods of time. Leaders need to be sensitive to when an effort is about to peak, so that they can move to the bargaining table when their strength is in the ascendant rather than in the decline.

Winning the Support of a Wider Public. To win the backing of a wider public, a group must be concerned with two images: its own and its adversary's. It must appear to be virtuous and victimized, while its target is seen as unprincipled and oppressive. Its tactics, therefore, must take both of these images into account.

The success of Martin Luther King, Jr., and the Southern Christian Leadership Conference was due in no small measure to its display of moral rectitude, particularly since its integrity so sharply contrasted with the hypocrisy of its adversaries. Self-discipline and righteousness may prove too burdensome for some protesting groups, but it is the price to be paid for widespread support.

Haggstrom develops a scenario for changing an opponent's practices, as follows:

The organization first searches for moral principles or rules that the practice violates and to which the opponent might be or might become committed. The organization then helps the opponent to commit himself to those principles, publicly, visibly, and sweepingly, without calling attention yet to the practice which the organization wishes to change. The organization may . . . lead the opponent to as firm and total a commitment as possible. The opponent may even be led to bear witness to his principles as he repudiates the "smear campaign" or "rumor campaign" he asserts has been launched to harm his reputation. . . . When the opponent appears firmly enough committed . . . the organization then applies it to the practice it wants changed and threatens a public exposé of the opponent if he does not apply the principle consistently. . . .[25]

The scenario perhaps underestimates the opponent. The latter may not read the script as the organization has written it. But its underlying principle is sound.

When groups use contest tactics to seek a change in values which are not clear or widely held, they risk arousing counterprotest of greater magnitude. The original complaint will then be overshadowed, and the practice confirmed rather than changed by the protest. Sleeping dogs are sometimes best left to lie and, as has been demonstrated in the case of fluoridation, some issues are more advantageously pursued quietly and politically instead of dramatically and publicly. The criteria are whether the proponents need public support to win their point and whether the values inherent in the issue permit an effective public case.

When the objective is to win public support, the substance and form of protests should be as closely related as possible. An example is the teach-in, which is credited with having started the peace movement in 1965. As Skolnick notes, the teach-in was "especially appropriate to that period when less was known about the war [in Vietnam] and when more militant forms of protest were unpalatable to many dissenters. The teach-in was by nature a form of hesitation between respectful inquiry and protest. . . ." [26]

Educational movements that press for changes for which the society is not yet ready ultimately give way to more virulent protest. Even then, the form and substance of the demonstration should be related, if the protesters hope to win the widespread support of, or simply to maintain the neutrality of, the public-at-large. In this context, an intervention at the Pentagon to prevent business-as-usual in the conduct of the war (which may fail) is a more effective tactic for winning

[25] Warren C. Haggstrom, "The Psychological Implications of the Community Development Process," in Lee J. Cary, ed., *Community Development as a Process* (Columbia: University of Missouri Press, 1970), pp. 110–11.

[26] Skolnick, *Politics of Protest*, p. 59.

peace adherents than an intervention to stop traffic in Washington, D.C. (which may succeed).

Although protesters violate normative behavior and the law, there are certain codes of conduct they must observe to gain support. They must be able to show that they have exhausted all legitimate channels to redress their grievances. They must, if they can, put the onus for polarization on their opponent. And they must take care that innocent bystanders do not suffer from their actions. If they do not follow these rules, they provide their opponents with the opportunity to "change the subject" by decrying their impulsive and unprincipled behavior. Attention is thus diverted from the substance of the protest to its form. This constitutes a failure in meeting the educational objectives of the action.

Target Vulnerability. A major task of the direct actionist or disrupter is to locate the "soft underbelly" of the target, his point of greatest vulnerability, while simultaneously protecting his own flank from counterattack. Haley comments on Jesus' tactical acumen in this regard:

> He made an audacious assault on the temple when he entered it and upset the tables of the money changers and dealers in sacrificial animals. . . . He did not violate the alter or intrude upon the Holy of Holies. . . . It was awkward for the priesthood to retaliate against him for his violent ways because he was quoting their own scripture to them, attacking a point difficult to defend.[27]

It is conventional wisdom that a man is hurt most in his pocketbook. Although like any truism, this statement is too broad a generalization, it does tend to hold up as a short-term tactical principle. That is, when economic sanctions are available, they are more immediately threatening than other kinds of sanction. From a long-range perspective, political challenge (i.e., threatening existing power arrangements) may be more unsettling, since changes in the distribution of authority can lead to changes in every other sector. The vulnerability of a target is further heightened when an economic or political threat carries moral authority as well.

Forms of protest vary in the degree they threaten opponents. Dem-

[27] Jay Haley, *The Power Tactics of Jesus Christ* (New York: Grossman, 1969), pp. 42–43.

onstrations are likely to be least threatening, noncooperation more so, and intervention the most alarming of all. This is so because the potential for halting normal operations increases in that order. The scope of the activity is also relevant. A massive demonstration may be more threatening than a limited intervention.

Small group studies suggest that the mere fact that one person can punish another is not sufficient to insure influencing the behavior of the latter. Not only must a target be aware of the demand and dissatisfaction, but two other conditions are necessary: (1) he must understand what he can do to avoid the punishment, and (2) if the threatened punishment is to be effective, he must believe that it can be carried out.[28] Both of these conditions are relevant in the use of contest tactics.

Alinsky offers a tactical rule which, while not as universally applicable as he suggests, is nevertheless an important starting point for direct action. "Pick the target," he says, "freeze it, personalize it, and polarize it." [29] He argues that in our complex and interrelated society, it is difficult to fix responsibility and identify an enemy. When protesters shift their attention from one jurisdiction to another, they dissipate their energies and diffuse their strength. The argument, in effect, speaks to the importance of focus, which, as we've suggested in earlier chapters, is relevant to many aspects of community work practice. Targets must also be personal rather than abstract in order to arouse the hostility necessary for contest tactics to be effective. City Hall is an inanimate structure, Alinsky points out, and corporations do not have soul or identity.

But action is not its own reward, and the dictum must be qualified. A target may be picked, frozen, and personalized, thereby generating action, winning a victory, and changing little. For example, the campaign to change racial segregation in the Chicago public schools focused its attack on the person of the superintendent of schools. Forcing the superintendent's resignation would then be considered a successful outcome, but it might or might not alter racial practices in the Chicago schools. Unless an organization can move from a per-

[28] Barry E. Collins and Harold Guetzkow, *A Social Psychology of Group Processes for Decision-Making* (New York: Wiley, 1964), p. 133.
[29] Alinsky, *Rules for Radicals*, pp. 130–36.

sonalized target as its starting point to an understanding of systems and roles, it may win only Pyrrhic victories.

A COMMENT ON VIOLENCE

The efficacy of disruption as a change technique stems in part from the threat of violence which is implicit in the tactic. Unfortunately, the threat may be realized, and direct action, begun peacefully, may end violently. Most violence stemming from political protests is unplanned and arises out of the spontaneous interaction of protesters and responding authorities.[30] It is for these reasons that a brief comment on violence is in order as we conclude this chapter on contest interventions, even though violence is proscribed for professional use.

Although one might wish it otherwise, violence may be the most effective means of political expression for groups which, for all practical purposes, are disenfranchised and do not have access to the levers of influence. Anthony Lewis has noted in *The New York Times* that "it took the explosion in Watts to make many white Americans begin to realize the desperate conditions of life in the urban ghettos of the North." [31] Nor are other examples of the utility of violence as a change mechanism rare. Nieburg points out that even the backlash of white counterviolence, threatening as it is, has drawn attention to the long-neglected needs of the American lower-middle class.[32]

There are, however, those like ourselves who would argue that although desperate people may sometimes understandably turn to violent means, and even benefit from its results, the costs are too high and the risks too great to justify its use. Apart from the price in human life and dignity, the danger of escalation, and the threat of repression which violent action provokes, there is the risk that the violent, however high-minded initially, will become brutalized in the

[30] This is a finding of the study conducted by Skolnick, *Politics of Protest,* p. 4.

[31] Anthony Lewis, "The Price of Violence," *New York Times,* September 18, 1971, p. 29.

[32] H.L. Nieburg, *Political Violence* (New York: St. Martin's Press, 1969).

process. As Genet has said: "If we behave like the other side, then we are on the other side. Instead of changing the world, all we'll achieve is a reflection of the one we want to destroy." [33]

For the above and other reasons, it is incumbent on the organizer to take what precautions he can to prevent direct actions from becoming violent ones. It is, of course, impossible to predict when violence will occur, although a contingency scenario for demonstrations, mentioned earlier in this chapter, can be developed to anticipate and prepare for its possibility. Although a large share of the responsibility for violence stemming from political protest must be borne by official action,[34] the demonstrators, if they are warned against provocative acts, can reduce its likelihood. There are, furthermore, some techniques by which marshals and others in a demonstration can help to contain those outbreaks which do occur. *The Organizer's Manual* suggests a number of them; for example, calming words, physically cordoning off those engaged in violent action, and moving away from the scene.[35]

Planned violence is another matter. As we noted in chapter 12, it is a tactic aimed at the reconstruction of the entire system. It is not, like direct action and disruption, a call to resist the immoral acts of legitimate authority, but the withdrawal of legitimacy from the sovereign authority. "The leap into revolution," to use Oglesby's words, "leaves 'solutions' behind because it has collapsed and wholly redefines the 'problems' to which they referred. The rebel is an incorrigible absolutist who makes one grand claim that the entire system is in error." [36]

Since a professional receives his sanction for practice from the larger society he serves and its legal and political systems, he is hardly in a position to act as if that framework is no longer legitimate. Morally, he may come to that conclusion, and it is difficult to argue that a moral basis for such a conclusion does not exist in present-day America. Whatever his *personal* commitments, however,

---

[33] Jean Genet, *The Balcony* (London, Faber and Faber Ltd., 1957), p. 56.

[34] Skolnick, *Politics of Protest,* pp. 3–4.

[35] O.M. Collective, *The Organizer's Manual* (New York: Bantam Books, 1971), pp. 116–17.

[36] Oglesby and Shaull, *Containment and Change,* p. 146.

professional sanction and professional values (e.g., to help people make *their* choices, rather than to impose *his* choice of the right solution) do not permit professionals, as professionals, to engage in revolutionary activity. Nor do we believe, in any case, that viable revolutionary alternatives exist.[37] If revolution is the goal and violence is the means, then community work is the wrong field and this is the wrong book.

Although we hold that community work can provide the means for improving social conditions, we recognize that it is, at best, a limited means and that the changes it can achieve are limited as well. Nevertheless, modest change ought not to be dismissed. All modern societies, even those which have experienced revolutions, must confront problems which require the levels of change amenable to community work intervention.

We hold, with Shaull, that "service in the framework of a particular institution does not necessarily demand complete subservience to it," [38] and that professional social reformers, such as community organizers, can be "in" but not "of" these structures. If, in adopting this stance, the professional, with his constituents, cannot at least contribute to the reformation of societal institutions which is required to transform America, he will have acted in a drama without purpose. We believe there is no other choice than to try.

[37] This point is discussed more fully in chapter 3.
[38] Oglesby and Shaull, *Containment and Change,* pp. 196–97.

INDEX